The Ice \ ___

Surviving the Soviet Break-up
and the New Russia

By Helen Womack

Published by

**MELROSE
BOOKS**

An Imprint of Melrose Press Limited
St Thomas Place, Ely
Cambridgeshire
CB7 4GG, UK
www.melrosebooks.co.uk

FIRST EDITION

Cover designed by David Pearce

ISBN 978-1-908645-58-6

Printed and bound in Great Britain by:
Martins the Printers, Spittal, Berwick upon Tweed

Helen Womack has had a 30-year career as a foreign correspondent, writing mainly from Russia. In the 1980s, she worked for Reuters and in the 1990s reported from Moscow for *The Independent*. Now freelance, she continues to cover Russian affairs while also spending more time in the West. Her home is in Filey, North Yorkshire.

ACKNOWLEDGEMENTS

Large parts of this book are based on articles that first appeared in *The Independent*. Thanks to the newspaper for permission to mine this material. Thanks also to *The Moscow Times* and *The Times* for permission to reproduce columns and use live quotes.

Special thanks to John Harrison, former editor of *Passport* magazine, who started out on the path with me and gave me the confidence to go the distance on my own.

Particular thanks to Jill Fairley for gentle but spot-on guidance in editing.

Thanks also to Michel Krielaars, Miranda Ingram, Meg Bortin and Olga Kadomtseva for reading the manuscript and encouraging me.

And finally, I am grateful to Jill de Laat, Ken Darke and the whole team at Melrose Books, who worked on the production of *The Ice Walk*.

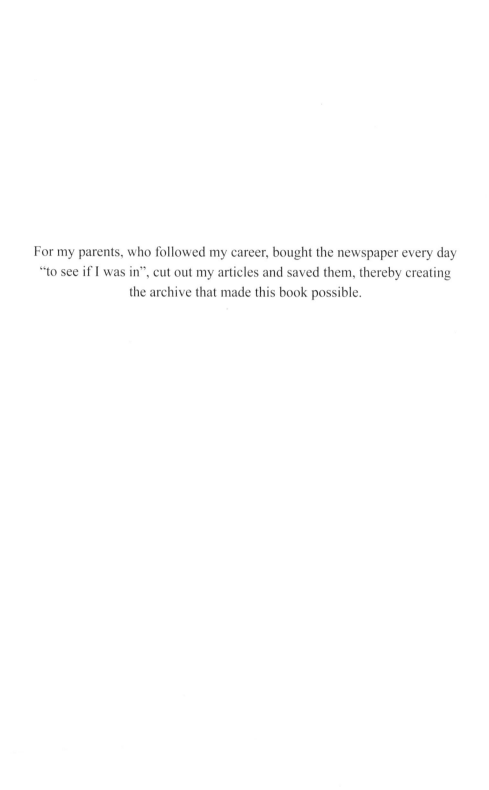

For my parents, who followed my career, bought the newspaper every day "to see if I was in", cut out my articles and saved them, thereby creating the archive that made this book possible.

"May you live in interesting times."
(Often referred to as the Chinese curse.)

CONTENTS

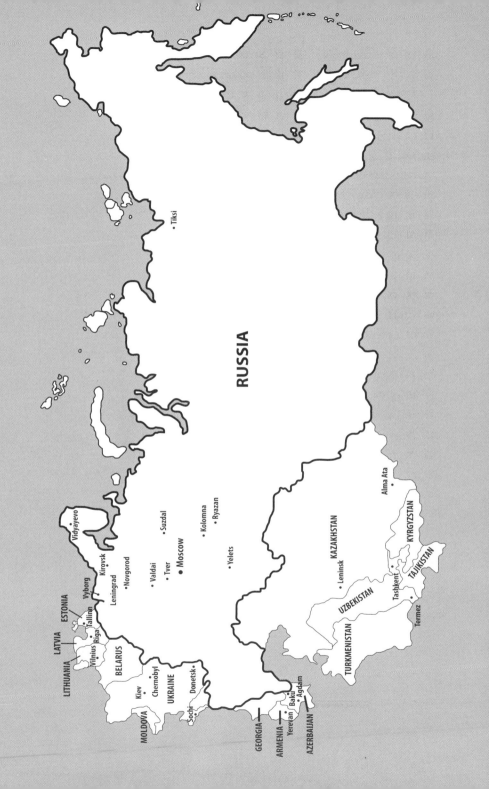

AUTHOR'S NOTE

I fell in love with Russia late one January afternoon when the sky was turning indigo and snowflakes were sparkling over Red Square. Perhaps if I had first seen the country on a cloudy day in November or a muddy one in March, I might have felt differently and headed straight for the airport. Then I would have spared myself half a lifetime of trying to understand Russian behaviour or what Winston Churchill famously called the "riddle, wrapped in a mystery, inside an enigma".

For me, unravelling the puzzle boiled down to two tasks: trying to work out what was real and what was *pokazukha* (a show put on for the benefit of outsiders), and trying to grasp what had changed and what was timeless or eternal about Mother Russia. "Oh, you must have seen so many interesting changes," friends in the West used to say. But often it was a question of *plus ca change, plus c'est la meme chose*.

I arrived in Moscow in 1985, the year Mikhail Gorbachev took over from his geriatric Communist predecessors. I stayed to observe the rule of three Kremlin leaders – Gorbachev, Boris Yeltsin and Vladimir Putin. In retrospect, I realise I was lucky to have lived through and witnessed one of Russia's periodic political thaws, when Gorbachev introduced *perestroika* and *glasnost* and Yeltsin tried to reform post-Soviet Russia.

These were "interesting times", both in the Western sense of being exciting and novel, and in the Chinese sense of being chaotic and unpredictable – what you wouldn't wish on your worst enemy. Pensioners picked through rubbish bins, looking for scraps; atomic physicists were reduced to selling cat food in kiosks; and concert pianists became estate agents in a desperate attempt to feed their children.

But businesses grew, the shops suddenly offered variety, travel became possible and there was the powerful tang of freedom in the air. The makers of *Kukly*, the Russian television equivalent of *Spitting Image*, were not afraid to make fun of Yeltsin and his cronies, week after week.

Then, in 1998, Russia defaulted on its sovereign debt and the game was up. It's my opinion that not long after that, a very quiet coup took place. The Federal Security Service (FSB) stepped in to restore their kind of order. Russia came to be ruled by a security mafia whose public face was Vladimir Putin.

To some he was fatherly; to others a new dictator. He catered to those nostalgic for the Soviet Union. Above all, he brought stability. The times became predictable, prosperous even; they ceased to be "interesting". And the period 1985–2000 was airbrushed out of history. Except that some of us remember (and kept our notebooks from that time).

THE ICE WALK

In Russia, spring is a wearisome battle with winter, which outstays its welcome like a tedious guest. February sees the frost release its grip, the birds begin to sing and the hours of daylight lengthen, but the snow continues to fall thicker than ever. The winter of 1999 was an especially long one and, between false thaws, the snow kept on falling until the end of March. Only on April Fools' Day did the sun shine suddenly hot, melting the snow and turning the parks to lakes and the streets to rivers. There would be no leaves or flowers for a further month and more snowflakes might yet swirl in the air, but it was clear that the new season had finally taken the upper hand.

"I can't stand being stuck in the city another minute," said my friend Vitaly. "Let's go out into the countryside."

It was too early, really. The roads to the *dachas* (country houses) would be swamps. My neighbours, still keeping their cars in their corrugated iron garages, looked at us askance as we polished up my red Niva jeep for the trip. "We'll stick to the main roads," said Vitaly. "We'll just go and see my sister in Kolomna. Maybe we will be in time for the *ledokhod* (ice walk)."

Kolomna, with its ancient kremlin and belching factory, was familiar to me, as I had made numerous visits to the Matveyev family. Vitaly's sister Natasha lived in an old house on Suvorov Street, overlooking the Oka River. One winter, we'd driven the car over the frozen river to the forest on the other side, where we'd spotted lynx tracks in the snow. Her riverside home would be the perfect place from which to see the "ice walk".

"You're too late," Natasha said. "The ice has cracked already. I heard it the other night. It sounded like a distant cannon shot. But we can go down to the river anyway."

If no icebreaker cuts through the ice, it breaks itself in a dramatic natural process and starts to "walk". After the first booming crack, the ice rears up, like a white horse, and breaks into smaller chunks. These fracture into ever smaller pieces that crackle and pop like breakfast cereal in milk. It's a thrilling sight. No wonder the Russians have a richer vocabulary than we do to describe the almost animal behaviour of snow and ice.

By the time we reached the river, it was half fluid, with icebergs sailing in a stately way down the middle. On one large floe, still attached to the bank, anglers sat on camp stools, drilling through the ice like demon dentists and fishing through the holes.

"Come on over," shouted one. "It's perfectly safe. The ice is still seven centimetres thick."

"They're mad," said Natasha. "They're only fishing to feed their cats."

Her brother ripped off his shirt and, like an ecstatic yogi, began rubbing his bare chest with ice crystals. Natasha gave him a disgusted look and led me off in search of pussy willow for Willow Sunday, as the Russians call Palm Sunday.

After lunch, Vitaly had to stay indoors, drying his boots and trousers on the radiator, so Natasha took me shopping. We went to a new honey shop, attached to an award-winning privatised factory that produced gourmet and medicinal honeys and mead. The head biochemist waxed lyrical about the bumblebees, which had just woken up and were flying to the willows.

"To me, that's the real start of spring," she said.

We left with a crate of different honeys – with walnuts, with ginseng, with propolis – and several bottles of alcoholic mead. Then it was on to a shop with sausages from a local factory that had adopted German *wurst*-making technology. Life in Kolomna certainly seemed more cheerful than when I'd first visited the declining, one-industry town in the early 1990s. In addition to the honey and sausages, Natasha added two sacks of potatoes from her own cellar and proudly filled the boot of the car with food for Vitaly and me to take home.

"In Soviet times, we country people had to take the train up to Moscow to buy food. I remember we would go all the way to Moscow just to buy salami. Now you come out to the country for it. That's the way it should be."

We left before it started getting dark. At midnight, I dropped Vitaly off at his house before driving on to my place, where I parked in a deep puddle. The neighbours' curtains twitched as I unloaded my share of the country cousins' booty. I would sleep like a log – after I'd had a cup of tea with honey and put my boots and trousers on the radiator to dry.

It had been a wonderful day, one which I would always remember. But I didn't fully register the significance of the ice walk for me personally until quite a few months later. My own happy and seemingly stable life was to become like that river, which was solid one moment and the next, breaking, rearing up and cracking all over its surface. I had married a Russian – married into Russia – but it didn't last and I was left with no choice but to go with the flow.

My meltdown was nothing, of course, compared to the terrifying ice walk experienced by Russians, who saw their country, the Soviet Union, crack, disintegrate and dissolve in raging flood waters. The thaw brought the promise of spring but for many, before the change of weather could become pleasant, there was the risk of simply going under.

And nobody thought to erect warnings on the riverbank: "Watch your footing. Danger of drowning. Life vests limited to the lucky few."

PART ONE

CRACKING

Red Wedding

The ceremony was set for 4.15 pm on 3 February 1987 at Moscow's Palace of Weddings Number One. My fiancé and I had no choice about the date or venue. The bureaucrat at the single registry office that handled marriages between Soviet citizens and foreigners gave us a slot three months on from the day of application. There was only one moment in time, one place in the world for my marriage to Constantine Gagarin. We gratefully seized the chance the Soviet state gave us, for we both knew it was a miracle we were marrying at all.

I used to tell myself the lack of choice in the old Soviet Union was a blessing. The months, even years, of planning for a traditional English wedding – the endless consideration of dresses, invitation designs, hotel menus etc – would have appalled me. Costya and I had only three months to organise a wedding within the limited scope of the Soviet shops. It was strange but the Communist set-up made me feel freer than my own free market system, free to concentrate on the main thing, which was that I loved Costya.

Having taken our booking, the bureaucrat at the Palace of Weddings gave us a wad of coupons with which to buy clothes and food for our reception. *Defitsit* was the word you heard everywhere in Moscow in those days. Shortages. In all the shops there were shortages of the most basic items, not to mention wedding luxuries. But along with Communist Party bigwigs and veterans of the Second World War, young couples were allowed to jump the queues for the inadequate supply of goods. The bigwigs had permanent privileges, of course, whilst ours was a one-off chance to go shopping in Vesna (Spring), the department store for the officially betrothed.

Here we bought Costya the first suit he ever possessed. He was vehemently against brown crimplene, so we took one in grey wool, even though it was a touch too tight for him. We also bought our ration of caviar

3

and smoked salmon and our entitlement to gold in the form of two simple rings. But the kipper ties were too revolting to contemplate, as were the meringue-like wedding dresses. In the end, I cheated a bit. Costya had no exit visa but wasn't I a free human being? Despite my fine theories about the improving effect of deprivation, I flew home. In Leeds, which seemed like Paris or Milan compared to Moscow, I bought a grey and red silk tie for my future husband and an off-the-peg, knee-length dress in cream silk for myself. My high-heeled shoes were lilac to match the delicate amethyst necklace that had belonged to my grandmother.

Back in Moscow, Costya and I began to make arrangements for the reception by going on an inspection tour of the city's restaurants. Many Russians choose to have their wedding parties in the privacy of their own homes. But I lived in a golden cage, a comfortable ghetto for foreigners, while Costya came from a closed town in Leningrad Region. We had nowhere to invite our guests except to a restaurant.

In 1987, before Mikhail Gorbachev allowed the opening of "cooperative" cafes in the first step towards private business, Moscow had only a handful of state restaurants, named after and serving the ethnic dishes of the 15 Soviet republics plus the socialist countries of the Warsaw Pact.

We sampled *lobio* (beans) and *khachipuri* (cheese pie) in the room where Stalin used to dine at the *Aragvi* Georgian restaurant. We also braved the stuffed bear at the entrance of the Restaurant Berlin to see what culinary delights East Germany had to offer. Finally, because the waiters were friendly and gooey chocolate cake was the house specialty, we booked our reception at the Prague on the Old Arbat.

On the day of the wedding, there were 30 degrees of frost. That is the temperature at which cats and dogs hop along on three paws to minimise contact with the frozen ground and nylon stockings can stick to your legs so that you have to have them surgically removed, or so my Russian friends used to tell me. I was never quite sure whether or not they were joking. The members of our party all wore heavy sheepskins over their best clothes for the short walk from the taxis into the Palace of Weddings.

Although we were on time, we were kept waiting. Mendelssohn's "Wedding March" sounded at 15-minute intervals for several other couples on the conveyor belt ahead of us before we too were summoned before the registrar, a woman with a chain of office like a mayoress. The experience was not quite as tacky as it sounds. The music was live, played by a small palm court orchestra that included a harp. The registrar managed to put feeling into words she must have pronounced hundreds of times. Costya and I both giggled when she congratulated us on forming a new "Soviet family". We exchanged the rings. I decided to remain Helen Womack, tempting though it was to become Mrs Gagarin, a relation in name if not in fact to the first man in space.

From the Palace of Weddings, we drove straight to the reception at the Prague, avoiding the usual patriotic ritual of laying flowers at the Tomb of the Unknown Soldier on the edge of Red Square. We drank champagne, ate sturgeon and kissed to cries of *gorko* (it's not sweet enough, kiss again). But, since the plates were not our own, we refrained from smashing the crockery to bring good luck in the traditional Russian way. (The next day, my mother slipped on the ice and broke her wrist, which Russian friends took to be an even greater sign of luck. She didn't see it that way.)

Our group was small, as Russians in those early days of *perestroika* were still quite nervous about meeting foreigners. Costya had gathered only his closest friends, most of them young men he had met while dodging the army by logging in Siberia. Plus their wives and girlfriends, of course. I was represented by my parents and aunt and uncle, who came from Yorkshire with armfuls of daffodils and a home-made English wedding cake. At the airport, customs officers had wanted to cut it open until my parents explained what it was. The guests called it the "concrete cake" because of its hard, white icing.

My relatives and new in-laws had common memories of the Second World War, which gave them something to talk about. The rest of us were children not of the war but of the Cold War. We had grown up with a fascination for the "enemy" on the other side of the Iron Curtain. Now here we all were, rapidly breaking the ice at our wedding party.

While we caroused, Igor Borisenko, a photographer from Tallinn, went round the table taking pictures of all the guests. Igor went on to become an award-winning film director, so perhaps the photographs have more than sentimental value now.

He zoomed in on Alina Habibulina, an actress who had been my witness at the registry office. She was married to a famous counter-tenor, who was building an opera career, defying his music professors who told him to "stop singing like a woman".

Costya's witness was his best friend from youth, Konstantin Vasiliev, fondly nicknamed Little Kostya. A railway worker, he was to go on to make a success as a small businessman. He was accompanied by his wife Ira, who was wearing an alluring midnight blue dress.

Our toastmaster was the eloquent Sergei Lakshin, son of a famous writer. He was with his wife Lyuba, a doctor. Then there was Mikhail Butov, a poet, with his girlfriend Vera, and Anton Yarzhombek, an icon painter, with his wife Tamara, a ceramic artist.

Svetlana Patsayeva came too. The daughter of a cosmonaut, she was herself a scientist. Her boyfriend Oleg was a scholar of Japanese, with a passion for haiku poetry and martial arts.

A rather sad figure on his own was Vadim, a biologist. His partner Marina had just emigrated as a Jew. In those days, if a person accepted an exit visa as a Jew, he or she had no right to return to the USSR. This did not trouble Marina because all her family had left with her. But Vadim could not go so easily because his parents wanted to remain in Moscow. The only way out for him was to marry a foreigner and leave the Soviet Union not as a Jew but as a spouse, in which case he could return to visit his parents. This he eventually did, making a marriage of convenience with an American to reach Marina in the US. Such were the lengths to which the totalitarian system forced people to go in order to live the lives they wanted.

Costya and I were luckier. We were together, just married and looking forward to the future. We had narrowly escaped the fate of the so-called "divided spouses" – couples who had been apart for years because the Soviet authorities frowned on mixed marriages and would not give exit visas to Russians married to foreigners or entry visas to foreigners married to Russians.

But times were changing. Thanks to Mikhail Gorbachev, a grand love affair was blossoming between East and West, making possible the small loves of individuals.

Costya and Helen on their wedding day

Costya and I had met one evening in December 1985, when the snow was falling in thick flakes on Strastnoi (Passion) Boulevard. The street name referred to the Passion of Christ, there being an old monastery nearby, but for us there would always be the other meaning.

I had gone out in need of fresh air after working late in the Reuter office translating a newspaper article about how Mikhail Gorbachev was cracking down on alcohol abuse. Vodka prices were going up to curb consumption, and new penalties were coming in for "hooligans" caught drinking in public places.

At the same time, walking towards me from the other end of the deserted boulevard was Costya, who had left a party where the vodka was running out. He told me afterwards that he had been hoping to find a taxi driver who would sell him black-market liquor out of the boot of his cab. But meanwhile, mistaking me for a Russian girl in my fake fur coat and being a cheeky lad, Costya decided to try his luck.

"You don't by any chance have a bottle, do you?" he asked.

"You leave me alone. I am a British correspondent," I replied in broken Russian, fearing a KGB provocation to get me drunk in a public place.

We stood staring at each other like two animals in the forest. Luckily Costya was joined at that moment by another party guest, Nikita, whose English was slightly better than my Russian. He explained the situation, calmed me down and invited me to the party. It was madness for me to follow two strange men to an unknown apartment at nearly midnight but I felt instinctively that they were not going to hurt me.

They took me through a dark yard into a doorway reeking of urine and up in a creaking lift to a small fifth-floor flat. The narrow living room was furnished with a green velvet sofa spewing its stuffing, and two or three wooden chairs. On the table were a few mandarins and a dish of *sukhariki* (nibbles of dried bread). The party had broken up for lack of lubrication and the host and hostess had gone to bed, but Costya roused them again to greet me. They turned out to be Seriozha, who was following his father, a well-known writer, into the world of literature, and Lyuba, a doctor.

Seriozha spoke French, which was also my best foreign language at that time. The two of us got carried away, talking about art, politics… everything under the sun. We had nothing to drink except diluted eau de cologne or tea. I chose tea but quickly got inebriated by the discussion. Nikita got bored and left, Lyuba went back to bed, and Costya sat in uncomprehending silence throughout the night.

Although I was talking to Seriozha, it was Costya I really liked and judging from his body language, he was attracted to me too. He asked me to go out with him and we agreed to meet the following evening outside a furniture shop on the boulevard. I took a pocket dictionary with me on the date. Costya's English was extremely limited, although he managed to express quite complicated ideas in the primitive language at his disposal.

"Costya no like now house," he said, meaning that he was not an admirer of contemporary architecture.

"Soviet Union covered in prick trail," was his description of a land under dictatorship and barbed wire.

On our first outing, he took me to see the "Forever Fire", the Eternal Flame down by Red Square.

Because of the language barrier, we learnt about each other slowly. It was nearly two weeks before I understood that Costya did not live in Moscow but was extending his stay so that he could see me. He was from Kirovsk, a town in Leningrad Region, which was strictly closed to foreigners because it had a factory that produced parts for submarines.

As a boy, Costya had lived in a wooden house overlooking the Kirovsk cemetery. His father, Policarp Ivanovich, worked in the timber industry. His mother, Lyubov Andreyevna, who had a degree in history, taught *diamat* (dialectical materialism) in a workers' night school. Since his mother was busy teaching, he was effectively brought up by his grandmother. She had lost 17 years of her life in one of Stalin's labour camps because in the 1930s, she had given a night's shelter to a priest.

The Soviet Union was still an atheist state when Costya was born in 1959. His grandmother, released from labour camp, baptized him secretly at home in a washing- up bowl. In his youth, Costya rebelled against the status quo by declaring himself a Christian whereas I, growing up in the West, had rejected Establishment values by briefly toying with Communism.

At 16, Costya left Kirovsk and took a place at a technical college in Leningrad. From this springboard, he tried to jump into theatre school but was rejected because he could not produce a satisfactory political essay. Asked to write on the subject of the wartime victory of the Soviet Union, Costya wrote, "The Soviet Union had a great victory, full stop." Nevertheless, he'd made it out of the backwater that was Kirovsk, and now had a colourful bohemian life in Leningrad.

To avoid prosecution as a "social parasite", he had a state job on paper. In reality, he lived like a bear, gathering food in summer and hibernating in winter. When the weather was warm and the days long, he would build *dachas* for private clients, strictly speaking an illegal business. When the frosts came, he would sleep by day and party by night. He had friends all over the Soviet Union and travelled to visit them, taking his guitar wherever he went. He wasn't an anti-Soviet dissident as such but his hippy lifestyle was subversive in its way.

The fact that he travelled protected us for a long time. Costya would come to Moscow to see me and then go away again, so the secret police, then called the KGB, never had time to latch onto us. We were both nervous of the KGB. There were days when I was so paranoid, I used to think my rabbit fur hat was bugged and the KGB were listening to my thoughts. Costya was more relaxed but he took the precaution of never visiting or telephoning me in "Sad Sam", the foreigners' compound on Sadovaya Samotechnaya Street, where the walls and phones were almost certainly riddled with eavesdropping devices. Instead, like spies, we used to meet on the street and agree the venue for the next date before we parted.

At the start of our courtship, we met several times outside the furniture store; then we decided to change the place of rendezvous to Mayakovsky Square. I remembered that we had a new arrangement but Costya forgot, so while I was waiting at the square, he was standing outside the furniture shop. I waited for an hour in the cold before giving up in despair. There were no mobile phones then, of course, and I didn't have an address or telephone number for Costya. All I knew was that he stayed with friends, somewhere in the general area of Belorussky Station.

The situation seemed hopeless. I went back to "Sad Sam", lay on the sofa and stared at the ceiling. After about an hour, I had an urge to go to Belorussky Station. I took a taxi and among the thousands of people milling about at the station, I spotted Costya in the rush-hour crowd. It was as unlikely as finding a needle in a haystack. After that, we were careful to exchange telephone numbers and addresses.

Costya continued to visit me in Moscow but we also started to meet in other Soviet cities. Naturally, I went to Leningrad and we also had little holidays together in the Baltic States. On each trip, I would check into the local Intourist hotel but in actual fact stay with Costya and his friends. Our favourite Baltic capital was Riga. Costya said that people from Leningrad would go to Riga just to get a cup of coffee. Perhaps that was an exaggeration of the shortages but Riga old town, with its cafes and fresh flower stalls, was certainly a world away from grimy Leningrad.

Back in Moscow, Costya and I tramped the streets, stealing kisses in doorways like teenagers. Friends were kind and took us in but we needed a place of our own. In those days, it was illegal to rent an apartment but Costya managed to borrow one. One warm May evening, in a worker's flat near a meat processing plant in the grimy suburb of Kuzminki, he asked me to marry him. He went down on his knees to make the proposal. Not lilacs but an aroma of boiled bones floated in through the open *fortochka* (little window). Yet for me, nothing could have been more romantic.

When I was engaged, I thought I should inform my employers at Reuters. Both Costya and I expected trouble from the KGB, which we were to get in full measure in due course, but I failed to foresee that my bosses were going to be less than sympathetic to our little East-West union. At first, the editors wanted to withdraw me to London for "losing my objectivity". I didn't blame them. They were only doing their jobs. Fortunately, the intervention of one progressive-minded German editor saved my bacon and Reuters decided not to cancel my Moscow posting.

Soon Costya and I had other problems. I got an early warning of this from Misha Butov, the poet who had been at our wedding. Misha and I sang together in a choir. At one of the rehearsals, he took me aside and told me that he had been called in by the KGB, who wanted to know the identity of my fiancé. It was incredible but that vast, supposedly all-powerful organisation couldn't work out to whom I was engaged. Misha refused to inform on me and as a result, lost the place he was hoping to get at film school. But the gods rewarded his loyalty as a friend because in the 1990s, he went on to win the Russian Booker Prize for his novel, *Freedom.*

As for the KGB, they didn't manage to find Costya until October 1986, when our marriage banns went up at the British embassy – a necessary formality before we could book a ceremony at the Palace of Weddings. In the banns, Costya's address became public knowledge: 4A Reidovy Peryulok, Kirovsk, Leningrad Region.

Armed with this information, the KGB sent army recruiters to Costya's home. No doubt they thought he would make excellent cannon fodder for the war in Afghanistan. He was nearly 27 and almost too old for conscription.

Costya had successfully dodged military service for the previous nine years. He never actually refused to serve but played on the essential laziness and incompetence of Soviet officials. Call-up papers would arrive through

11

the post every spring and autumn and in these seasons, Costya would sneak off to Siberia or wherever. He would return when he reckoned that Colonel Rakitin of the Kirovsk recruitment office had had time to fill his quota for the six months ahead. "Sorry I'm late, Sir," he would say, and Rakitin would wave his hand and promise to include him in the next batch. This went on, year after year, and Colonel Rakitin went to his grave without ever managing to recruit Costya.

Fooling Rakitin was one thing but now the KGB were on his heels. Fortunately, Costya was not at home on the morning the press gang arrived, and his father tipped him off to stay away from the house.

The next thing I knew the telephone was ringing in my flat in "Sad Sam". It was six o'clock in the morning and it woke me up. The guard at the gate told me I had a visitor. I went out into the cold and saw Costya standing there with a rucksack on his back. "I'm moving in with you," he said. The guard could not actually prevent this, as I was free to invite guests, but Costya had to show his passport at the security booth before I could welcome him in. Most Russians, of course, would not have revealed their links to a foreigner by identifying themselves in this way but Costya had nothing to lose.

I took him into the flat, which was just an ordinary Western-standard apartment, with living room, bedroom, spare bedroom and fitted kitchen, but to Costya it seemed like a palace. He drank a Coke from my fridge and said it was his first.

That day, Costya crossed a line and became a dissident, joining a small community of Russians who had claimed asylum inside "Sad Sam". Once they had entered, they were stuck; they risked arrest on the street if they tried to go out again. Their lives became like that of anti-Communist Cardinal Jozsef Mindszenty, who sought asylum and lived in the US embassy in Budapest for 15 years.

Among the refugees in "Sad Sam" was Lyuda Yevsyukova, whose brother Sima was in an Arctic labour camp because he'd refused to do military service lest he learn state secrets that would prevent his family from getting permission to migrate to America. What enraged the Soviet authorities was that the Yevsyukovs were not Jews and still they wanted to leave the country – the height of disloyalty!

12

Sima Yevsyukov returns from labour camp

The others – Lena Kaplan, Matvei Finkel, I can't remember all of them now – were members of the "divided spouses" group. They had married Westerners but been separated because their partners were not allowed to stay in the Soviet Union and they were denied the right of exit. In some cases, they had not seen their loved ones for years. It looked as if Costya and I were about to find our names at the bottom of that sad list.

In desperation, I went to see the British consul. He took me into a small, padded room where he said the KGB could not overhear our conversation, and listened with concern as I told him our story. To this day, I do not know exactly what the British did but Margaret Thatcher was due to visit Mikhail Gorbachev in Moscow and I imagine the diplomats preparing the meeting suggested to the Russians that it was not in their interests to have another human rights case. So we had a wedding instead. Benefiting from the chemistry between Maggie and Gorby, Costya and I were able to become man and wife.

13

Now a married man, Costya reported to the army recruitment office in Kirovsk, where an officer took his "military ticket", the document all Soviet men carried to show whether they had served or been exempted from the army, and burnt it in an ashtray in front of him. "Now that you are married to a foreigner, you are no longer fit to serve the Fatherland," the officer said.

Other officials promised that Costya would be allowed an exit visa to visit Britain later in the year.

That should have been the happy ending to the story, but it wasn't. We fell into a new trap through our own youthful foolishness.

We'd already had a lovely, modest wedding but we decided to gild the lily by throwing a huge housewarming party for all our friends. We were starting married life in a new flat in the October Square compound. This was still reserved for foreigners but the atmosphere was more relaxed, as there was a greater mix of nationalities including Yugoslavs, Chinese and Africans. If "Sad Sam", with its Anglo-Saxon contingent, resembled an Ivy League or Oxbridge college, then October Square was more like a modern, international university.

Costya's eyes nearly popped out of his head when we went to the *beriozka* (hard currency store) to stock up on booze for the party. The system of segregated shops really was as iniquitous as apartheid in South Africa. Along with our wedding certificate, Costya had been given a document saying he was legally entitled to carry dollars in his pocket. He had become an honorary foreigner in his own country, a "white" because of his association with me. We bought wine, beer and spirits and all kinds of food, unavailable in ordinary Soviet shops.

Our party got underway and soon became merry. The British consul dropped in to wish us well. He'd asked me what the dress code would be and I'd said casual, so he arrived in a T-shirt and jeans. The Russian guests might have been poor but they came in their best clothes. They refused to believe this could be the consul. "He's so scruffy," they kept whispering.

More guests arrived. My American friend and colleague, Meg Bortin, came with a home-made, tiered chocolate cake topped with a model of St Basil's Cathedral. Other Western journalists attended and there were dozens of Costya's friends from all over the country.

14

While I was chatting to guests in the back room, Costya came in and said he was going out for a walk with Genya, a rock musician from Leningrad. About half an hour later, the telephone rang. It was Costya. In a shaking voice, he told me he'd taken my brand-new red Volvo and crashed it into another car. The other driver was not hurt but there was some damage to his Lada. The GAI (traffic police) had breathalysed Costya and not only found him over the limit but also discovered that he did not possess a driving licence; indeed he did not know how to drive a car. We were in deep trouble.

After a miserable honeymoon in Ukraine, we returned to Moscow to face the music at the traffic police headquarters.

At the interrogation, it rapidly became clear that the GAI inspector was less important than his pudgy, leather-jacketed "translator" and the leather jacket was far more interested in me than in Costya, who was sent outside to sit in the corridor.

I then had one of the most frightening experiences of my life – an interview with a recruiting officer from the KGB. He leered and introduced himself as Sergei. We talked for what seemed like hours. I could not just get up and leave, because Costya had committed an offence. It was like a debate with the Devil. I knew if I made one false step, I would be damned.

"We could send your husband to jail for three years," Sergei said.

"Charge him then, and we'll get a lawyer," I replied.

"I'm sure there's no need for that, Ms Womack. How would you like to go to parts of the Soviet Union that other correspondents cannot visit? You could go and see your new in-laws in Kirovsk. You'd like that, wouldn't you?"

I said I didn't want any privileges other correspondents didn't have.

"We do have this," Sergei said then, pulling out a thick file. "Let's see, February 12, Helen Womack arrived in Leningrad, checked into the Astoria Hotel, didn't stay the night; March 25, Helen Womack went to Tallinn, registered at the Hotel Viru, didn't stay the night. And in Riga, I see, you were in trouble with the local police for visiting a *dacha* outside the city limits. We could call that spying. We could send an official protest to the Foreign Ministry and have you expelled."

"Do it," I said.

Again he softened and switched on the charm.

"You love Russia, don't you? I'm sure if the Soviet Union was in danger, you would want to help us, wouldn't you?"

"Certainly," I said. "If I see a fire, you can be sure I'll call the fire brigade."

And with that, the KGB gave up and washed their hands of me. The GAI fined Costya 400 roubles (the Soviet rouble had artificial parity with the pound) and deprived me of my driving licence for two years.

I was furious with Costya. He was mortified. But we still had reserves of love and we put the disaster behind us.

As for the driving ban, the KGB did me a favour. Forced from the world of comfortable cars, I descended into the metro and saw how ordinary Soviet people lived. I went on to make my name and my living walking with the *narod* (people) rather than with *vlast* (power) and describing life from the citizens' point of view.

THE KOMMUNALKA

With my mother-in-law, Lyubov Andreyevna

Being married to a Russian was the best way to gain insight into Soviet society and the living conditions of ordinary people. Having a Russian mother-in-law who didn't speak English beat any intensive language course, and Costya also widened my experience by introducing me to his many friends.

One I came to like particularly was Oleg Schwarz, who lived in a mindboggling *kommunalka* (communal apartment) in what was then Leningrad.

Oleg's apartment was on Ulitsa Pravdi, or Truth Street. A marble staircase

17

led up to a heavy wooden door, behind which were six rooms, all with high, moulded ceilings. Before the Bolshevik Revolution, the grand apartment had belonged to a single, bourgeois family. After the Communists came to power, appropriating private property, workers' families were crammed into the space the rich people had occupied. There was one family in each of the six rooms.

In his satirical novel *Heart of a Dog*, Mikhail Bulgakov described how a professor, who had created a proletarian monster by transplanting a human heart into a dog, lived to regret it when a Communist housing committee came to take over his spacious apartment. Oleg and his family were not proletarian brutes but decent working class people, still living with the grim consequences of Communist housing policy.

Oleg was a wry, kindly character, a joiner and maker of scenery for the theatre. He wore very thick, tortoiseshell spectacles. In his thirties, he still lived with his parents – father Ernst Richardovich, an ethnic German, and mother Polina Ivanovna, originally from Siberia – in one of the six rooms.

Ernst Richardovich would begin the day by going out onto the balcony and throwing a bowl of ice-cold water over himself. Then he would come in and start lecturing the family about the need for law and order. Polina Ivanovna would try to keep the peace by changing the subject but as often as not, father and son would end up having a row. Oleg, an anarchist at heart, would retreat to his narrow bed behind a curtain, the only private place he had, to read a good book. The family all read copiously. It was the only way they could escape from each other.

I remember we paid a visit to the Schwarz family one 7 November, celebrated in Soviet times as the anniversary of the October Revolution in 1917 (when the calendar differed from our modern one). The year would have been 1986, I think. Oleg met us with some good news.

"I've moved out of my parents' place," he announced with a bitter laugh.

What this really meant was that he'd left the large room with maroon striped wallpaper, where Polina Ivanovna and Ernst Richardovich slept, ate and watched TV, and gone one door down the corridor to the little blue room occupied by a neighbour until his recent death.

Oleg's cramped living conditions had not been conducive to a love life.

He did once have a Lithuanian girlfriend called Rita but she migrated to America, after which he started drinking more vodka than was good for him. Now, if he wished, Oleg could bring a woman back to share the single bed in the corner of his own room. But so far he'd limited himself to getting the dog he'd always wanted, a poodle he called Bely (Whitey) in a play on his own surname, which is German for black.

Oleg's room was sparsely furnished. A photo enlarger that looked as if it belonged in a museum was piled with other junk on top of the wardrobe. Apart from this, there was an armchair and a table covered with literary journals such as *Novy Mir*. Oleg was reading Anatoly Rybakov's *Children of the Arbat*, an expose of the Stalin era, that was finally seeing the light of day with the relaxation of censorship.

Like the majority of Soviet citizens, Oleg was benefitting from *glasnost* but his material standard of living had improved hardly at all. There were long waiting lists for self-contained flats in high-rise apartment buildings and it would be years before Oleg could hope for anything better than the *kommunalka*.

As the former Russian capital, built by Peter the Great using European architects perhaps including Oleg's own ancestors, Leningrad had more communal apartments in rambling old buildings than other, more modern Soviet cities. The *kommunalka* may have seemed romantic to Western visitors like me but the claustrophobia and lack of privacy must have been hard to bear. Oleg said one poor woman had hanged herself in her room some years before.

While being forced to share, the residents tried to maintain their separate dignities and there was a strong sense of property. In the narrow bathroom, which served six families, there were six shelves. The Schwarz family kept their soap on the top shelf and warned visitors against using the neighbours' toiletries by mistake. Likewise, it was important to know the demarcations of the kitchen, with its six stoves and crockery cupboards. In the *kommunalka*, you were welcome to borrow but shouldn't help yourself without permission.

The system was carried to absurdity in the tiny toilet, where six light bulbs were connected to six switches, leading to separate electricity meters.

Only the pile of paper strips torn from *Leningradskaya Pravda* and used as toilet paper seemed to be for common use. And of course, there was always a queue for the loo. As you approached it, you would see old Mr Vasilyev in his vest and braces furtively open the door of his room, swear under his breath that you'd beaten him to it, and close the door again.

Residents of the Kommunalka

The flat-dwellers showed consideration for each other by discouraging friends from telephoning after 11.00 pm and by generally trying to avoid noise. But inevitably, in this microcosm of Soviet society, somebody was having a birthday party when someone else had to work the next morning. The best time for a drunken binge, therefore, was a prazdnik (public holiday).

On 7 November, we arrived early with plans to watch the Leningrad Revolution Day parade on local television. There was a great commotion at the door as muddy boots were exchanged for slippers, and coats removed and taken to the curtained-off cubicle where Oleg's parents slept.

Despite Gorbachev's anti-alcohol drive, there was vodka on the table and the men were already sampling it by mid-morning while the women were still drinking tea. Polina Ivanovna or Tyotya Polya (Aunt Polya), as we called her, made cabbage pies and the Siberian *pelmeni* (dumplings with both beef and pork) for which she had a reputation in the *kommunalka*. Uncle Ernst got out the family photo album, full of fair-haired characters with Russified German names, and showed us a crackly home movie of his canoeing holiday in Siberia in 1976.

By afternoon, the women had started drinking too and soon everyone was voluble. Oleg began to recount some of the gruesome things he'd learnt about Stalin through his reading. He should have known better. The merry mood abruptly changed and he found himself in a row he'd had at least a hundred times before, a row that was widening the generation gap in millions of families across the Soviet Union.

"You can't blame Stalin," cried Aunt Polya at the top of her voice. "He knew nothing of the killings; it was the evil people all around him." At nearly 60, she'd been a lifelong member of the Communist Party and was too old to discard her beliefs.

Uncle Ernst stepped in to restore order. "I will not have a word against Stalin said in this house," he said, banging his fist on the table. His attitude was incomprehensible to Oleg since the ethnic Germans had suffered particularly under Stalin, being deported en masse to Siberia lest they collaborate with the invading Nazis.

To avoid any more unpleasantness, Oleg, Costya and I got up and walked out onto the street, joining the thousands strolling along the banks of the River Neva in honour of Revolution Day, or perhaps just escaping from their own domestic tensions. We stayed out into the night, watching the fireworks.

Costya and I kept in touch with Oleg and saw him every time we visited Leningrad. In the early 1990s, when reformist mayor Anatoly Sobchak was in power, aided by the then unknown Vladimir Putin, Oleg and his parents were moved out of the *kommunalka* and allotted a self-contained flat in a high-rise block in an outer suburb. Oleg didn't like it much. He said it was soulless. He was still living with his mother and father, only now they were all together in a modern box, like sardines in a tin.

Out of nostalgia, I went back to look at the derelict mansions where the *kommunalkas* had been. Eventually they would be taken over by real estate developers and re-converted into fine flats for the rich but at the time of my visit in 1992, they were occupied by squatters.

The courtyard of number 14 was littered with broken bottles, human excrement and a dead cat. At the top of the stairwell, a couple of men in their twenties and two teenage girls who had dropped out of college were smoking marijuana. They said they were living without gas or running water but strangely the telephone was still connected. They earned a crust by busking and also took food coupons from the city authorities.

"There's a Russian saying," said one of them, "take whatever is given." And he blew his nose on a dirty towel.

Uncle Ernst would have had plenty to say about that.

All these years later, I still remember the Schwarz family with fondness. Sadly, in the mid-1990s, Oleg and his mother, together with the dog Bely, were run over by a drunk driver on a zebra crossing. Aunt Polya and the dog died instantly. Oleg hung on for some weeks in intensive care before also dying.

He never lived to marry or have a flat of his own. His self-contained accommodation was a grave in the Kirovsk cemetery. I think of all the opportunities that I have enjoyed compared to the relatively narrow life Oleg was forced to live in the great *kommunalka* that was the Soviet Union.

Oleg Schwarz

UNDERGROUND

In Soviet times, it seemed everything was forbidden. The first word a child learnt was *nelzya* (don't, you can't, you shouldn't, you mustn't). Everything normal was naughty. You couldn't trade or travel or even read what you wanted.

One of my strongest impressions from that period was being at an intellectual's flat where a *samizdat* (illegal, self-published) translation of George Orwell's *1984* was being passed round among the guests. It was written by hand in a school exercise book and the person who had risked jail to produce it had even added his own illustrations and maps. Several people wanted to borrow it and the rule was they could have it for one night before passing it on.

From this, I understood that Russians were like water: they always found a way around obstacles. Sure there were shortages but the black market flourished. And there was a whole secret cultural life that went on underground, hidden from the authorities – art exhibitions in forests, poetry readings and rock concerts in private flats.

When Mikhail Gorbachev launched his policy of *glasnost* (openness), the underground artists began cautiously to emerge into the light of day. They popped up, one after another, like moles breaking the surface of the soil or, as the Russians would say, like mushrooms after rain.

The birch trees of Moscow's Bitsa Park were suddenly hung with paintings and lampshades at a new open-air art and craft market. For a number of years, a small band of determined, unofficial artists had been breaking the law by selling their work there. But when the city authorities sanctioned the market and even allowed an announcement about it on state TV, hundreds of artists and thousands of buyers flocked to the woods to enjoy the show. Of course, Costya and I were among them.

24

What a change this was from the atmosphere a decade earlier, when the KGB had famously sent bulldozers in to smash down the easels of a group of painters who had tried to hold an avant-garde art exhibition in a field.

Like all good markets, Bitsa had a smart end with fancy goods at high prices, and a scruffy end with lots of junk and perhaps a few genuine bargains.

I remember chatting to a man who was selling handmade ceramic animals for a few roubles apiece. Incredible as it sounded to my Western ears, the police had previously bothered to confiscate these small, harmless items but the raids had stopped and he was confidently trading, making more money in a few hours than he could in a month at his day job as a manual labourer.

Nearby, portrait artists were vying with each other to make instant sketches of customers on brown paper. Sharks were also trying to sell badly-made, overpriced lampshades but the free market was working because nobody was buying them.

The paintings were mostly innocuous landscapes of varying degrees of artistic merit but the occasional, more controversial religious or psychological pieces crept in. Some were copies and one woman proudly walked off with a Modigliani for the equivalent of 10 quid.

Redzhepov Rakhmet, from Turkmenistan in Central Asia, was selling poster-style paintings. He told me that before the appearance of the market, he used to sell his pictures through private contacts.

"Expensive and soulless," one Russian standing next to me said, but I noticed that a foreign diplomat was quick to snap up a few examples of this trendy work. Money was changing hands as on an eastern bazaar and nobody at this stage of the game foresaw that in exchange for allowing enterprise, the authorities would soon introduce the concept of income tax.

Pensioner Anatoly Solovyov, one of the founders of the market, was selling miniatures of churches and country scenes, making a good profit, although a lot less than he would have been paid if his work had been accepted in a state art shop. He said that like many of the painters in the woods, he was a professional in the sense that he had an artistic education, but he wasn't in the official Union of Artists.

Back then, to be an official artist meant to belong to the appropriate artists' union and to toe its politicised cultural line. The rewards were a good salary, a *dacha* and the chance to travel abroad. To be an underground artist meant to work as one pleased, limited by lack of access to facilities and, if one didn't hold down a state job or if one criticised the state too strongly, facing the risk of prosecution as a "parasite" or "anti-Soviet element".

Being a counter-culture sort of guy, Costya already knew quite a few of these "alternative" artists and he invited them to our home. Before I knew it, our little flat had become the centre of the hip *tusovka* (crowd who hang out) and the booze flowed freely. It was great fun but unlike the rest of the arty set, who could sleep in until midday, I often had to get up to do the early shift at Reuters, which was tough. On the other hand, I suddenly had some amazing contacts, giving me cultural stories of which other Western correspondents could only dream.

One of them was a film actress who called herself Masha-Larisa-Borodino-Waterloo and showed off shamelessly. But in a more thoughtful moment, she said to me, "Many artists effectively spent their lives on strike. Now the distinction between official and underground is starting to blur. I am living with one foot underground and one above, working on my own projects but taking those state contracts that attract me."

"We are coming out from underground," the poet Tatyana Sherbina said when I went to visit her in her book-crammed apartment. Friends had told me Sherbina was regarded as one of the best living Soviet poets. Her work had been published in the West and *samizdat* editions of her slim volumes had passed from hand to hand in Moscow for years.

"Those underground publications were technically illegal," she said, "but I was never prosecuted, probably because my work was not all that anti-Soviet."

She wrote secretly in childhood because her mother had told her that poetry brought only trouble. In 1980, she did receive an offer of official publication in the Soviet Union.

"But my position was, 'Let them publish Brodsky and Pasternak first'," she said, referring to two great, banned poets. Publication in 1980 would have involved too many compromises in Sherbina's writing, which wove cultural themes from past and present, Russia and abroad.

By 1987, when I met Sherbina, Brodsky and Pasternak were published and she was locked in negotiations with the editors of *Ogonyok* (Flame) magazine about the small cuts they wanted to make to her verses when they brought out a collection of her work the following year.

"I see myself now neither as an official nor an underground writer," Sherbina said. "I am independent."

The same approach was taken by theatre director Boris Yukhananov, for whom words like "underground" and "dissident", with their ring of struggle against the system, implicitly took that system seriously. He preferred the word "parallel", suggesting he lived in a world of his own, not in conflict with the system but just different to it.

"The political climate doesn't affect me," he said. "It's like the sky above me. The sun may shine or it may rain but I am the same."

Underground artists

Boris was a colourful character, who used to wear jodhpurs, high boots and a beret over his long, black ringlets. It was with him and other "parallel" people that I attended the first unofficial Soviet film festival, held in a variety of obscure clubs in Moscow in November 1987.

"This is like the 1970s, when we used to meet for underground rock concerts," he said in a conspiratorial tone, as we congregated at a metro station to be shown the way to a friendly physics institute, where one of the showings was to take place.

On the way, I chatted to one of the organizers, director Igor Aleinikov, who was to die tragically in an air crash in 1994, when the pilot of an Aeroflot flight en route to Hong Kong allowed his children to play with the controls in the cockpit. Back then, Igor was full of promise, making films with his younger brother Gleb.

"The festival's going well," Igor enthused. "We had some problems because various cinemas refused to host it and the city council phoned wanting to know what we were up to. But we have always managed to find a venue."

Arriving at the institute club, we found it already filling up with film fans. The people in the audience – fringe artists united by their contempt for the conventional – were as entertaining to my eye as the movies themselves. They crammed onto benches or sat on the floor and roared their approval of experimental films they could never have seen at the official cinema.

Parallel cinema was not amateur movie-making but attained a professional standard equal to that of the official film industry; it was just that the themes were different.

We watched Yukhananov's *Game in Ho*, ho being both the sound for laughter and the letter X (Kh) in the Cyrillic alphabet, suggestive of a common Russian expletive. The film was about two Jewish friends visiting a series of Moscow apartments and arguing all the way about the plans of one of them to migrate to America. Boris said it was the dilemma of his generation.

The film captured the bohemian atmosphere of Soviet artists' flats, where guests packed themselves round tiny kitchen tables covered with bottles of vodka, half-eaten sausages, ashtrays and cockroaches. Going one better than official "socialist realism", the film also included an erotic scene with actual prostitutes from the National Hotel.

The Aleinikov brothers offered a confronting film called *The Cruel Illness of Men*, which included a homosexual rape scene shot late at night in an empty carriage between stations on the metro to ensure that passengers didn't alert the police. They also showed two comedies mad enough to match Monty Python. In *Tractor*, voices began ponderously describing the agricultural machine glorified in so many Soviet films before speeding up to a satirical frenzy, using more and more absurd and obscene language. A similar technique was used in *Monstrum Exosse*, where squiggles of disgusting-looking plastic mess were described as in a nature documentary.

Underground was fun, of course, because it gave unorthodox Russians the thrill of defying the grown-ups. But in the clear light of day, it became obvious that not all underground artists were equally talented; there was a lot of pretentious rubbish and not too many jewels. Now a wider audience was able to view, listen and judge for themselves.

Oleg Usmanov, the lead singer and double bass player in a 1950s-style band called Mister Twister, became popular, playing rock and roll hits such as "Let's Twist Again" and "Rock Around the Clock", as well as Russian songs. A Yugoslav journalist heard the band and was so impressed that he promoted them on Yugoslav radio and demanded to know why the Soviet Ministry of Culture was ignoring their talent. Soon after, they were given airtime on Soviet state television and toured the country.

Believe it or not but at one time, even jazz was condemned as decadent, let alone rock and roll. In the 1950s, volunteer police would go round slitting the tight trousers of *stilyagi* (teddy boys). During his tour of the Soviet Union, Oleg was thrilled to find some of these old rebels, still alive and rocking. "We met an old *stilyaga* during our visit to Rostov-on-Don," he told me. "He's about 50 now but he's still got his teddy-boy suit and hundreds of rock and roll records. He's young at heart."

Oleg enlivened the Soviet music scene for a while but some Russian rock musicians shot to even more serious stardom. Boris Grebenshchikov of the band Aquarium ended up mixing with the likes of David Bowie, George Harrison, Julian Lennon and Peter Gabriel. When I met Grebenshchikov, or BG as he was affectionately known, in Leningrad in 1987, he was still living in a shabby apartment and was grateful to receive a gift of tea from the West. But it wouldn't be long before his lifestyle changed dramatically. Fans and journalists were continually knocking on his door.

"I had to throw some strangers out physically at four in the morning after my last concert," he said. "I have not slept for three weeks. I have no time to write new songs and I hardly ever see my wife and son. I will have to get a press secretary and a lawyer, like Bowie."

With rock star Boris Grebenshchikov

YOOF

We found them at 3.00 am at the airport terminal, the only place open and serving hot meals. They were quietly eating dumplings and drinking tea. It was hard to believe they were the new menace of Moscow. But their motorbikes were lined up outside and soon they would be zooming off again into the night, scaring careful drivers by riding on the wrong side of the road.

They were the *rokkeri* (rockers), raising hell, defying the police and provoking public complaints. The Moscow press had been full of the antics of this new youth group, which made the Komsomol (Communist Party Youth Movement) look like a knitting circle by comparison.

According to some reports, swarms of up to a hundred bikers had been seen whizzing at 85 mph or more up and down Moscow's wide and, by night, largely deserted avenues. My Spanish colleague Pilar Bonet and I wanted to ride with them, although we hoped to persuade them to go on the right side of the road and at a reasonable speed.

Despite their fearsome reputation, we easily got talking to the *rokkeri* in the canteen and found them surprisingly courteous – apologetic even.

"We know we're a nuisance and the people who complain about us are probably right," said a guy in his early twenties, who introduced himself as Volodya. "But we love going fast on our bikes; we just can't help it."

Volodya was a mechanic, all oily-handed. He said he'd been fooling around with bikes since he was 13 and it looked like he hadn't seen much soap in that time. Other rockers joined the conversation. They said they routinely broke the speed limit; it was no fun otherwise. I knew the police called them "suicides" and that year, 1987, statistics showed there had been 61 accidents involving motorbikes, in which 5 people had been killed and 67 been injured.

Full of dumplings and warmed by the tea, the rockers left the terminal. They were heading off in a convoy of about 10 bikes to their club, a rented garage in the Silver Forest suburb.

"I'm never scared when I ride with Volodya because he doesn't drink like the others," said his girlfriend Lyuda, 17, as she climbed up behind him on his Czechoslovak-built Jawa.

As for me, my heart was in my mouth when another rocker called Anton offered me a seat in his rickety sidecar but he took off at a sedate 40 mph for my benefit and I managed to enjoy the ride. We all made it back to Silver Forest in one piece.

At the garage, where Volodya repaired bikes and prepared them for official motocross competitions, the wreck of a machine belonging to someone called Vlad was being wheeled in. Vlad himself, we learnt, was in hospital, recovering from injuries he'd suffered after riding through a red light and hitting a car. The rockers seemed to regard injury as an occupational hazard. "When I broke my arm recently," said Volodya, "I rested for three days, then rode around wearing the pot."

They cracked open a bottle, turned on some loud Russian rock music and started questioning me eagerly about the life of bikers in the West, as if I was an expert on that subject.

"We don't have the right clothes," complained one called Lyosha. "We can't get the leather gear and boots here." The bikes themselves were also a problem, being scarce and expensive, he said.

"I'm saving up for my own bike," said Lyuda. "I'm sick of riding pillion. I want to ride for myself."

Misha recounted how he'd recently covered the 700-mile route from Moscow to Krasnodar in the south and said altogether he'd clocked up 50,000 miles the previous year.

And so we talked until dawn, when the booze ran out and the rockers either went to work, like Lyuda, who was a shop girl; or went to bed, like vampires retiring to their coffins. They were friendly guys, unlike another gang whose members were gaining notoriety for wearing checked trousers and beating up punks, hippies and other young people influenced by Western trends. Or so the magazine *Ogonyok* alleged.

They were called the "Lyubers" because they came from the satellite town of Lyubertsy, just outside Moscow. A police chief, Major-General Vladimir Goncharov, said the Lyubers were a figment of journalists' imagination but when I went out there, the number of young men walking down the streets in checked trousers testified to the existence of a youth sub-culture of some sort.

I approached one teenager, who said his name was Pasha and he was 16. He proudly acknowledged he was a Lyuber and led me through a maze of backyards to a metal door painted with the figure of a body-builder and the word Malysh (infant). "Come this way," he said. "The trainer and the older guys are working out now."

Behind the door, narrow steps led down to a network of cellars, which had been converted into a weight-training club. Misha, Semyon, Sergei and other youths aged between 16 and 22 were lifting dumb-bells in time to the music of the Russian rock group, Mashina Vremeni (Time Machine).

Misha, the oldest, was the instructor. He was a member of the Komsomol and had just come out of the army, having finished his military service. He said the club had been founded illegally 10 years earlier but he was putting it on a proper footing by getting it registered with the local authorities. He proudly showed me nine little rooms, fitted out with all kinds of weight-training equipment that the members had paid for themselves.

The old Soviet authorities didn't like young men who did body-building or martial arts outside the context of the army because it was thought they might pose a threat to the regime, but it seemed that Mr Gorbachev's reforms were benefitting not only cultural but also sporting types.

Misha said about 20 youths trained regularly at the club while others, less committed, drifted in and out. Five similar clubs were functioning in Lyubertsy, which made the town quite a mecca for body-building.

Misha objected to the *Ogonyok* article, saying it gave a false impression that youths from Lyubertsy were violent. "Our group is only interested in sport; in making the male body strong and beautiful. We do not go into Moscow to beat up punks and hippies, although we don't like them." But he said the club couldn't control youths who had latched onto the culture surrounding body-building and did travel by the *elektrichka* (suburban train) into Moscow, sometimes getting into fights with other gangs in the capital's cafés and discos.

One such youth might have been Igor, who I spotted in the local department store with his tartan-clad girlfriend, Sveta. She was helping him to choose checked material for a new pair of trousers.

"I'm into sport – boxing, athletics and other kinds. Sure, we go to Moscow," he said with a leer. I asked him why the Lyubers picked on punks and hippies. "So they don't insist on their rights," was his reply.

There was certainly something of a problem because in April 1987, a group of about 500 people demonstrated in Moscow against what they called the violent behaviour of the Lyubers, and school authorities even warned parents to keep their kids at home at weekends to avoid gang fights.

But the youths at Malysh said they were only "upholding the Soviet way of life" and for them that meant clean living, hard work, loyalty to Russian rather than Western rock groups, and alcohol only on special occasions.

Semyon, 18, who was going into the army, said 18 months of body-building had given him self-confidence and dignity as well as the rippling arm muscles which he cheerfully flexed. "I am preparing myself so it will be easier to do my military service." He added that he supported Gorbachev "because he is attacking drunks and parasites who will not work". Probably the effects of Gorbachev's *glasnost* on the cultural sphere would have appealed to him less.

Some journalists sought to explain the mystery of the Lyubers by suggesting they might be organised by elements opposed to the liberalisation going on in society. One Moscow artist told me that two busloads of Lyubers had been taken to an exhibition of avant-garde paintings that had been previously banned. Apparently the Lyubers had been told to scrawl negative comments in the exhibition visitors' book. It was the kind of dirty trick that, years later, the pro-Putin youth group Nashi would play on Kremlin opponents.

The young men at Malysh said they knew nothing about that. Their philosophy was "live and let live".

Riding with the rockers, with Spanish colleague Pilar Bonet

AFGHANISTAN

Costya and all the other Russian men of my acquaintance did everything they could to avoid military service. When I was sent to Afghanistan in 1988, they joked that I was doing their military service for them. In fact, I was one of the first Western journalists to see the war from the Soviet positions. For most of the decade that Afghanistan was occupied by Soviet troops (1979–1989), Western reporters could only get access to the country by going in over the mountains from Pakistan with the Mujahideen. But when Mikhail Gorbachev decided to withdraw Soviet forces, Western correspondents were able to see Afghanistan for the first time alongside the Russians, and through their eyes.

I made two trips to Afghanistan. The first was a kind of recce. In April 1988, the Soviet Foreign Ministry (MID) invited a small group of Moscow-based correspondents to go the capital, Kabul, which was safely in Soviet hands. We were shown barracks and I particularly remember the empty beds, with black ribbons laid across the top blankets, in memory of those who would not be going home to their families. We also went to Mikrorayon, the officers' suburb, which was built like all the grey housing estates across the Soviet Union. It was here I heard a tale about bored Russian housewives, who had disguised themselves in burqas to go shopping at the bazaar. The story had it that their white hands and feet, protruding from the burqas, had given them away and they were lynched by a mob. But I couldn't confirm the facts and working for Reuters, of course I never reported urban myths and rumours.

It seemed that both my employers and MID were satisfied with this first, exploratory trip to Kabul because in May 1988, I was asked to go again. Our small group stayed in luxury at the Intercontinental Hotel, or Inter-Con, as we called it. There was a press conference with the commander of Soviet forces, General Boris Gromov, after which I passed the time walking in the city. I remember seeing a Russian tank, or personnel carrier (APC), stuck in the river, surrounded by jeering Afghan kids. I also had quite a frightening experience in a back alley when I suddenly found myself being followed and surrounded by a crowd of curious children. I don't suppose they would have done me any harm but a local intervened to shoo them off.

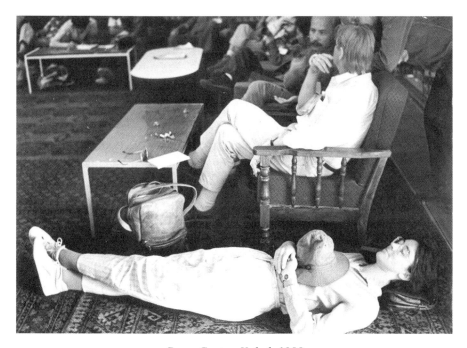

Press Centre, Kabul, 1988

A few days into the second visit, I was approached by my MID minder and told there was a chance to ride in the first convoy to be leaving Afghanistan. The word "embedded" was not fashionable in those days but the Russians were offering journalists from a range of countries and of course the main news agencies the chance to ride with their forces. The convoy was to leave from Jalalabad in the east. MID warned us that outside the capital, they would be powerless to protect us. If we chose to go on the journey, we would have to be ready for possible battle conditions because the

Mujahideen had not accepted a ceasefire and might shoot at us.

I consulted my editors in London and of course they wanted coverage but they didn't put any pressure on me. They assured me my career would not suffer if I preferred to stay in the relative safety of Kabul. I thought about it. I was newly married to Costya and he had been against me going to Kabul, let alone Jalalabad. For myself, I was afraid and excited in equal measure. I was in my early thirties, with enough experience not to do anything too silly but with the confidence and energy of a person still in youth. I said "yes" and then to my disappointment, the Russian army said "*nyet*".

The chosen journalists, who included four women, were all assembled on the tarmac at Kabul airport, waiting for the military flight to Jalalabad. The Russian officer in charge took one look at our group and said, "I'm not taking those women." We girls protested, saying we had a job to do. I was rather more vocal than the other women, who came from Germany, Sweden and Spain. I remember arguing that if women could give birth, they could go to war, and feeling rather foolish after I'd said it.

"Get on that plane then," commanded the officer.

"Now what have we got ourselves into?" the four of us whispered. A part of me had been secretly hoping to avoid this test of courage.

The plane took off, shooting out flares to deflect the Mujahideen's heat-seeking Stinger missiles. The women didn't sit together in a sisterly group but mixed with the men. I found myself sitting next to Marco Politi of Italy's *Il Messaggero* newspaper. He took my hand.

"I'm sorry; it's a bit sweaty," I said.

He laughed, and that sealed our friendship.

The night air was full of the scent of flowers and the stars twinkled benevolently, or so it seemed to my heightened senses, when we landed in Jalalabad. We went straight into a press conference at our hotel. Nearby, we could hear the sound of desultory shelling. In Moscow, Costya read the wire reports in the Reuter office and worried on my behalf.

I spent the night in a small room shared with the Swedish woman and some other Scandinavian colleagues. They offered me whisky to calm my nerves but I preferred fear and a clear head. Before dawn, I stood under a trickle of water from the rusty shower. Outside, I could hear what sounded like the chirp of frogs and the early call of the *muezzin*. I remember soaping my legs and wondering in a strangely detached way whether I would still have them the next day.

We attended a dawn ceremony on the parade ground at which the Soviet soldiers were congratulated by their officers for having "fulfilled their international duty". Then we were taken to the convoy of tanks and APCs and allotted our vehicles. Marco and I were put on an APC manned by pro-Soviet Afghan soldiers, who spoke no English and little Russian. We had hoped to be with Soviet boys, with whom we could have spoken Russian. I can't say whether there was a deliberate policy to limit Western journalists' communication with the conscripts or whether this just happened in our case.

We were told that the road ahead, running through the mountains to Kabul, was mined and that there might also be snipers along the way. We could choose to sit inside the APC or on top of it. Inside, we would be safe from snipers but goners for sure if we ran over a mine. On top, we could perhaps roll to safety from a mine blast but would be easy targets for the snipers. We preferred the fresh air of sitting on top.

Crowds of Afghans gathered by the roadside to wave goodbye to the convoy and they threw bouquets of flowers at the departing troops. Among the flowers were other small gifts. As we set off, I was hit in the mouth by a piece of dried camel dung. I was lucky it wasn't a nail. In my case, nothing worse was to happen in the pullout from Afghanistan and it turned into a wonderful adventure, one of the highlights of my life.

Withdrawal from Afghanistan, 1988

The ride, through spectacular mountain scenery, was exhilarating. Occasionally, the Mujahideen did shoot at us but they were in the distance and every time their little puffs of gun smoke came from the mountainsides, Soviet helicopter gunships clattered up, like giant locusts, to protect the convoy. We relaxed. The movement of the APC was gentle – "like a gondola", said Marco – and at one point, we even fell asleep. When we woke, the Afghan soldiers offered us packed lunches of flat bread and hard boiled eggs, washed down with water. Water…

Suddenly I understood why the Russian officer at Kabul airport hadn't wanted to take women on the trip. It had nothing to do with sexism; it was purely a practical consideration on his part. The men, you see, could urinate whenever they wanted over the sides of the moving vehicles. But under Mujahideen fire, the convoy wasn't making any comfort stops for the ladies. I crossed my legs and tried to visualise arid landscapes. All my previous thoughts of mortality were driven away by this desperation.

And then, for some reason, the whole convoy ground to a halt. I think one of the vehicles ahead of us must have broken down. I seized my chance, jumped down from the APC and hurried behind a rock. I prayed the convoy wouldn't start up again, leaving me with my knickers down in Mujahideen-held territory. Fortunately, it didn't.

In their history of the war in Afghanistan *Vtorzhenie* (Invasion), the Russian authors D. Gai and V. Snegirev seem to refer to me when they remember the trip from Jalalabad. It's interesting to see how memory works and how we interpret things from our different points of view.

"Heat, dust, exhaust fumes," writes Gai. "In our convoy, just a little way ahead, Afghan tanks and personnel carriers were moving. On one of them, a Western lady journalist was sitting – either an Englishwoman or a Swede, relatively young, dark-haired, speaking Russian with a dreadful accent, energetic and elbowing her way through everywhere, as we say. On the eve, she had literally begged our representatives to allow her to make the journey from Jalalabad to Kabul. She said she was writing a book about Afghanistan and wanted to be able to add her personal impressions. All attempts to dissuade her and arguments about the dangers and difficulties of the 150-km way were in vain. The stubborn reporter got her way, although for some reason she sat not on a Soviet but on an Afghan personnel carrier – perhaps it had something to do with her notion of ethics?

"Now she's having a really bad time. The convoy has stopped because of the latest block. Taking advantage of the pause in our movement, Afghan soldiers are carrying her in their arms to a spring of water bubbling from the mountainside and letting her drink and wash herself. This revives her, the Englishwoman or Swede, and she cheers up and with determination gets back up on the personnel carrier. Good for her. We quietly envy her: how nice it would be to get down now and have a drink and a wash at the spring. But we haven't received an order and without an order we're categorically forbidden to leave the vehicles."

The rest of the ride to Kabul was uneventful, at least for me. Not far from the city, in a place where the Soviet officers evidently felt safe, soldiers and journalists alike were allowed to dismount from the convoy and go swimming together in the river. We arrived in Kabul by evening.

I don't know where the soldiers went then but the journalists and officers ate dinner, served by busty Ukrainian waitresses, and we hacks retired to our hotel.

The next day, the soldiers who had done their "international duty" had to listen to more tedious speeches from the top brass at another Soviet farewell ceremony, this time on the much bigger parade ground in Kabul. We journalists stood to the side and at quite a distance from the men, who were lined up with their vehicles.

One young man on top of an APC cheekily caught my eye and threw a bouquet of flowers in my direction. He must have been nearly the length of a cricket pitch away from me. Normally I am clumsy, myopic and hopeless at sport but because of lack of sleep and the joy of still being alive, I was in such a state of flow that I stretched out my right arm and caught the bouquet in one hand, like an ace cricketer. The convoy erupted in applause. It was a moment with a poster-like quality – the returning soldier and the girl, a symbol of life and hope.

After that, the convoy left to trundle on for a further four days, up through the Salang Pass to the border with Soviet Uzbekistan. MID did not waste the journalists' time with this monotonous journey. Instead, we were fast-tracked up to Mazar-i-Sharif, where we saw the blue-tiled shrine of Hazrat Ali. I remember the disturbing experience of trying to interview some burqa-clad Afghan women, who peered out at me through the little cloth grilles covering their eyes.

Then we were flown by military plane to Termez in Uzbekistan to prepare the welcoming party for the troops. As on the first plane to Jalalabad, we sat in two long rows, facing each other while hanging onto overhead wires for support. The central gangway was filled, floor to ceiling, with red paper flags for the arrival ceremony. I felt we were in a flying wastepaper basket, highly inflammable.

A Soviet officer opposite me lit a cigarette. I had been quite brave up to this point but now all my adrenaline had run out and I was my real, cowardly self. I started to cry.

"Please put that cigarette out," I said.

Fortunately, without any display of machismo, he did.

"Thank goodness you said that," whispered an Afghan officer sitting next to me. Evidently, he had been too afraid to say to his superior what many of us had been thinking. We landed safely.

With our load of red flags, we were ready to cheer when the convoy finally rumbled across the bridge over the Amu-Dar'ya River. In Termez, the local Uzbek women had prepared a huge open-air feast of *plov* and water melon.

Unfortunately, I couldn't sit around enjoying it for long because I had a story to file. Magic happened to me throughout my time in Afghanistan and it didn't desert me at that crucial moment. I had a two-kopeck coin in my pocket. I found a public telephone box. I knew the Reuter Moscow bureau would be closed at that hour, so I rang the photographer at home and got him out of bed. I dialled the number once and got straight through to break the news that the first Soviet soldiers had come out of Afghanistan.

I didn't think then how the withdrawal from Afghanistan would lead indirectly to the break-up of the Soviet Union; how years later Western forces would be fighting the Afghan warlords they had financed and supported. Like the ordinary Russian soldiers, I was just grateful I had survived and glad to be going home.

FIRST IMPRESSIONS OF ENGLAND

In 1988, Costya and I moved to London. We settled in Hackney and while I started a new job at *The Independent*, he went to college to improve his English. You could still surprise Londoners by being Russian in those days and the newspaper was keen to publish Costya's first impressions of England:

The first thing that struck me as I peered from the window of the airplane at Heathrow was the number of cars snaking along to the airport and parked in rows. I realized that to live as an Englishman, I had to get a car. My wife and I had saved money while we lived in Moscow, so we went to buy one.

"Certainly, Sir. That will be six thousand pounds. You can have it on Thursday," said the smooth-faced salesman. It was as simple as that. A rival salesman had tried to seduce me into buying another make by offering me a free, talking alarm clock.

My friends at home would have wept to see those showrooms and the garages, stocked to the roof with spare parts. In the Soviet Union, you wait about three years to buy a new Lada and spare parts are almost impossible to obtain except on the black market. The choice and ease of everyday life in the West delights me. But at the same time, I feel Britain is very decadent. Soon this country could become a huge rubbish heap. The future belongs to empty, undeveloped places like Siberia, where I used to go logging.

We put learner plates on the car and set off to tour Yorkshire. It's beautiful in the north but we have settled in

44

London where I hear people in the shops speaking worse English than me and I do not feel alien. Yorkshire people are friendly but they don't know much about Russia. When a shop assistant in Scarborough asked how to spell my surname, I said, "Gagarin, you know, like the spaceman."

"Sorry, love, I don't watch the news," she said.

We drove all over the Yorkshire moors, spotting grouse and rabbits. The rabbits are something new for me because in Russia, they only exist as domestic animals. We have wild hamsters instead.

It was good to experience the countryside with my wife who, as a foreigner, was restricted from travelling to wild places with me in the Soviet Union. But the English countryside is somehow disappointing. I am surprised that commercialisation has spread, even to remote villages. Whatever is picturesque is turned to commercial advantage. Also, there seem to be a lot of private forests and you can never go far without meeting somebody; when I went on holiday in Russia, I could walk for days in the forest without seeing a soul.

But I like the freedom. Nobody has asked me to show my documents here, not even when I went to hire a bicycle in Thornton Dale. I just paid a £10 deposit, with no proof of identity, and rode away over the Yorkshire Wolds. The rule seems to be that if you have money, you can have what you want. For this reason, I think the West demands more self-discipline than the Soviet Union.

One Western experience I will not choose to repeat is going to a rock concert. I was shocked to see how the fans at a Pink Floyd concert in Manchester mindlessly idolised the group and how the event was so stage-managed and phoney.

Now I have the chance to read Solzhenitsyn legally for the first time but I have not yet done so. I am reading less than I did in Russia and getting a little fatter because I am going to pubs in the evenings and coming home with my favourite Indian

45

takeaways to watch television horror movies such as The Fly. Many of them are silly but they amuse me because such films do not exist in the Soviet Union.

Pubs, of course, are fantastic, representing a whole culture that has no Soviet equivalent. After sampling a few brews at the Leeds Beer Festival, where I won a bottle of stout for throwing a rubber ring over a dummy of Mrs Thatcher, I decided Theakston's Old Peculier was best.

In a pub near Harrogate, a friendly man called Rick taught me how to play darts but really I am more addicted to fruit machines. My wife said I was spending too much on gambling, so we went out and bought a home computer as a more long-term investment and now I want to explore the world of computers.

One thing impressed me – that in a provincial city like York, we were able to buy not only a computer but also a special program so that I can write in Russian on it. The difference between the standards of living in Moscow and the Soviet provinces is vast; town and country seem to enjoy more equal facilities in England.

The computer was paid for with one from my baffling new collection of plastic cards, which give me access to our joint bank account. Does this make me a yuppy? I still do not fully understand this word. Money fascinates me because you spend it differently in the West from the way we do in the Soviet Union. It is strange to me, for example, that a pair of jeans costs only £20 here compared with at least 100 roubles (£100) in Russia. On the other hand, we pay £650 a month rent for a terraced house in Battersea. I do not know how I will explain this to my friends in Russia, who pay 10 to 20 roubles a month for their state accommodation. I also wonder how I will convince my stubborn Uncle Ernst in Leningrad that I do not need a propiska (residence permit) to live in London.

Since I believe that life depends essentially on inner

development rather than the environment, I think I can be as happy here as I was there. One thing does hurt me, though. It seems that relations between people are cooler in the West than in Russia, where our poorer standard of living means we have to look after each other more. Could I, for example, turn up late at night, uninvited, at an Englishman's house and sit at the kitchen table, nibbling whatever food happened to be available and talking until dawn?

Costya in a pub in Edinburgh

PART TWO

BREAKING UP

1989

The thaw in Moscow made possible an extraordinary political spring across Eastern Europe. In 1989, like icebergs breaking away from the ice shelf, the countries of what had been the Warsaw Pact slipped one by one from the grip of the Soviet Union and floated off towards their own independent futures. Poland had already been going its own way with the Solidarity trade union. Now the Berlin Wall fell and Czechoslovakia celebrated its Velvet Revolution. It was mostly a peaceful process. The exception was Romania, which invaded our living rooms on Christmas Day that year.

I was at home with the family in Yorkshire. We switched on the TV and heard the news that Nicolae and Elena Ceauşescu had been tried by a military court in Bucharest, put up against a wall and shot. The Securitate, Ceaucescu's vicious secret police, were sniping from the sewers and gun battles were going on at the airport.

"I hope to goodness you don't have to go to Bucharest," my father said.

"I'll probably have to," I replied. I'd recently joined *The Independent* as one of their specialists on Eastern Europe, so Romania was my patch. But I was still at home on Boxing Day to enjoy my mother's mince pies.

A day or two later, a call did come from the office and I flew to Budapest, from where I took a train to Bucharest. To be honest, I was frightened. It was good not to have to fly straight in to what might still be a battle but to have a slower entry into the country, enabling me to judge the situation somewhat through the train window. By the time I arrived, the shooting had mercifully stopped. Other colleagues had been heroic; I was mopping up.

The editors now wanted the human interest stories – the accounts of poor Romanians queuing for their ration of chickens' feet; the shocking revelations coming out of the country's orphanages. The West had called Ceauşescu the "maverick of the East bloc", implying some independence from Moscow, but it turned out, in its autonomy, the Romanian regime had been the most brutal.

Having been in Moscow, where *perestroika* was in full swing, I was used to dealing with confident, talkative Russians. It came as a shock to see how cowed and fearful the Romanians were. In addition, there was the language barrier. Luckily, I found a family of ethnic Germans who took me under their wing. The eldest daughter and her brother helped with contacts and showed me round Bucharest, speaking to me in German. The girl gave me a gift of a hand-knitted dress. Some months afterwards the family moved to Germany, which was the dream of most ethnic Germans in Romania at that time.

I went out news gathering each day – demonstrations, student meetings and the like – and in the evening filed a report to London. All foreign journalists had to share one telex machine and there was always a long queue to use it. Mindful of the queue, I typed as fast as I could, barely noticing that there was no key cap over the letter T, just a metal spike. The letter T crops up rather often in texts. By the time I'd finished typing, my left index finger was ripped to shreds and bleeding – an occupational hazard of covering revolutions.

The highlight of the trip to Bucharest was gaining access to Ceauşescu's residence. This was not the giant, ugly House of the Republic but a smaller villa where he actually lived. Guides told us he had 365 pairs of curtains – a set for every day of the year. And for his wife, Elena, fresh orchids were flown in regularly from Singapore because she despised humbler flowers such as roses or daffodils.

What struck me most was the juxtaposition of priceless items, such as Ming dynasty vases, with cheap plastic souvenirs. I particularly remember a tasteless toy hedgehog on Ceauşescu's desk.

At one point, I realised the guides had gone on ahead, leaving me alone in the bedroom of the dictator's daughter, Zoia. In her wardrobe, I saw rows of silk shirts and bell-bottomed trousers. I rifled through her drawers, finding letters, contraceptive pills and another hedgehog. The temptation to pocket the hedgehog was almost overwhelming but I resisted, which was lucky because we were searched by revolutionary guards on the way out.

On the editorial desk in London, the appetite for stories about the excesses of the Ceaușescus was almost as insatiable as the greed of the dictator and his wife. We published the menu for Elena's 70th birthday party, the year before the revolution.

The litany of gluttony read: "Caviar, black, Manchurian and carp; Swiss cheese, cream cheese, salami, ham, salted fish, turkey breast, paprika with sweet cheese and dill, tomato and aubergine salad, wild mushrooms, meat in aspic, vegetable rolls, roast beef, butter and lemons". And those were just the hors d'oeuvres. The roasts were "turkey, venison, pork and beef with chips, mashed potatoes, quince puree, sauerkraut, apples, beans, carrots, peas and cauliflower". And for dessert, there was "birthday cake, fruit roulade, fruit cake, melted-sugar cake, ice cream and nuts and fruits of all kinds".

When we'd finished exposing the "king and queen", we dug dirt on the rest of the "royal" family, with the help of the newly freed Romanian press, which was having a field day. Son Nicu, who as Minister for Youth had been responsible for giving young Romanians an utterly deprived and fun-free start to life, was revealed as a con man who had graduated as a pilot without being able to fly. The local papers also published a letter from Ceaușescu's sister-in-law, who'd tried to hide from the revolutionaries in a peasant's cottage, in which she revealed in ungrammatical Romanian where she'd stashed her money.

Almost more than their decadence, the Ceaușescus' ignorance and lack of culture seemed to outrage ordinary Romanians. They said the surviving clan members should be made to pick at the packed ice on the pavements with their fingernails, or worse, join the food queues with everyone else.

The vulgar palaces and hunting lodges of the Ceaușescus were there for all to see but as for the stories about them, it became difficult to know where fact turned into fairy tale. One story doing the rounds – and sourced to a doctor – said Nicolae Ceaușescu had had transfusions of children's blood in a vain attempt to stay young. It sounded like some Translyvanian vampire fantasy but he did brainwash orphans to become his bodyguards, ban all research on AIDS with the result that a frightening number of cases of the disease were coming to light, and deprive the elderly of the right to medical treatment.

The people had been terrified of him but in private they had laughed. The Romanian jokes I heard weren't as achingly funny as Russian anecdotes but it was good to know these downtrodden folk had not had their sense of humour completely erased.

Teacher: "Tell me the blessings of socialist man."

Pupil: "He has food, drink, clothes, anything he wants."

Teacher: "Very good. Nine out of ten."

Pupil: "If you give me ten out of ten, I will tell you *who* this man is."

I must say I enjoyed my assignment to Bucharest. Indeed, I was having the time of my life when word came through from London that Andreas Whittam Smith, co-founder and editor of *The Independent*, was so transfixed by the Romanian story that he was coming out to Bucharest to see things for himself. This is the last thing a working journalist usually needs – a "state visit" by the editor, who gets in the way and requires entertaining.

But the boss was great; he mucked in and worked with me. Together, we got an interview with Silviu Brucan, a Gorbachev-style reforming Communist who briefly took over until the Communist Party itself was outlawed. Mr Brucan said the interim government had found "100 per cent chaos" after the fall of Ceauşescu. The dictator had not only doctored the weather forecasts so as not to have to switch on the heating in the apartment blocks but he had also left false economic statistics, leading Romanians to believe they had substantial grain supplies when in fact the cupboard was almost bare.

Romania would continue to be interesting for a long time but my stint there was a short interlude. By 1990, I would be back in Moscow, where I'd stay for the next decade. The East bloc satellites had spun off into their own space. The collapsing Soviet Union remained the big story.

CHERNOBYL

As a young journalist, I was good at talking to people but not always sharp enough at judging the significance of news. I had been on duty in the Reuter office in Moscow on 26 April 1986 when radiation was detected over Sweden. Big deal, I'd thought, and done nothing about it. That was a serious mistake because I'd managed to miss the world's worst nuclear accident, unfolding at Chernobyl in Ukraine. Other news agencies had got onto the story before us – something that Reuters didn't like.

In my defence, others had missed it too. My colleague Tony Barber had been in the Ukrainian capital of Kiev when the explosion occurred but he'd only found about it on his return to Moscow a few days later. By then, we'd all learnt about Chernobyl and its dangers, so Tony had gone off to get tested for radiation at the American embassy. The test had revealed a patch of radiation on the seat of his trousers because he'd been sitting on a park bench at the time of the blast.

Gorbachev's lack of *glasnost* had really been to blame, of course. He'd allowed openness about Stalin's repressions and all sorts of other controversial subjects but had played for time and hidden from the people of Kiev the minor detail that clouds of radiation were filling the air when they were marching in their May Day parades, four whole days after the accident.

"Naturally, we can regret, today, after the fact, that we did not grasp everything more quickly," Gorbachev was to say later.

We'd all been slow to cotton on but we found ourselves living with the fallout from Chernobyl for years afterwards and the consequences of the disaster inevitably became a theme of my reporting.

In September 1989, when I was on the desk at *The Independent* in London, I made a short trip to the Soviet Union to meet a scientist who had some extraordinary photographs. His name was Vladimir Shevchenko and he was head of the Laboratory of Ecological Genetics at Moscow's Vavilov Institute of General Genetics. He had just been on an expedition to the closed zone around Chernobyl. His photos showed that the area was beginning to reap a disturbing harvest from the nuclear fallout, as monster trees were springing up there.

As a scientist, Dr Shevchenko was cautious and meticulous, anxious to avoid creating a scare. He stressed that only certain plants and trees growing very close to the power station had suffered; that the mutations were mostly "one-off injuries" to existing trees and wouldn't be passed on genetically; that no hasty conclusions should be drawn about animal and human life. But still his pictures were shocking.

The area immediately around the destroyed fourth reactor had been cleaned up but several plots of land in the zone had been left "dirty" so scientists could observe the long-term effects of radiation. In these plots, Dr Shevchenko and his colleagues found wild raspberries and strawberries with pale or patchy leaves owing to chlorophyll loss, dwarf plants, firs that had thickened and grown darker, pines whose needles had twisted, baby oaks with misshapen leaves up to eight inches long, and mountain ash whose finger-thin leaves had swollen and grown bulbous.

Dr Shevchenko took seeds from the small plants and tried to grow them in his greenhouse in Moscow. He discovered the next generation of seedlings also had the chlorophyll deficiency and many of them shrivelled and died. But the other phenomena were temporary and shouldn't blight the species in future, he said.

The giant leaves, for example, were the result of radio-stimulation. The thickening and darkening of the fir foliage was a defence mechanism. In nature, fir trees do grow bushier where conditions are harsh.

He had one particularly impressive picture of a pine sprouting a candelabrum of grossly enlarged branches. Many of its neighbours had simply died, he said, for the pine is the most sensitive of trees. It is as vulnerable as a human being to high doses of radiation, and 1,000 roentgen will kill it.

By contrast the oak, even when young, is pretty sturdy but its leaves, normally crisply cut in a symmetrical pattern, lose their shape and grow round as a result of radiation. "See here," said Dr Shevchenko. "The fine line of nature has been broken."

He hadn't published his photographs anywhere, not even in the Soviet scientific press. I persuaded him to give them to *The Independent*. We published them exclusively and my success in getting this scoop helped me to secure a posting as a correspondent for the paper in Moscow.

"Time to pack up; we're going back to Moscow," I told Costya, who initially wasn't too pleased to be leaving London. But he quickly adapted and in no time we were back in the USSR.

One of my first assignments then was to go to Byelorussia, which if anything had been even more badly affected than Ukraine by Chernobyl because the clouds of radiation had drifted on the wind in a northerly direction. In April 1990, in the city of Gomel, I saw not trees but children poisoned by radiation.

Dr Stanislav Zdota, deputy director of Gomel regional hospital, took me to see his young leukemia patients – Dima, aged 8, with bloated face, trying not to cry; Olya, 5, thin and pale; Sveta, 10, staring at the ceiling. The wards were full of these poor children. Was there a definite link between their illnesses and the Chernobyl accident? "There's no proof, there's no proof, but we have our intuition," said Dr Zdota, and he heaved a huge sigh.

Before Chernobyl, Gomel was famous for two things – producing tooth powder and raising former Soviet Foreign Minister Andrei Gromyko, known to the world as Mr Nyet because he nixed the West's initiatives. The city was pleasant enough, with pear trees in blossom and chickens scratching in the lanes between the wooden houses of the old town. But I had never seen a sadder place.

"Does it smell of radiation?" a young man called out to a girl, sniffing a flower on Lily Lane.

At the market, people too poor to afford uncontaminated tomatoes from Azerbaijan picked through the day's remaining local wares – seeds for sowing in irradiated allotments, and plastic garlands for tombstones.

It was hard to believe that Gomel had once been a tourist destination, popular with Poles from over the border. In 1990, it had few visitors.

Locals discovering that I was staying at the hotel brought me flowers and chocolates. "Come again; please come again," they begged.

Apart from the high-rise suburb of Valatava, which was contaminated, Gomel itself was said to be relatively free of radiation. "Only five curies per square kilometer – we're supposed to be grateful for that," said Dr Zdota, sneering at the "acceptable norms" of pollution set in Moscow.

Beyond the city, the countryside was peppered with "dirty spots" – Bragin, Khoiniki, Dobrysh, Vetka, Chechersk – right up to Mogilev in the north and across the republican borders to Zhitomir in Ukraine and Bryansk in Russia. All these areas lay outside the 18-mile exclusion zone, which was drawn with a pair of compasses around Chernobyl, as if radiation fell in a perfect circle. People living in the zone itself were evacuated. Pripyat, the dormitory for the power station workers, was a ghost town, its flats having been abandoned in various states of disorder as people had rushed to safety. But the irradiated villages of Byelorussia were still inhabited and agriculture continued there.

The government of Byelorussia said at the time the health of a fifth of its population was jeopardized and over 100,000 people should be evacuated urgently. In Ukraine, the Green leader, Yuri Cherbak, said altogether four million people were living with radiation; and 85 villages in Byelorussia, 19 in Ukraine and 14 in Russia should be evacuated without delay.

In Moscow, the authorities were not entirely idle. An order went out that luxurious sanatoria used by the bureaucrats of the *nomenklatura* should be made available to Chernobyl victims. But the Kremlin was treating Chernobyl as a rather bad industrial accident rather than a catastrophe on a global scale. The truth was, it didn't have the funds to evacuate so many people.

And ordinary citizens didn't want to be evacuated either. The ones I spoke to said Byelorussia was their home, however unsafe, and they preferred to stay. What they did want was reliable food supplies.

In a sausage shop in Gomel, a woman started to shout when she was shown a certificate from the supplier, guaranteeing the salami was free of radiation. "How can I trust that?" she demanded. "There should be a Geiger counter here so I can measure for myself but the government doesn't produce them because they are not profitable."

People also wanted regular medical checks and medicines and equipment to save both adults and children, who were falling ill with increasing frequency.

The immediate death toll from the Chernobyl blast had been a mere 31, mostly firemen, and a further 200 had suffered acute radiation sickness at the time. But Mr Cherbak said 1.5 million Soviet citizens, including 160,000 children, received a significant dose of radiation to the thyroid gland, and cases of nuclear-related cancer were expected to explode. The total number of people in and beyond the Soviet Union who have died over the years as a direct result of Chernobyl will probably never be known.

The only thing that could help the sick was sophisticated diagnostic equipment, available from the West for hard currency. They also needed medicines that would give the sick at least an even chance of survival – 50 per cent of leukemia patients should, in theory, achieve a five-year remission, the doctors said.

Dima needed a bone marrow transplant, beyond the possibilities of Soviet medicine. But luckily this boy, who wanted to be a mathematician, had been picked to go with a small group to Israel in the summer of 1990 – if he survived that long.

"It's a solution for one individual," said his doctor, Tatyana Chernoshei.

Little Olya, who came from the Urals but had happened to be visiting her grandmother in Gomel at the time of the accident, had an equally poor prognosis and no foreign trip in sight. Her ward was spotlessly clean; her nurses could not have been kinder. But there was nothing else they could do for her.

This was not to mention the poor prospects for adults with leukemia, who took second place. "We give everything to the children," said Dr Chernoshei. "This means depriving adults who should also have a chance to fight for their lives."

Charities were virtually non-existent in the Soviet Union, since the state was supposed to provide everything, and Gomel looked with more hope for foreigners to help them than local organisations.

"Go and write your article," said Dr Zdota. "Let the English know there is such a place as Gomel." I did, and I don't know if anybody read it. But I discovered an interesting thing when I bought a house in the small seaside town of Filey on the North Yorkshire coast in 2002. Apparently, for years a former nurse called Lillian Whitely and her husband Brian had been holding fund-raising suppers in the local Chinese restaurant and using the money to send lorry loads of medical supplies to Byelorussia. And on the beach at Filey each summer, you could see pale Byelorussian children, playing on the windswept, eight-mile sands.

WHAT ABOUT THE WORKERS?

Gorbachev was still in power and the Soviet Union still intact when Costya and I returned to Moscow in 1990, but the atmosphere had changed in the time we'd been away and it was like coming home to a different country. The joy of the early *perestroika* period, when everything opened up and Russians revelled in new possibilities, had been replaced by a pervading sense of discontent.

Some citizens were unhappy that Gorbachev had gone too far with his reforms, such as those who found the withdrawal from Afghanistan a national humiliation. Others thought he wasn't going far enough, for example the people in the Baltic States, who wanted total independence. Everyone grumbled at the lack of improvement in their basic living conditions. In the populist Boris Yeltsin, who rode on public transport and made lightning visits to shops to check the food queues, Gorbachev had an emerging rival.

The problem was that Gorbachev had done nothing about the economy. He hoped to make Communism work better when what was needed was a move to the free market.

It's a truism that China succeeded by quietly restructuring its economy behind the façade of an unchanged political system. Gorbachev did the opposite. He delayed economic reform and gave people political freedom first. He tore down the red curtains of Communism to reveal the economic disaster behind. The result was that people saw the mess and complained about all the things the command economy was failing to provide.

Some of the bitterest complaints came from coal miners in the Arctic, Siberia and Ukraine. They saw on television lively debates coming from the All-Union Congress of People's Deputies (parliament), whose members included the dissident physicist Andrei Sakharov, freed from internal exile in 1989. The debates might have excited Muscovites, who walked around with radios pressed to their ears to hear the latest arguments, but this great talking shop cut no ice with the miners, who didn't even have any soap to get washed with at the end of their shift.

In the summer of 1989, there was a wave of miners' strikes from Vorkuta in the Arctic to the Siberian Kuzbas and the Ukrainian Donbas. Past Soviet leaders would have used force against strikers but Gorbachev tried to meet their demands. In a historic decision, he recognised their right to strike, acknowledging as nonsense the Soviet notion that workers in a workers' state would never go on strike against themselves.

But other promises were broken and it wasn't long before the miners were forming their own independent trade union, going on strike again and calling for Gorbachev's resignation.

It was during this second wave of industrial unrest that I went to Donetsk in Ukraine to see for myself how the miners of the Donbas lived.

Their working lives were hell, of course, and not unreasonably they expected some earthly reward for their toils. But when the miners finished their shifts, they returned home to two-room cottages without indoor toilets or running hot water; to tables laid with the meagre fruits of their wives' queuing. Vodka, pigeons and choral singing were their comforts in a hard, dangerous life that made me think of Wales or south Yorkshire half a century earlier.

During my visit, the miners voted for a mass departure from the Communist Party, declaring it could no longer claim to be the champion of the working class. They were angry that little had changed since their dispute in 1989, except that they had started to get free soap at the pithead bathhouse.

"Soap doesn't solve our problems," growled miner Nikolai Bobrakov, pushing aside a plate of slops dished out to him for 20 kopecks (20 pence) in the canteen at the Sixth Capital mine. "When my father was a miner, he could buy a Pobeda (Victory, type of saloon car) with his wages. I can barely feed my family."

This wasn't so much because of low pay as because of the general state of the economy. Soviet miners, long regarded as the aristocracy of the proletariat, actually earned a fair bit more than most other workers but in

1990, the money was nearly useless because the shops were all but empty. At the same time, the miners feared the introduction of market reforms, not only because prices would rise but also because the growth of private business would erode their wage advantage over other workers. It seemed a selfish argument until I saw the terrifying underworld in which they spent six hours a day, five days a week. Then I thought they deserved every rouble they earned and a whole lot more.

Lyubov Nikitevna, a woman as broad as a wall and with a voice like a klaxon, dressed me to go down the Sixth Capital mine, opened in 1912 and still offering rich seams of coking coal, although at increasing depths.

"Don't be afraid, my little rabbit!" she bellowed as she tightened the waist of the white pyjamas that went under my coarse grey miner's jacket and trousers. "I worked down there until the 1950s, when they threw the women out. Oh, how we cried when we had to leave the mine."

I found her nostalgia hard to understand as I entered the cage, equipped with a helmet and a bottle of oxygen which, in the event of a gas leak, would keep me alive for five hours seated or 45 minutes running.

Once at the bottom, my eyes never left the broad back of Vladimir Ampilogov, the mine director who, at the surface, had seemed a typical grey Communist official, opposed to the founding of the independent miners' union. In the depths, he was a beacon of kindness and competence, leading the way past many dangers.

"We are superstitious; we don't like to talk about it," he'd said when I asked, before setting off, about health and safety in the mines. In the week of my visit, six men were killed in accidents in other pits in the Donbas regions.

The cage took us 350 metres down the main shaft to a world of cold winds and infernal noises. Further we could only go by lying flat on our backs, dead still, on the conveyor belt which went down to 600 metres and tropical heat.

At the coal face, I was offered the chance to crawl on my belly for 40 minutes through a tunnel three feet high, but I must confess I backed out after two minutes, which was probably fortunate. The miners said a Czech journalist who had visited the pit a few weeks before had succumbed to claustrophobia half way through the tunnel, when it was too late to go back, and had had to be dragged to the other end.

On the return journey to the surface, we had to jump on a moving conveyor belt going steeply upwards, making sure to land chest down and head first, so as to be ready to spring off again at the top. I fell and landed feet first, not daring to turn and unable to judge the moment to leap. The director grabbed me by the seat of the pants and the scruff of the neck, saving me from riding up to the coal chute.

Never have I been so glad to see a cloudy sky as I was when we emerged again on the surface. We swilled several jamjars of water from a standpipe before going to the bathhouse for showers with soap (but no shampoo) and a feast of tea and mushy-pea pasties. I had walked in the mine for just two hours but I was exhausted, every muscle in my body aching.

The miners were paid an allowance for the trek before and after the six hours of work at the coal face, during which they were expected to hack out about four tonnes of coal. The mine produced 444,000 tonnes of coal a year, I was told.

After the visit to the mine, I went to see the colliers' white-painted brick cottages. Outside one, miner's wife Nadia Harlamova was sitting with her invalid mother-in-law, Antonina Sergeyevna, admiring the strawberry patch. Inside, there were sofa-beds to maximise space in the two small rooms. An old-fashioned coal-fired stove heated pans of water for washing. The toilet was a wooden privy in the garden, next to the chicken run.

Nadia's husband was away, helping to build a block of flats under a scheme by which the Ukrainian government provided the finance and the mine supplied the labour. He was being paid a pittance but at the end would have the right to occupy one of the flats, with his wife, mother and young son.

There would be no garden, no strawberries and no chickens but there would be an indoor toilet and bathroom with hot and cold running water.

I asked Antonina Sergeyevna if she would miss the village. "Yes," she said, "but I would rather have the hot and cold running water."

LEMON PIE

Perestroika created a huge appetite in the West for details of how ordinary Soviet people lived. Mainly, with our *Schadenfreude*, we wanted to know *how badly* ordinary Soviet people lived. I could describe what Russians did or did not have for breakfast and be sure the readers in Britain would lap it up. There was fascination mixed with sympathy for the contents of a poor man's fridge: one plastic bag of sweaty carrots, a jar of vinegar from which the last pickled cucumbers had been eaten, and two packets of butter. The same man, I informed my avid readers, had sold his wedding ring to buy washing powder to wash his children's nappies.

We knew there were shortages in the Soviet Union, of course. When Margaret Thatcher had come on her first official visit in 1987, I was with her when she toured what looked like a relatively well-stocked food store. I was never a fan of the Iron Lady but I had to admire her thoroughness and scepticism when she turned to me and asked, "Is there always this much food here?" Of course, my answer was no.

But by 1990, the pressing question had become: are the Russians actually going hungry? This grew to be an obsession with my editors. Looking at the empty shelves of the state shops, you might have thought that *golod* (starvation) was as real as in Africa. But I knew my Russian friends always managed, somehow, to put food on the table and something in their stomachs.

Those with dollars were now legally allowed to go to the *beriozka* (hard currency stores) that had once been the exclusive domain of foreigners. Behind venetian blinds were unheard of luxuries – bananas, coffee, cornflakes and cat food. One Saturday afternoon, I watched husbands push trolleys while wives loaded them up with instant coffee, toilet paper, muesli and family packs of chocolate bars. Customers who had literally only one or two dollars in their pockets queued patiently for sweets or a can of soft drink – anything so long as it had the magic of Western wrapping.

It must have been the same addiction to anything Western that enabled a woman I saw on the Rizhsky market to do a roaring trade selling "second-hand" Big Macs from MacDonalds, which had just opened its first outlet in Russia on Pushkin Square. She queued for the burgers and then resold them for double the price on the market. "Real MacDonalds," she cried, "only two hours old."

At what should have been the other end of the social scale was Yeliseyevsky's, the Russian equivalent of Harrods' Food Hall. Before the Bolshevik Revolution, it had been a cornucopia. The shop still had its beautiful old wood panelling and chandeliers but now it was run by the state and you could catalogue its entire contents in two minutes: cigarettes, brandy, frozen chickens, ribs, four kinds of tinned fish, jars of tomato juice and pickles, lard, baby food, one kind of cake and bread. At least it had the merit of being within the reach of the average Russian, as the prices were all subsidised.

I monitored the food situation regularly because I knew it was one of the best social and political barometers. I used to go shopping with two Moscow housewives, Tamara Lavrienteva and Irina Benditovich, and in May 1990, for the *Independent on Sunday*, we set off to buy groceries for their families. We had 60 roubles (£60 at the official rate) between us but with the best will in the world, we only managed to spend 24. We spent three hours visiting 13 "produce" shops, as the state food shops were unimaginatively called, but the list of things we failed to find was far longer than that of our purchases. Missing from the food basket were meat, eggs, rice, dairy products, cheese, fruit and beetroot, the latter essential in Russia to make *borsch* (beetroot soup).

Sometimes the necessary items were simply not there; other times they lay tantalisingly on a distant counter but the queues were so long that we gave up the attempt to reach them. Some items were on sale *v nagruzku* (in a bundle) – in other words, in order to get something good and fresh that you wanted, you also had to buy something stale or rotten, thereby boosting the state's sales figures.

In one shop on Solyanka Street, we found a single piece of beef (mostly bone and fat), a tray of pork fat, a dish of kidneys and a pile of tinned fish that Irina pronounced inedible. But there was some margarine and she grabbed a pack. "We'll make lemon pie," she said, "that is, if we can find the eggs and the lemons. The way we live, we can't plan anything. We have to be spontaneous."

So we began the search for the other ingredients needed to make the lemon pie. After scouring a number of shops, we managed to find flour and sugar but we never did find any eggs or lemons. We could make dry pastry but the pie would have no filling. The readers loved it. Like Oliver Twist, the hungry editors wanted more. The problem was that soon after the lemon pie story, Irina migrated to Israel.

Tamara stayed in Moscow, however, and it was to her I turned when we really needed to pin down the facts about "Russian starvation". After food-rationing was introduced in December 1990, the British press went wild with stories about "hunger and possible political repercussions". My own newspaper, while writing accurately about supplies, carried a misleading photograph of Muscovites queuing in the snow outside St Basil's Cathedral.

This prompted an angry letter from a reader. "The implication was that these were frozen people waiting for food when anyone who knows Moscow would be aware that it showed people queuing for communion at the cathedral," wrote Disgusted of London SE10. I could only share her disquiet at this lapse in our professional standards.

Tamara

Tamara and I went back to Solyanka Street with the same amount of money we'd had on our earlier shopping expedition with Irina in May. Some things that had been available then had disappeared but other products were on sale instead. There was more fruit because the harvest was in. The assortment was not very inspiring but it was a long way from the starvation rations of besieged wartime Leningrad, when people boiled leather, ate dogs and rats and licked the glue from the back of wallpaper.

"There's an assistant behind that counter," said Tamara hopefully as

68

we entered one shop. "That means she's got something to sell." The shop, which last time had had butter and scraps of meat, was offering herbs, jars of apple sauce, inferior Turkish tea and "coffee drink powder". Tamara already had those but she bought a bottle of lemonade, some salt and a bag of "cornflakes", which turned out to be very hard, sweet crisps – a danger to teeth.

In another shop, we found scrappy meat but 30 people were queuing for it, so we moved on. In any case, Tamara didn't have a ration card because she hadn't had time to fill out the necessary paperwork to get one.

In a third store, there were bad pomegranates and mouldy grapes but good apples, carrots and beetroots, which Tamara bought. Later, she would send her husband Anton with a rucksack to fetch the heavy potatoes and onions. And however bad the situation got, there was always bread in the bakeries. We bought some black bread, two white loaves and two sweet buns and went home to take stock of our ingredients.

Having spent 15 of the 60 available roubles, Tamara had everything she needed to make *borsch* that night. "Fine for a vegetarian," she said, "but my children should have protein: milk, eggs and cheese."

This was not to mention the clothes and other things the family needed. That winter, Tamara was sharing a pair of boots with her mother. "When it's not my turn to wear them, I sit at home," she said.

Other basic commodities appeared and disappeared from the shops without any apparent rhyme or reason. One week, there would be a shortage of matches; then soap would be like gold dust. The latest *defitsit* (in short supply) item was shampoo. "Imagine how horrible you feel," said Tamara, "after washing your hair with household soap. You want to curse the Soviet system. It's such a little thing but it has such a big effect."

Hearing these stories of deprivation, of lack of variety and limited nutrition if not starvation, well-intentioned people in the West started offering help to the Russians. It was the beginning of a wave of what the Russians called "*gum-po*" (humanitarian aid). Before organised deliveries and charitable initiatives got going, my own readers at *The Independent* simply sent parcels of food to our office in Moscow. I didn't really know what to do with them.

I felt I couldn't just hand them to Russian friends like Tamara or I would risk being accused of nepotism. So on 24 December 1991, I decided to play Good King Wenceslas and went out onto the snowy streets, looking for poor people to whom I could give the boxes.

I saw a woman approaching with a pram and gave one to her. She was astonished, delighted and effusive in her thanks. But an old woman to whom I offered another box said, "It may be Christmas for you but it's not Christmas for us yet (Russian Orthodox Christmas is on 6–7 January). Keep your box. We don't want your charity."

This was a real eye-opener for me, as I understood for the first time that Russians felt humiliated by Western aid. They didn't want our pity, our charity or our "know-how". They had their own "Russian way" and would doggedly follow it to their own version of salvation.

THE BALTS

On an Aeroflot flight to Vilnius in May 1990, I sat next to a young woman called Snezhana, who came from Tiksi on the Arctic coast of Siberia. She was clutching a bag of rather smelly Lena River fish and a "Lithuanian" passport – actually a Soviet passport that she had covered with green card. For she was in fact of Lithuanian origin and since her Soviet-occupied country had just declared independence, she was going home to the land of her ancestors. The fish, she said, was to help break the economic blockade that Gorbachev had imposed on the Lithuanians as punishment for their political impudence.

What would she do when she landed? Snezhana said she would try and find a Lithuanian family who wanted to swap their flat in Vilnius for her apartment in Tiksi, surely one of the most God-forsaken places on the planet. "I know it's a bit of a long shot," she admitted. "I will probably just have to abandon my flat in Tiksi and start in Vilnius from scratch."

It seemed an unlikely story until Snezhana explained that her family had been among the hundreds of thousands of Baltic nationals deported in cattle trucks to Siberia after Stalin annexed Lithuania, Latvia and Estonia in 1939. Snezhana was determined to settle again in her homeland. "There are too many Lithuanian graves in Siberia," she whispered.

In the early 1990s, there were too many Lithuanian graves in Lithuania as well.

Having waved goodbye to Snezhana at Vilnius aiport, I travelled on to the republic's second city of Kaunas to meet the widow of a Lithuanian worker who a few days earlier had set fire to himself in a dramatic act of protest on Moscow's Red Square.

Stasele Zhemaitis said she suspected nothing on 25 April when she set off for work, leaving her husband Stanislovas to do the household chores, as he had recently been laid off from his job as a driver, due to Gorbachev's oil embargo against Lithuania. When she came home, she found a note on the kitchen table.

Dear Stasele, forgive me if there was anything bad in my life. I can't go on. The occupiers have turned off the tap and are sending in the paratroopers. People are left without work. I leave my wedding ring to our youngest, Rasa. With love and respect to you all. PS: I have gone to Moscow to burn myself on Red Square. Stasele, take the two months' wages of 500 roubles (£500) I am owed from the Erdvytes Co-op.

Stasele said she was surprised to see her husband's ring, which he usually did not take off. As for the note, she simply couldn't believe it, so she did nothing. In any case, there was little she could do because Stanislovas was already on the train. The next evening, Lithuanian television reported that a 52-year-old worker from Ezherelis, near Kaunas, had died of burns in Moscow's Sklifosovskaya Hospital.

His elder daughter Vaiva and her husband Saulius heard the news. "I guessed it was my dad," said Vaiva, "because the details fitted together." She saw in retrospect that a visit he had paid some days earlier, when he had played for a long time with the couple's young child, had been his farewell. "Obviously he wasn't just depressed or he would have committed suicide at home," said Saulius.

This harrowing story convinced me that the Lithuanians were not going to back down from their declaration of independence and revert to the Soviet constitution, as Gorbachev was demanding. Indeed, parliament had just chosen as national leader a romantic musicologist with impeccable anti-Soviet credentials, preferring him over a pragmatic engineer who might have negotiated with Gorbachev. The new President was Vytautas Landsbergis and he defied the Kremlin until January 1991, when Moscow's patience snapped.

I was back in Moscow when Soviet Defence Minister Dmitry Yazov ordered 1,000 extra paratroopers into Lithuania, ostensibly to round up deserters and draft dodgers. Clearly a crackdown was underway. Thousands of Lithuanians, singing nationalist anthems, gathered round parliament to protect it. The situation looked ominous. I remembered that two years earlier, Soviet troops had killed demonstrators in the Georgian capital of Tbilisi with sharpened shovels. Was something equally terrible about to happen in Vilnius?

On 12 January Soviet troops stormed two buildings: the old Communist Party printing works that had started to promote the cause of independence, and the offices of Lithuania's new National Defence Organisation. Both were encircled by tanks.

Then on the fateful night of 13 January, Soviet paratroopers backed by T-72 tanks moved in on the broadcasting centre and in the melee opened fire on unarmed civilians, killing 13 of them. Eyewitnesses said about 20 troop carriers had come round the corner of a narrow street to find a tightly packed crowd blocking their way. They illuminated the crowd with their powerful projectors. "Then the soldiers suddenly started shooting at us to make a path," said Aunas Romanavicius, a student who suffered a bullet wound to the leg.

"We announce that normal programmes are interrupted because of brutal military force..." said Lithuanian radio before it was cut off. The official Soviet version of events was that the crowd had hurled stones and the troops had retaliated in self-defence.

Undeterred by the killings, tens of thousands of Lithuanians massed outside parliament and stood their ground, linking arms, singing songs and lighting bonfires to keep warm through their nightly vigils. Inside, volunteers as young as 16 guarded President Landsbergis, who turned his office into a bunker and vowed to defend Lithuanian independence to the death. Foreign Minister Algirdas Saudargas, on a visit to Poland, set up a government in exile. The Lithuanians were expecting to be attacked and occupied all over again.

On the orders of my editors in London, I was soon on another plane to Vilnius. I arrived in time to go with mourners up the wooded hill to the Antakalnio cemetery, where 9 of the 13 victims had been buried.

"Before the army attacked us, our politicians argued a lot amongst themselves," said a young woman called Donata, who had brought a candle to add to the sea of wreaths on the snow-covered graves. "But this tragedy showed we are united on the essential things."

"The Communists do not respect human life," said Arturas, a young engineer. "They have murdered millions of people, so what are 13 more?"

Above the freshly dug graves was a wooden crucifix, carved by folk sculptor Ipolitas Uzkurnys. In his studio in Vilnius, he was carving 13 small oak figures of Christ, the Man of Sorrows, to give to the bereaved families.

Mr Uzkurnys cursed the Russians but was hardly more forgiving towards the West, which was tied up at that time with the first Gulf War and distracted from the Baltic crisis. "So you will write an article," he snapped at me. "Your soul does not hurt. If your brothers and sisters had died, you would have written a whole book."

Most of the 13 who died by the television tower were young. This was because youths were standing together, holding a street disco with a boom box, while the older generation of protestors were standing apart, singing folk songs, when the tanks arrived and targeted the younger group.

One of the victims was Loreta Asanaviciute, born in 1967. She had tried to run away from an armoured car bearing down on her but didn't make it and fell under its wheels. The lower part of her body and the top of her legs were crushed but she remained conscious for several hours. Before she died, she was reported to have asked doctors whether she would still be able to have children.

The 64-million-dollar question was whether Gorbachev, who had won the Nobel Peace Prize in 1990, had personally ordered the attack on the broadcasting centre. The official Tass news agency said Lithuanian state radio and television had been "turned into a mouthpiece of disinformation and slander. This gave rise to the wrath and indignation of working people". The general opinion in Lithuania was that of course Gorbachev must have known.

But Gorbachev, after staying silent for 24 hours, told parliament in Moscow that he had only found out belatedly about the tragic events. "We did not want and do not want this," he said.

Marshall Yazov went on to blame General Vladimir Uskopchik, the commandant of the Vilnius garrison. "You understand," said Yazov, "he lives there, he knows this Lithuanian propaganda and, under the influence of his emotions, he gave the order to take the radio and television immediately to put an end to this propaganda."

Evidently, a battle was going on in Gorbachev's soul and he couldn't decide whether to heed his hardline or liberal advisors. Meanwhile, the situation in Vilnius remained volatile.

I visited the besieged parliament, where through one narrow gap correspondents were being allowed to enter and see President Landsbergis, like Santa Claus in his grotto. An old woman guided me in past the rubble and coils of barbed wire. "How can you all be so in love with Gorbachev in the West?" she demanded. The barricades were plastered with caricatures of the Soviet leader. One showed him as a butcher, standing in a pool of blood and forcing the small bodies of the three Baltic States through a mincing machine.

Inside, Landsbergis was holding talks with the visiting Foreign Minister of Iceland, the first Western country to recognise independent Lithuania. All around, nervous youths sat on sandbags, nursing hunting rifles. Molotov cocktails were also at the ready in case of attack by Soviet troops.

Fortunately, it didn't come to the storming of parliament. Washington exerted its influence and by the end of January, Soviet troops began pulling out. In February, the Lithuanians held a referendum to underline their determination to be independent. Citizens were asked to vote *taip* or *ne* to independence. Since Lithuania was a homogeneous society, with only a tiny Slav minority, nearly 90 per cent voted *taip*. Gorbachev, who was planning his own poll on preserving the Soviet Union, declared the Lithuanian vote illegal.

The situation in the other two Baltic states, Latvia and Estonia, was potentially more complicated because there ethnic Balts and Russians lived in almost equal numbers. But when the Latvians, shocked by the deaths in Lithuania, erected barricades in the old town of Riga, they were joined by Russians, Ukrainians, Poles and Jews, who also wanted democracy. They were calling Gorbachev not Gorby but Gory.

At night, the civil defence of Riga took on the appearance of a street party. Rock groups, jazz bands and folk choirs entertained the thousands who kept watch round giant log fires. The Lutheran cathedral opened its doors to provide shelter and sandwiches. Despite the huge numbers, there was not a scrap of litter. I watched, fascinated, as a woman carefully swept up three cigarette butts while all around her, young people danced and a male-voice choir made a mist with their collective breaths.

Soviet troops did not attack the barricades in Riga. Only one man died in the Latvian capital during the Baltic crisis, shot by Soviet soldiers because he got in the way of their trucks.

Neighbouring Estonia tiptoed even more discreetly to the door marked "exit from the Soviet Union" and suffered no casualties at all in early 1991.

"We know we will not leave the Soviet Union through war," said Prime Minister Edgar Savisaar. "We will not buy ourselves out of the Soviet Union with money. We can only manoeuvre free from the union by wisdom and cunning."

Not realising that the whole Soviet Union would soon be cracking up, the Estonians thought their independence was still a way away. When I interviewed Foreign Minister Lennart Meri in Tallinn in March, he was advocating a subtle approach whereby Moscow should be persuaded it would receive more food supplies and other economic advantages if it let the Baltic States go free. The way to independence was through Moscow's stomach, he said with a twinkle in his eye.

Mr Meri was a delightful man. He told me that the Foreign Ministry budget was so small that on his official trips abroad, he did not eat every day.

"Literally?" I asked.

"Yes," he said. And then he told me some more stories from his life.

His father Georg had been a diplomat representing independent Estonia in Paris and Berlin before the Second World War. In 1941, he returned to Estonia and soon after he and his family were rounded up in the middle of the night by the KGB and carted off to Siberia. Georg Meri, who as well as being a diplomat was an international authority on Shakespeare, was sent to a labour camp. His wife Alice and Lennart, who was 12 at the time, went to a village near Kotlas, west of the Urals, where they chopped wood in the forest.

Mrs Meri had carried into exile several of her husband's silk neckties. These not only helped her and Lennart to survive but were also instrumental in giving the young man a start in his career. Mrs Meri traded the ties on the local market for some eggs, which she counted in her mother tongue, Estonian. The market traders were astonished to hear her using a language similar to theirs, for they were Cheremis, one of 22 Finno-Ugric tribes ethnically related to the Estonians. After the war, Lennart became an anthropologist and specialised in small ethnic groups such as these, writing books and making documentary films about them.

THE GIRL FROM MARS

A down-to-earth girl from Mars made the news in May 1991 by becoming the first British cosmonaut to join the Soviet crew on the orbiting space station *Mir*. Helen Sharman, then 27 and a chemist from Sheffield, had worked as a chocolate technologist for the confectionery company Mars – indeed, she'd help to develop ice-cream Mars bars. So that was a gift to the headline writers of the British press, whose cynical correspondents were bussed out to the Baikonur launchpad to watch her blast off in a tin can of a rocket, little changed since Yuri Gagarin's historic flight 30 years earlier.

Helen had been chosen from 150 candidates to spend eight days on *Mir*, conducting experiments and bringing glory to Britain and much-needed cash to the Soviet space programme. But the mission was dogged with problems from the start. The cost of her flight was five million pounds but British businesses, hit by recession, failed to come up with enough sponsorship money for her. Malicious tongues said Helen would have to appear on chat shows for the rest of her life when she returned to Earth to pay for her ticket to space. Resentment at Britain's failure to cover the costs bubbled up in the Soviet press. Some Russian journalists said the hard-pressed Soviet Union was subsidising her ride, or at the very least losing profits it might have made by carrying a cosmonaut from a better-paying country.

"Now now; now now," General Igor Kuriny, chief political officer of the Ministry of Defence, rebuked us journalists as we tried to get more mileage out of this scandal at the first press conference in Baikonur. "Some things are priceless," he said, "such as strengthening international cooperation."

We hacks were in an irreverent mood, having been cooped up in Moscow too long, covering the serious political events of that year. We made much of the fact that the famous Baikonur was actually a tawdry little town called Leninsk, the real settlement of Baikonur being 620 miles to the east across the steppes of Kazakhstan. Using such pathetic disinformation, the Soviet Union had tried to mask the real location of its secret sites.

We gave Helen rather a hard time when, ahead of her flight, she came out of training to talk to us from behind a glass screen. This was to protect her from the risk of infection but it did nothing to shield her from our trivial and unscientific questions. She'd had muesli for breakfast, she disclosed. Yes, she was taking a present from her father: a butterfly brooch. No, she wasn't taking a mascot. Inevitably, someone asked her how she was feeling. We wanted her to show some emotion, some sense of the enormity of her adventure, but she was sternly downbeat about the mission.

"I am not going into infinity," she said in her flat Yorkshire accent. "I am going into lower Earth orbit. I have been training hard. If there is an emergency, I know what to do. What have I got to be frightened of? People are only afraid of the unknown."

While Helen completed her preparations for the flight, we visited the Baikonur cosmodrome and watched the Soyuz TM-12 rocket in which she would travel being shunted out of its hangar and erected on the launchpad. The red and silver craft was surprisingly small – only 85 feet high – and reminded me of the rockets used by the Thunderbird puppets in the old television series.

Major-General Alexei Shumilin, who guided us round the site, was confident the Soyuz would serve Helen well. The pad had already seen 335 launches, he said, pointing to a row of stars painted on one of the rocket supports, commemorating flights going back to the first manned mission by Gagarin in 1961. The old, tried and tested technology was her best guarantee of a safe return trip to *Mir*. And, of course, she would be with two experienced cosmonauts: Commander Anatoly Artsebarsky and Engineer Sergei Krikalyov.

Nobody wanted to dwell on disaster before the departure but it was impossible not to bring up the question of past accidents, about which Soviet officials were starting to be more open. One of the main sights of Leninsk was an obelisk in memory of about a hundred workers who had died in a launchpad explosion in 1960. Because of an error by Field Marshall Mitrofan Nedelin, a missile had blown up and those nearby became human torches, some perishing in scalding tar as the tarmac melted, we were told.

In 1971, there was also an accident in space. The cosmonauts Volkov, Dobrovolsky and Patsayev died in their Soyuz-11 craft when their computer failed to alert them to an open hatch door on re-entry. Actually, I already knew about this because my friend Sveta Patsayeva, one of the guests at our wedding, was the late Viktor Patsayev's daughter.

But most missions were successful, the officials stressed, and the Soviet Union's record with its permanently-manned station *Mir* was impressive. Unless she was very unlucky, the worst Helen was likely to suffer was a bout of space sickness. Apparently the Japanese journalist Toyohiro Akiyama, who had been to *Mir* the previous December, was ill for three days until he adapted to weightlessness.

There was still time to kill before blast-off, so I decided to explore the town of Leninsk, which had been closed to foreigners. And what an instructive tour this was: perhaps more than any town I visited, Leninsk opened my eyes to Soviet reality. I had assumed the space city, at least, would be modern and well-supplied; but here too people had to queue for food whilst condensed milk, meat and butter were available only on production of a ration card. The specialists who worked in the space programme's back-up industries lived in jerry-built blocks and had to boil their water or risk contracting hepatitis from the tap supply. In the central hotel, helpful staff apologised for the broken toilets and failure of the lights.

The local Kazakhs were also disgruntled. What benefit would Kazakhstan reap from Helen's flight, they asked me. Why, when cosmonauts from 17 non-Soviet countries had flown from Baikonur, had there not been a single Kazakh crew member? Why couldn't the space chiefs put a satellite in orbit so that villages in the Central Asian republic could at last receive television? To be fair, this state of affairs was rectified when Tokhtar Aubakirov was picked for a mission in October 1991 and became the first Kazakh in space.

But back to Helen; her moment of heroism was approaching. We gathered at the launchpad with bated breath. I, for one, was no longer taking the mickey. I imagined myself in Helen's shoes.

She smiled and waved on the steps of the spacecraft. Minutes later, with a great roar and trailing a blinding flame, the rocket sliced the air. Building to a speed of 18,000 miles an hour, it quickly disappeared into the clouds but its thunder could be heard – and felt in the chest – for a long time afterwards.

"Sweet Blast-Off for Woman from Mars," was the headline on my story in *The Independent.* The space chiefs said the lift-off had been technically smooth.

Helen's parents, who had come out from Sheffield to support her, expressed relief. They had seemed as cucumber-cool as their daughter before the take-off but now her physicist father John Sharman said, "Phew! I don't think I could go through that again." At last the hacks had the emotional angle they were looking for.

ESCAPE TO THE COUNTRY

My friend Tamara introduced me to Vitaly Matveyev. She knew I sang for a hobby and thought I might like to meet him because he was a pianist. Vitaly was home alone the day I went to see him and we did indeed click musically, so much so that I agreed to have singing lessons with him. He told me his family was away in the village and I didn't think much more about it. We had a quiet cup of tea and made an arrangement for my first lesson.

So I was completely unprepared for the cheerful bedlam that met me on my second visit to Vitaly. His kids were back from their summer holidays – all six of them! His wife Marina was not quite a Soviet "hero mother" because for that honour a woman needed to have 10 kids, but she and Vitaly were certainly what the Russians called a "many childrened family". Because I went every week for my singing lessons, I got to know them pretty well.

To say they were a musical family only began to describe them. Marina's father, Anatoly Sergeyevich Dyomin, was professor of French horn at the Moscow Conservatory. As a child, he'd seen all his relatives die in the Siege of Leningrad and had been taken into a children's home, where he'd learnt to play the horn. His wife Miryukha, originally from Siberia, had been a cellist in her day.

Marina had also played the cello before embracing motherhood full-time. She and Vitaly had four boys: Dima, Kirill, Danil and Fyodr. For most struggling Russians, that would have been enough but they had also adopted two girls. Lera had come into the family from a children's home when she was eight. Masha, abandoned as a baby, was the newest member of the family and still only crawling.

They lived at Karetny Ryad in a prestigious block of flats allotted to artists from the Bolshoi Theatre. Despite this, they were among the poorest people I knew. Vitaly supplemented his tiny wages as a musician by mopping floors at the local library. He was a Bob Cratchit figure, working for Scrooge in the form of the miserly Soviet state. I gathered his family was largely dependent on humanitarian aid.

Marina, Dickensian in both her jollity and wiles, was very resourceful, however. Once I went to see the family and found them all tucking into ice-cream cakes. Marina had heard that a consignment of the cakes had been delivered by foreign aid donors and the sell-by date was running out. She acted swiftly to make sure that not only her own family but all the neighbours topped the list of "most deserving" and received the cakes before they melted.

The dollars I paid for my singing lessons helped the family. The money was nothing to me but made a difference to their budget and diet. I also played Santa Claus to the kids at Christmas. They were fantastically generous to me in return. Marina sewed me the most gorgeous wine-red velvet dress for my first concert with Vitaly in 1991.

More than anything, though, I was grateful to the family for getting me out of Moscow and showing me real life in rural Russia. I'd travelled quite widely in the Soviet Union but up to that point,

Singing with Vitaly

all my trips had been made in groups guided by the Foreign Ministry. The authorities were convinced we foreigners were all dangerous spies, and correspondents were not allowed to go outside the capital without giving prior notice to the Foreign Ministry so that a KGB tail could be arranged. But the rules were changing.

Vitaly, Marina and the kids spent their summers in Valdai, an exquisite lake district halfway between Moscow and Leningrad. All winter, imprisoned in Moscow, they would pore over photographs of this paradise and reminisce about their last holiday until the time finally came to make another escape to the village of Terekhovo. Here their poverty ceased to matter and they were the lords of the forests and the fields. In the early summer of 1991, they invited me to join them there. They had gone ahead by train; I followed them up in my Volvo.

The family was all staying at Granddad Dyomin's house. Anatoly Sergeyevich and Miryukha had bought the wooden cottage from a local peasant called Petya some 20 years earlier. They'd paid him secretly at the time but had only recently become official owners, with the change in property laws. Anatoly Sergeyevich admitted he'd neglected the house, saying he was a musician, not a handyman.

The house tilted alarmingly and rats invaded it in winter until Vasya the cat was brought in in summer to sort them out. The six kids slept together in one room while Marina and Vitaly made a bed in an alcove behind a rag curtain. It might have been a Viking hut had it not been for the crackly black and white television on which the kids watched *The Muppet Show* in the evenings. The main discomfort was having to go into a cold field if you needed the toilet in the middle of the night, but the stars were breathtaking.

I wondered where I was going to sleep. Marina put me with her brother Sergei and sister-in-law Irina, who lived in a separate house, and I had a comfortable bed to myself. Sergei and Irina were both doctors with something of a hippy lifestyle. They'd tried to go into farming, taking over a herd of cows from an obsolete collective farm, but they'd failed spectacularly, partly because of inexperience, partly because of local hostility, and gone back to work in medicine, accepting that village life could only ever be a temporary break from Moscow.

Their tumbledown holiday cottage had once been a prayer house for the Old Believers, a branch of the Orthodox Church which resisted 17th-century reforms. In the corner where the icon should have stood, Irina had stuck up a poster of the Indian god Krishna. The villagers would no doubt have attributed the couple's lack of agricultural success to this act of sacrilege. Irina blamed the unwelcoming locals. "They gave us the evil eye," she said.

I was beginning to detect a degree of tension between the *dachniki* (holidaymakers who came into the village and rented the cottages as summer *dachas*) and the permanent rural population. In fact, Terekhovo was struggling to avoid the fate of scores of Russian villages that disappeared each year as the collective farms collapsed, the young moved away to the cities, and the elderly died out. In summer, the village resounded to the shouts of children from Moscow and St Petersburg, catching frogs in the meadows, swimming in the lake and hanging out in the bus shelter. But in winter, only six souls remained, the youngest already 65.

"You should go and talk to the old people before it's too late," said Irina, so I did.

In one cottage, I found 80-year-old Alexander Vasyukin, who remembered collectivisation in the 1930s, when the Communists had come to confiscate his father's farm. "They made lists of all our possessions, right down to the curtains and tea towels. Then they threw us out," he said. Mr Vasyukin had had no option but to join the collective farm where, although he steadfastly refused to join the Communist Party, he was put in charge of a brigade of 30 labourers. He was still known in the village as the "brigadier".

Apart from him, seven other old people had lived in Terekhovo all their lives. They were known by the diminutive, affectionate form of their names – Dyadya (Uncle) Grisha and his wife Praskovya; Dyadya Petya, his sister Baba (Old Mother) Katya and sisters-in-law, Baba Nina, Baba Tanya and Baba Manya. Nina and Manya were too frail to cope all year alone and went to their city relatives in winter when the snow drifted up to roof level.

I rather assumed they would help each other but was told they mostly sat at home in isolation, meeting only at the counter of the mobile grocery van once a week. They gossiped, of course, and the main subject of their malicious tale-telling was 75-year-old Dyadya Petya, alias Pyotr Mokin. Legend had it that he was very mean and buried his money in the garden; that he was so jealous of his late wife Ekaterina that he put a thread across the door so that he knew when she went out; that he lost his eye not during the war but when he fell down dead drunk in the hay and was butted by a bull.

Dyadya Petya I absolutely had to meet, but it wasn't easy because he was cussed as a Yorkshireman. I found him scything grass at the bottom of the village. "Hello," I said.

"How do I know you're not a spy?" was his gruff response and he demanded to see my passport. I showed him and in a return gesture, he took out his glass eye and held it out to me on the palm of his hand. After that, we got talking.

Unlike the brigadier's family, the Mokins, with 12 mouths to feed, had been "poor folk". Petya went more willingly than his neighbours to the collective farm, where he managed a brigade for two years. "But I was illiterate," he said. "I only finished three classes, so they replaced me. I didn't mind; it was OK on the collective farm. We all tried to fulfil our tasks."

Petya told me he only received his internal passport or identity document when he retired. In Communist times, collective farm workers had been tied to the land and had to get permission from the village council if they wanted to travel within the Soviet Union. "Rather like us foreign correspondents," I joked. Now I understood why he had wanted to see my British passport.

His wife Ekaterina had died three years earlier. "She was an excellent worker; she won an Order of Lenin," he said. With Ekaterina gone, Petya had found it difficult to control his two sons and the younger had died of drink, a not uncommon fate in the Russian countryside. Petya was mostly alone now, looking after his few sheep, tending his garden and cooking. His hearing was poor but he managed with his one eye.

"What happened?" I asked.

"Wounded by the Nazis outside Leningrad," he said.

After Petya, I went to see Manya in her cottage. At 84, she could no longer chop wood or carry buckets of water from the well on the yokes that were still a common sight in rural Russia but she was lively-minded, chortling from under a red headscarf. In her time, she'd been an excellent needlewoman. Green tomatoes ripened on the cloth-covered table. She got out a jar of home-made blackcurrant jam and started force-feeding me.

"Hey, what are you doing in here?" came Vitaly's voice from the doorway. "You're supposed to be on holiday, not interviewing people." It was always hard for me to switch off from journalism mode. I guess I was born with the inclination to observe, more important in a journalist even than the ability to write. And I was a sucker for jam.

"So what do you propose?" I asked.

"I'm stoking up the *banya* [Russian equivalent of the sauna]," he said.

After that, I allowed myself to relax with my hosts. We steamed ourselves in the *banya* or went hunting for bilberries and mushrooms in the woods. Miryukha suggested I went out in the rowing boat on Lake Uzhin. "I never thought I would find a place as beautiful as Lake Baikal [in Siberia] until I came here," she said. The boys wanted to go with me but there wasn't room for everyone so Dima, the eldest, politely gave up his place, allowing me to go out with Kirill, who showed me where the beavers lived and gave me a water lily.

All I could offer in return was to give the kids rides in my Volvo. They took it in turns to sit between my knees and steer while I kept control with my feet on the pedals. Even Granddad Dyomin couldn't resist this entertainment and I handed over the car keys to let him drive. My Russian was quite good but I still had problems judging the weight of words. The kids roared with laughter when I said to him, meaning would he like me to switch on the heated seat, "Anatoly Sergeyevich, would you like me to give you a hot arse?"

The village was a place of fun and freedom. It was hard to drag myself away but I sensed that events were calling me in Moscow. Unlike the *dachniki*, I couldn't afford the luxury of a long summer holiday, especially not that year.

THE COUP

Very early on the morning of 19 August 1991, Costya and I were woken by the ringing of the doorbell. On the doorstep was our friend Kostya Vasiliev, or Little Kostya, as everyone called him to distinguish him from my much taller and fatter husband. Little Kostya was clearly distressed; close to tears in fact. Whatever was the matter?

He'd just arrived on the night train from Leningrad. On the radio in his compartment, he'd heard an announcement that President Gorbachev had fallen ill while on holiday in Crimea and was being replaced by something called the GKChP (State Committee for the State of Emergency). In other words, there had been a hardline coup against the father of *perestroika.*

Little Kostya and Ira

What really upset Little Kostya was the fact that he and his wife Ira were due to go to London at our invitation; we were all going to have a holiday in England together. And now it looked as if that trip would have to be cancelled. Or on the other hand...

I put the kettle on and we sat in the kitchen, discussing in all seriousness the possibility that Little Kostya and Ira might escape to London and stay there. "But what about Katya?" I asked, referring to their daughter, who was three years old at the time.

"She could stay with her grandmother until it's safe enough for us to come back and get her," said Little Kostya, rather unconvincingly.

We were crazy, of course; mad from the shock. Perhaps Little Kostya had misunderstood the radio announcement. I turned on the television. A cellist was playing Bach – rather a bad sign, I thought, at quarter to eight in the morning.

At 8.00 am, the cellist gave way to an announcer in a grey suit, who appealed to the Soviet people on behalf of the newly-created GKChP, "A mortal danger hangs over our great homeland. Every citizen feels a growing uncertainty about tomorrow and deep alarm for his children's future. The crisis of power has had a catastrophic effect on the economy. Millions of people are demanding the adoption of measures against the octopus of crime and scandalous immorality. The pride and honour of the Soviet people must be fully restored."

"The trouble is," said Costya, "this will strike a chord with a lot of poor, ordinary people." He and Little Kostya had been planning to go into business together. "We can say goodbye to that now," said my husband.

The hardliners had been grumbling and rumbling against Gorbachev for some time. The last straw for them was Gorbachev's plan to head off any more independence demands like the one from Lithuania by loosening the Soviet Union and creating a more voluntary "Commonwealth" among the 15 republics.

On the television, traditional balalaika music was playing to accompany idyllic shots of the Russian countryside. This was followed by fast pop music and pictures of young Muscovites. It was almost like a Western commercial and the message was clear: this coup is for you too, young man on your skateboard; young woman licking your ice cream and swinging your long blonde hair. Finally, the television settled for showing a production of the ballet *Swan Lake*, which would for ever afterwards be associated in the minds of Russians with the GKChP and their wretched coup.

Tanks, which had been waiting on the outskirts of Moscow since the small hours, didn't start rolling into the centre until about 10.00 am. I went out and just round the corner from our building saw the first of these vehicles – two armoured personnel carriers on Petrovka Street.

Although the GKChP, consisting of grey bureaucrats and military and KGB bosses, had outlawed demonstrations, knots of protestors were gathering. I followed a group that swelled as it marched down Tverskaya Street to the edge of Red Square. These demonstrators formed a human chain and persuaded the commander of a column of tanks heading for the Manezh to turn back.

I made for the Manezh, under the Kremlin walls, because it was here that anti-Communist and anti-Gorbachev demonstrations had been going on for months, turning Boris Yeltsin into the rising political star. Yeltsin was now President of the Russian Federation, the biggest of the Soviet Union's 15 republics, which made him almost as powerful as Gorbachev, who was Soviet President.

On Manezh Square, several hundred people stood in the pouring rain, listening to speeches. A wild-eyed young man called on the crowd to hijack trolleybuses to build barricades. None of the protestors reacted. Neither did the stony-faced special police, who were blocking access to Red Square itself. "Are you going to shoot us?" a man asked. "We don't have weapons," growled one of the visibly armed Black Berets.

"Russians are famous for their patience but they're not going to lie down and take this *putsch*," fumed a man in the crowd. "I'm going home to feed my dog but I'll be back."

I decided to go home too and feed my cat. I was out reporting again a couple of hours later, by which time the action had moved to the banks of the Moscow River, to the Russian parliament or White House, as it was known.

There, in front of a small crowd that morning, Mr Yeltsin had stood on top of a tank and called for resistance. Because I'd followed the crowd to the Manezh, I'd missed this historic moment but a journalist can't be in two places at once. It didn't matter because Yeltsin's speech would be on all the wires for me to read later.

Terror would strike the land if the coup against Gorbachev was allowed to succeed, Yeltsin said. "Soldiers, officers and generals, the clouds of terror and dictatorship are gathering over the whole country. They must not be allowed to bring eternal night. Soldiers, I believe in this tragic hour you can make the right choice. The honour and glory of Russian men of arms shall not be stained with the blood of the people. In this tragic moment for Russia, I appeal to you: do not allow yourself to be ensnared in a net of lies and promises and demagogic calls to 'military duty'. Think of your loved ones, your friends, your people."

Yeltsin, guarded by loyal elite police, said he was ordering the army and KGB in the Russian Federation to obey his orders over Soviet ones. In effect, Yeltsin was declaring the sovereignty of Russia. Other republics backed Yeltsin, although Azerbaijan hedged its bets in a mealy-mouthed way, calling the coup a "natural consequence of the politics that have brought chaos to the Soviet Union".

Yeltsin took a huge gamble but it paid off. Crowds of Muscovites gathered at the White House and started to camp there. That evening, 10 tanks flying the red, white and blue Russian tricolor came over to Yeltsin's side and helped to strengthen the barricades. Lithuanians were also present in large numbers, showing solidarity and sharing their experience of resistance with the Russians.

Over the next three days a pattern developed. By day, tens of thousands gathered to defy the GKChP. By night, the defence dwindled to a smaller hard core of men in bandanas, who sat round log fires, guarding the White House. Alcohol was banned. The parliament building was most vulnerable from 6.00 am, when the night shift went home to sleep, until about nine in the morning, when the daytime defenders started to gather again.

Before the coup, the huge pro-Yeltsin demonstrations had been dominated by the middle-aged. Now, suddenly, young people were involved. A woman called Valentina explained why. "We were the Khrushchev generation, who remembered the thaw at the start of the 1960s. When Brezhnev came, we carried that light secretly until we could bring it out again. That is why we followed Yeltsin from the start. How wonderful that the young have finally joined us!"

I got talking with a woman called Olga, who had taken time off work so that she could join the struggle. "Nobody I know supports the junta," she said. "I choose my friends carefully and I'm glad to say I haven't been wrong about any of them. The emergency shows us clearly who is who.

But I've heard strangers say things that astonish me. For example, I saw a young couple on the street and overheard the woman say, 'What's it got to do with me?' I think that's terrible."

Olga put her finger on what was troubling me. The resistance was thrilling, of course, but compared with the intense emotion and obvious national unity that I had seen in Lithuania earlier in the year, something was missing. For a country the size of Russia, there were simply not enough pro-democracy demonstrators. At most, about 300,000 were standing up for their freedom. But was the whole country really behind them?

Nevertheless, the demonstrations were enough to scare the members of the GKChP, who started to lose what little nerve they'd had in the first place. One of the enduring images of the *putsch* became that of coup leader Gennady Yanaev's hands trembling when he spoke at a press conference. Soon the tragedy of the August coup turned into a farce and the hardline plotters were seen fleeing to the airport. But not before three young men lost their lives in the grotesque and unfortunate business.

I joined the masses who followed their coffins at a state funeral on 25 August. Mr Gorbachev, restored to power, named the three Heroes of the Soviet Union. Mr Yeltsin begged forgiveness from their families that he had not been able to protect them. After the eulogies, the bodies were carried in a huge procession from Manezh Square down Kalinin Prospekt to the White House and on to the Vagankovskoye cemetery. It had rained throughout the coup but the sun came out for their burial.

Huge portraits of the dead men preceded the coffins, like icons being held aloft. First came a picture of Ilya Krichevsky, a 28-year-old architect and music lover who, when the junta's tanks had been trying to smash through a barricade on the Garden Ring Road, had jumped onto a tank and tried to reason with the driver. The commander shot him in the head and his body was carried for several yards on top of the tank.

Dmitry Komar and Vladimir Usov, two Afghan war veterans, tried to retrieve his body but were crushed to death as the tank rolled on regardless. Afghan veterans played a prominent role in defeating the coup. That the once-obedient Soviet army had little stomach for the crackdown and chose the democratic side, was due to the bitter legacy of the Afghan war.

It was impossible to count the endless stream of people who followed the coffins, carrying flowers according to Russian tradition in even numbers for the dead (a bouquet of odd numbers is for the living). The mood was sombre, especially as the procession passed over the bridge under which the killings had happened.

"It was a terrible, barbarous act," the woman next to me whispered.

Krichevsky was Jewish, and a rabbi read from the Kaddish while Russian Orthodox priests said requiem verses for the two other men at the cemetery. "He never said goodbye," said Krichevsky's mother Inessa. "For almost two days, we weren't sure he was dead." He'd done his military service in the southern city of Novocherkassk, where the Soviet army slaughtered striking workers in 1962. "He knew the history of Novocherkassk," she said. "The fertile soil was there. He did what he thought was right."

A Jewish prayer shawl was placed over his coffin on top of the Russian flag. As friends piled flowers on the plinth, one stopped to scribble from memory two lines from a poem Krichevsky had written:

> *Don't torture yourself with the hope,*
> *Don't soothe yourself with the hope*
> *That you will die as you wish*

That anyone had to die was tragic but the fact that Jews and Christians buried their dead together had a powerful unifying effect in a society that was still deeply anti-Semitic. For the state funeral, the Krichevskys agreed to bury their son on the Sabbath, which they would have preferred not to do.

Flags from other republics, including Lithuania, Georgia and Ukraine, fluttered alongside the Russian flag and the funeral seemed to express the hope that as the Soviet empire collapsed, a new ethnic harmony might be achieved.

"Our ethnic troubles were artificially created by the Communists," said Bella Tumyan, a Georgian woman. "Now we will all be independent and cooperate with each other."

That was wishful thinking, as it turned out. In fact, the trouble between ethnic groups in the Soviet empire and between Christian Russia and its

Muslim regions was only just beginning.

Mr Gorbachev's return was also rocky. A colleague at *The Independent* put it very well when he wrote that a coup is like a heart attack; you might survive it but it leaves you vulnerable.

Gorbachev was back in power for the time being but it wouldn't be long before Russia, Ukraine and Belarus pulled the carpet out from under him by announcing they were creating a new union called the Commonwealth of Independent States. The Soviet leader would be left as President of nothing very much, with little choice but to dissolve the USSR and resign, which he was to do with as much dignity as he could muster on Christmas Day 1991.

History was happening all around. With the benefit of hindsight, I can say that in my opinion, the big mistake Mr Yeltsin made in the autumn of 1991 was not to dismantle the KGB, as other East European countries did to their secret police. There was a moment when he could have done it. Straight after the coup, angry crowds had toppled the statue of Felix Dzerzhinsky, the founder of the Cheka, which was the forerunner to the KGB. They were clearly ready to get rid of the organisation as well. But Mr Yeltsin, perhaps thinking the time might come when he would need a secret policeman himself, did nothing except in due course to rename the KGB the FSB. He thus missed a historic opportunity to give post-Soviet Russia a fresh start in life.

SCHOOL

Marx, Engels and Lenin still glared down from the walls at Moscow's School Number 202 but when I paid a visit in autumn 1991, the 16-year-olds of the 11th grade were learning about Lech Walesa and the rise of Polish Solidarity. This was a departure from the Soviet national curriculum, which had remained unchanged since 1917, and taking responsibility for it was an energetic young history teacher called Svetlana Andreyevna.

"Why were there strikes in Poland at the start of the 1980s?" she asked the class.

"Because of price rises, Miss."

"And did the Soviet Union help Poland at the time?"

Silence.

"Only with tanks," she said, having explained how General Wojciech Jaruzelski, under pressure from Moscow, had "normalised" the situation.

"Why was our country against Solidarity?" she continued.

"Because it was a threat to the socialist camp?" offered one boy timidly.

"Yes, that's right. And why are the Poles finding it easier to reform now than we are?"

"Because they have a higher standard of living."

"Yes. We've had 70 years of Communism while they only became Communist after the war. And what are our relations with Poland like now?"

"Friendly?"

"Good. That's right; now we don't interfere in other countries. OK, there's the bell. Next week we'll do Hungary."

The Russian photographer working with me that day was gobsmacked. "I remember how they taught us about '68 in Czechoslovakia," he said. "The trouble was all stirred up by Western imperialists and the Czechs appealed to our brave boys to go in and help them. Of course, I believed that version when I was a teenager. I had no other information."

The photographer and I were visiting the school only a few weeks after the defeat of the hardline coup in Moscow. Gorbachev was still clinging to power but it was clear he was much weakened and on his way out. He was by that time highly unpopular with his own people. Yet what was happening at the school showed his real legacy. In years to come, I thought, historians would judge him more kindly and Russians would appreciate that despite all his faults, he had given them the most important thing: freedom.

Down the corridor from the history class, Inga Zamuruyeva, the literature teacher, was allowing the 15-year-olds to digress from the set text – Turgenev's *Fathers and Sons* – to a discussion about the characteristics of a "strong man".

"Does he have big muscles?" she asked.

"He should be able to feel, to be tender," said one eager girl at the front of the class.

"He shouldn't show his emotions," a boy growled.

"Watch out for him, girls," Mrs Zamuruyeva joked. "And what about a strong woman?"

The girls, outnumbering the boys in this class that had chosen to study the humanities, chorused back their suggestions.

"In our Soviet life she is strong but ideally she should be weak."

"The modern woman should stand up for herself and have opportunities."

"The power of woman is her weakness. She should be pretty and tender. She should be a slave to men."

At this Mrs Zamuruyeva, a 29-year-old specialist in Slavonic languages from Minsk, put her hand to her forehead and groaned.

Mrs Zamuruyeva's choice of Turgenev was not radical; Russian classics had always been taught in schools. The difference was that now more time could be devoted to them since teachers no longer had to pay equal attention to mediocre Soviet texts such as *Malaya Zemlya*, the late Leonid Brezhnev's account of his own bravery during the Second World War. The other new element in the lesson was the feminism, a philosophy that had barely taken root in conservative Soviet society.

Literature and history were the most ideologically sensitive subjects in education. Teachers of science, which was more or less neutral regardless of who was in power, had an easier time. But under Gorbachev, teachers of the arts had had to overturn all their thinking. Some of the older ones had not been able to cope and had retired early.

"Now we can say at school what we used to say at home around the kitchen table," said Mrs Andreyevna, a former member of the Komsomol (Communist Youth League) and graduate of the Krupskaya Teacher Training Institute, named after Nadezhda Krupskaya, Lenin's wife. "In education, we're always a bit behind events because you have to let the new thinking filter through yourself before you can pass it on to the children."

The frank lessons about Eastern Europe had been going on for two years but teachers were not yet talking about the recent coup in Moscow.

"Thank goodness the coup happened during the holidays," said Mrs Andreyevna. "What was I going to tell the children? The headmaster and I had a long discussion about it. We decided it was a fascist coup. I went to the meetings outside the White House; the headmaster was on the barricades. It was like childhood, terrible and exciting all at once. Of course, when school started again, the pupils wanted to know all about it. I told them our country had become like Latin America."

The youngsters in the history class, who would leave school in the summer with a general certificate of education, were fired up about politics in a way they had never been before. A boy called Leonid thought Yeltsin was capable of reform but a far-sighted lad called Alexei said Russians would soon get sick of him too. Did any of them still admire Gorbachev? Gales of laughter met that question.

The group also discussed what should be done with Lenin's body in its mausoleum on Red Square. Some were for giving it a Christian burial but others said it should be left on display because tourists liked to go and see it.

The portraits of Marx, Engels and Lenin remained on the classroom wall, it turned out, because headmaster Vladimir Prosvirkin, who also trained at the Krupskaya Institute, believed Russians shouldn't repeat their past mistake of wiping out the bits of history that didn't suit them. "I was a member of the Communist Party," he said, "and I always had my doubts. I still do. But we mustn't now skirt past Communism, because it did happen.

Without a past, we won't have a future. That's why I'm against taking down monuments. I'm for reform but against destroying history."

For this reason, the school intended to maintain its museum of Second World War battles, although Mr Prosvirkin wanted to add exhibits illustrating other aspects of Russian history as well. But as soon as he got hold of a can of paint, which like everything else at the time was in short supply, he was planning to erase Lenin's slogan from the staffroom wall: "Our school should give young people the basics of knowledge and ability to work out for themselves a Communist point of view."

The teachers, who said they were saved from complete brainwashing by the brave teachers who went before them, might have been free to express themselves at last but they were still stuck with the old textbooks. The history books had been updated to cover the atrocities of the Stalin era but they still failed to tackle Lenin as a mere mortal rather than as a god.

"The children get tired of just listening to me," said Mrs Andreyevna. "But I have nothing to show them. Of course, we use the newspapers quite a lot."

Mrs Zamuruyeva opened a cupboard and produced an anthology of Soviet literature. "You see – all socialist realism, a one-sided biography of Gorky. I want large numbers of Nabokov, Aksyonov. If I get one copy from the library I'm lucky, but that's no good because I have 40 in the class."

Mrs Zamuruyeva earned 560 roubles a month (then realistically worth about £11). "I could earn 10 times more if I gave private lessons," she said, "but what would become of these children? They're so sincere and fresh. They protect me from the hardness of the outside world."

She clearly had many fans among the girls in the 10th grade. "I try to encourage the children to dream," she said, "but I fear many of them will have problems afterwards, when they start work. Sometimes I blame myself for having widened their horizons."

If Soviet children previously had to cope with the contradictions between the Communist ideology they were taught in school and what they learnt from life experience and their disillusioned parents at home, then by the early 1990s the problem was often the other way round. School had started better to mirror life but some parents, particularly of the older generation, still clung to Communist orthodoxy.

But the real problem was that the new generation faced grimmer social conditions and an uncertain future. "My generation struggled with propaganda," said Mrs Zamuruyeva, "but these kids are under much more pressure. They are confused. They came into a world where all the adults were accusing each other of lying. All I can offer them is common human values. I want them to be self-confident human beings."

Lively they certainly were. When Mrs Zamuruyeva cancelled the rest of the morning's lessons so the kids could talk to me, we discussed everything under the sun.

The 10th grade had wide-ranging ambitions. Some wanted to be teachers, others were aiming at a career in the law. Several were attracted by the idea of running their own businesses. Either before or after university, the boys would face the difficult choice of performing military service or risking punishment if they evaded it.

The young people all dreamed of travelling. Had any of them been abroad?

"I've been to Tallinn," said Irina to roars of laughter.

"That counts," she shot back. "Estonia's abroad now."

What they really wanted was to go to America, France or Britain. Their conceptions of the UK were amusing – England conjured up Sherlock Holmes, fog, towers, men in top hats, and little houses. A girl called Anna asked an unusual question: "Would a teacher in Britain treat all the children in the class equally, regardless of what their parents did for a living?"

We talked about the US. One girl said America was "quite jolly during the day but dangerous at night". None of them had been to America, of course, but the American way of life had to some extent come to them. Olga had a holiday job as a cleaner at Pizza Hut. Irina was thinking of washing cars so she didn't have to ask her parents for pocket money. "Why should I be ashamed of that? People will feel nice to get a clean car and I will be working."

The teenagers complained that they only got one hour a week of tuition in a foreign language – either English or French – while they still had to spend two hours a week on civil defence lessons. They no longer prepared for war, with the boys learning how to handle rifles and the girls doing first aid. Now their tasks were defensive and involved only gas masks, they said.

Retired Colonel Vladimir Filatov, in charge of civil defence, defended his discipline. "The Cold War may be over but the children still need to know about war. Look at Iraq; look at Yugoslavia," he said. But this old paratrooper, who had spent years living in hostels between postings to Lithuania, Mongolia and East Germany, was a rather sad figure. He wished he could retire, he admitted.

In the staff room, the teachers were meeting to discuss ideas for developing the school. Plans were passed round. The headmaster was talking about creating a winter garden in an unused passageway, with a small menagerie. "We could have a lemur," he said, warming to his theme.

"Yes," said one of the teachers, thinking about her 560-rouble salary and the impossibility of acquiring books. "We could have a lemur. But how would we feed it?"

PART THREE

FULL FLOOD

FREE MARKET MADNESS

Helen interviewing

Anticipation and anxiety were in the air in equal measure when Boris Yeltsin moved into the Kremlin at New Year 1992. Russians had long told me that all they wanted was to lead "normal lives" like we did in the West, by which they meant they wanted to go shopping. Mr Yeltsin, with his willingness to grasp the economic nettle at last, was their best of hope of reaching consumer paradise. But they all knew the way forward to the free market was going to be agonisingly painful.

Towards the end of Gorbachev's rule, Russians had lived in one kind of cloud-cuckoo land, where the shops had been virtually empty and many people had more useless money in their pockets than they could find goods to spend it on. On 2 January 1992, Mr Yeltsin, advised by a group of economic shock therapists known as the "boys in pink pants" because of their ridiculously young age, abandoned the system of state subsidies and freed prices at a stroke. Costs immediately skyrocketed and the rouble plunged. Russians soon found themselves living in a different kind of economic madhouse.

Average workers with very little money gazed at and drooled over unaffordable goods in shop windows, as if they were treasures in a museum. The minority with access to the magic dollar – foreigners and increasingly a new class of rich Russians – became inflated fat cats who could scoop up anything from luxuries to, ultimately, factories and the country's natural resources at what to them were laughable prices.

At the peasant food markets, which had always been relatively expensive, dominated as they were by traders from the Caucasus and Central Asia, prices reflected the full cost of production and transport. Here a rich businessman planning a romantic dinner for his girlfriend could have bought steak, vegetables, salad, fresh fruit ahead of the Russian season and a bunch of flowers for 500 roubles, which was all of two quid at the new exchange rate. But someone working for the near-bankrupt state would have had to spend their entire month's salary for that one meal.

The unfairness was staggering. Under Communism, Russians had been used to a plodding life where the basics were guaranteed for all. Now a gulf was opening up between the haves and have-nots. The worst hit were pensioners and people with higher education in white collar jobs, such as teachers, doctors and nurses, scientists and artists, who might reasonably have expected middle class living standards but were suddenly plunged into deep poverty.

A study in November 1992 showed that an old person living without support from relatives would be eating only bread, potatoes and the occasional egg. The cheapest meat cost 200 roubles (80 pence) compared with two roubles before price liberalisation. A kilo of oranges cost the same.

Russians scrambled every which way to survive. The low paid never used the peasant markets, of course, shopping instead in the slightly cheaper state shops, but prices had risen there too. They coped by living off their stockpiles for as long as they lasted, growing food at their *dachas* and in many cases taking second jobs to supplement their incomes. The poorest pensioners collected glass bottles to recover the deposits, or worse, trawled through litter bins to find scraps of food.

So-called "commercial shops" popped up, selling imported clothes, food and drink. If you had money, you could satisfy quite a few of your needs and desires at these fledgling shops, many of them really only kiosks, but you had to be careful. A bottle of brand-name perfume might have seemed like a snip at 600 roubles (£2.40) but it would almost certainly have been a fake. German chocolate biscuits might have been genuine enough at the equivalent of 30 pence a box but what about that time when the kiosk owner sold you Greek-made "Danish" beer with a 1989 sell-by date? Alcohol was the most risky; a bad bottle could be fatal. This was the Wild East, where Russian entrepreneurs were starting to make money and there was no consumer protection against poisoning or being ripped off.

Poor Russians knew they should avoid the "commercial shops" like the plague. Cosmonaut Anatoly Artsebarsky, who earned 15,000 roubles (£60) for a five-month stint in space, could on returning to Earth have blown it all on a leather jacket brought back by a *chelnok* (shuttle trader) from a buying trip to Turkey. But a surgeon earning 1,200 roubles (£4.80) a month would still not have had enough after two month's work to afford a dildo at 2,500 roubles (10 quid).

Such was the degree of absurdity in the new free market, where advertising was to become the new propaganda. That in turn spawned a new kind of Russian joke, the advert joke.

For example: Three criminals are preparing to go to prison for life. The first decides to take a mouth organ with him. "Life's a long time," he says. "Perhaps I'll become a musician." The second decides to take some paint and brushes. "Life's a long time. Perhaps I will become a great painter." The third announces that he will take a box of tampons. "What?" cry the others. "Well, it says here on the box that with these you can go swimming, do skiing, play sports…"

Super-healthy yoghurt was being advertised with the catchphrase: "Not all yoghurts are equally good for you". So the joke went: A man is weeping and laying flowers on his wife's grave. The inscription on the headstone reads, "Not all yoghurts are equally good for you."

If you didn't laugh, you would cry.

While hurting the weakest, the new conditions forced Russians to work harder and brought out the latent talents of those who could adapt. Andrei, who was earning a pittance as a language professor in a state institute, started giving private lessons and quadrupled his income to the equivalent of 130 quid – six times the salary of a government minister (on paper, at least). With the money, he was able to hire a baby sitter, paying her a small wage that supplemented her student grant, and redecorate his flat. He bought a new duvet and bright red duvet case, sewn from scores of Pioneer or Young Communist neck scarves. "What a marvellous example of economic conversion," he joked.

Corruption had been a problem in the old Soviet Union but the 1990s really saw the rise of the "brown envelope" culture, where any problem could be solved for a bribe. Respectable people like teachers and doctors began to take money under the table, and who could blame them when, officially, they were so poorly paid?

For foreigners, of course, life was not bad at all. I always had enough to eat and plenty of money left over for clothes and fripperies. I often found bargains in the state sector, which still produced some goods of remarkable quality. For 1,400 roubles (£5.60), I could buy a set of beautiful wooden puppets that would make an original present for someone back home in England. And in a dress shop on Dmitrya Ulyanova Street, I saw women's spring coats, tailored in duck-egg blue wool with black collars, for only 1,900 roubles (£7.60). You could even get a natty little suitcase to go with your Easter outfit – admittedly not leather – but costing only 20 roubles, just over 10 pence.

Rents were going up, though. Russians who had country *dachas* as well as city apartments, or perhaps through inheritance not one but two flats in town, quickly grasped that they could rent out one home to a foreigner and live in the other themselves. For a three-room flat in the centre of Moscow, Costya and I paid a thousand US dollars a month, which I thought was a bit steep.

"Oh, but look at the rents in London and New York," said the landlord, who lived at his *dacha* and would never need to do a day's work again as long as we kept paying him.

"Yes, and look at the cockroaches and the clapped-out lavatory," I felt like saying, but another landlord might have been even more grasping. At least the flat was cheaper than the Metropol Hotel, where a single room for one night cost an outrageous 300 dollars.

With time and more healthy competition, it was predicted, the absurdities would iron themselves out. But in the early 1990s, Russians had almost no experience of the free market. Unaware of the value of things, they simply plucked prices out of the air, as one German businessman's story illustrated.

He'd been on a trip to Siberia to visit a factory that made safes. "Look at these fine safes; to you, only $167,953 each," said the Russian manager.

"But that's nonsense," said the German. "A safe in the West, even of the best metal, would cost no more than $400. Where did you get that figure from?"

The Russian disappeared into a back room and returned triumphantly with a catalogue. "See here, see here," he said, stabbing his finger at the page. He was pointing not to the price of the safe but to its serial number.

Bridal Business

Western women like me, who married Russian men and stayed in Russia after the fall of Communism, can probably be counted on the fingers of one hand. Perhaps I exaggerate a bit but the human tide certainly went the other way in the 1990s, when Russian women sought husbands in the West. It was as if a whole generation of Russian women gave up on their menfolk, whom they perceived to be drunken and lazy, and looked for comfort and self-development with Western men, on whom perhaps some of the lessons of feminism had rubbed off. Well, at least Western men did the washing-up.

In 1992 I went back to the satellite town of Lyubertsy, previously famous for its thugs in checked trousers, to visit one of the many dating agencies that were starting to spring up.

The agency, called Nakhodka (Lucky Find), aimed to match Western bachelors with willing spinsters from Russia. It worked in cooperation with a Los Angeles entrepreneur, who rejoiced in the name of Ron Rollband. Together they formed a US-Russian joint venture called Matchmaking.

The venture had had a rough ride with the Moscow press. One magazine painted a picture of exploitation all round. The women were gold-diggers, the men were middle-aged losers and the business was making a shameful profit out of them, it alleged.

In fact, I thought the agency looked rather innocent when I paid a visit. Sharing its premises with a knitting circle, it had floral curtains, a samovar and a puppy. This was of course before the age of computers and internet dating, and the manageress, Yelena Solovkova, sat behind a desk piled high with photograph albums. She opened an album at random.

"Look, this is not a supermarket of brides; these are completely normal girls," said Ms Solovkova, a psychologist by training. Women stared from the photographs – some bold, some shy, some young, some middle-aged, some in their best dresses, some showing a leg. Nina looked about 25 and had green eyes and beautiful long hair. She wore a swimsuit. In the caption under the picture, she said she loved housework.

The agency had been operating for a couple of years and had about 3,000 women on its books. As well as providing a photograph, they had to fill in a form giving their biographical details and vital statistics and write a brief description of the man of their dreams. To join the queue, they paid 350 roubles (£1.40) – not an insignificant sum in those economically straitened times – and then waited in the hope of receiving a letter from an American pen pal, to be found at the other end of the operation by Mr Rollband.

He was a practitioner of the not-very-funny one-line joke. "I thought Russian women either looked like tractor drivers or the tractors themselves," he'd quipped on his last visit to Moscow. But he claimed to be performing a social service, saving the men from monstrous, emancipated American career women, and the Russian women from the "hell" of life in a collapsed Communist country.

About five times a year, he brought his potential bridegrooms over to Moscow on package holidays. They paid $3,500 for the flight, a "banquet" where they would meet the woman of *their* dreams, and the use of a flat, translator and driver.

At the banquets, the women outnumbered the men three to one. The average age of the Russian ladies was 27 while the American guys were 47 on average. Champagne flowed and a lot of promises were made at these parties but not so many marriages took place afterwards. Ms Solovkova was a little cagey about the poor record. "We lose track of the clients after we have introduced them," she said.

She was outraged at suggestions made in the Moscow press that the joint venture promoted sex tourism. "I have never seen any prostitutes among our applicants," she said. "I am a psychologist and I think I should be able to tell."

"It's not fair to say that all our girls are necessarily looking for rich men," she went on, "although of course there is an element of that. Some fill in their application forms and do not even use the word 'love'. They want to see the world, have a nice house. It is understandable because many live in very poor conditions here. And so what? It is the right of every person to seek what they want."

Some of the women were well educated professionals who had failed to find men they felt matched them intellectually. Some had been disappointed by Russian men, with their macho refusal to try and understand their partner's point of view. Others were plain or shy.

But Mr Rollband's clients would have been wrong to assume that Russian women were more passive than their Western sisters. "Russian women are obedient at first but not for long. A lot of relationships break up because the American men underestimate our women," said Ms Solovkova.

Sitting with the manageress was Galina, 29, who worked as an assistant in the Nakhodka office while also hoping to find the partner of her life. She said she'd filled in an application six months earlier but still not heard anything from America. Her photo wasn't in any of the albums because she thought she wasn't photogenic enough and it was prohibitively expensive for her to go and have a good portrait photo taken in a studio.

Divorced, with a five-year-old daughter, she clearly lacked self-confidence. She sat in a hand-knitted jumper and grey skirt, her hands folded on her lap. She complained that the application form was too concerned with statistics and didn't give her a chance to describe her personality.

So how would she describe herself, I asked.

"I am quiet; I am modest – no, I shouldn't say that about myself, should I? I am looking for somebody who is independent, strong and reliable. Western people are more confident than we are, it seems to me; maybe I am wrong. What do you think?"

Galina was reluctant to speak of her ex-husband but it seemed Russian men had let her down.

"Maybe it's my fault. I can't say all Russian men are bad. I just seem to attract the wrong kind. They promise a lot but do little."

Did this mean she had given up hope of finding love at home in Russia?

"Oh no," she said, and a twinkle suddenly appeared in her eye, transforming her into a beauty. "I'm looking here, I'm looking there, I'm looking everywhere. Maybe in England? Why not? I am ready to try anywhere."

HOT SPOTS

The collapse of the Soviet Union created a number of "hot spots" of ethnic conflict. This was a term (*goryachi tochki* in Russian) that the Foreign Ministry in Moscow used, as if seeking to downplay these local wars; to suggest they were insignificant flare-ups on the vast map of the superpower. But the wars were real enough to the people who lost their loved ones in them.

From 1988 to 1994, Christian Armenians and Muslim Azeris fought a nasty little war over the mountainous territory of Nagorno-Karabakh. Each side accused the West of bias in favour of their enemy. It was difficult for correspondents trying to be fair; a minefield for objective reporting.

In February 1992, news came out that something terrible had happened in Khojaly, an Azeri settlement in the disputed enclave, mostly populated by Armenians. Hundreds of Azeri bodies were said to be strewn across a snowy mountainside. Were they battlefield casualties? Or had there been a massacre?

With a group of Moscow-based correspondents, I flew to the Azeri border town of Agdam, to which refugees from Khojaly had fled. We arrived in the middle of the night, tired and in need of refreshment, but instead of being taken to lodgings by our Azeri hosts, we were bussed straight to the town's mosque to see a grim display. Four hideously mutilated corpses were laid out for our inspection.

"When Armenians get killed, you simply report it," said the soldier guiding us. "When our people die, you say they were 'allegedly' killed. You come here and show sympathy but we know you will go away and write something different."

Before we arrived in Agdam, Armenian officials had denied that civilians had been killed in the fight for Khojaly and said the Azeris were not only exaggerating the death toll but staging a show to make it look as if a massacre had happened. I didn't know what to believe.

Disoriented at three o'clock in the morning, I didn't know what to make of it at all. My rational mind said, "Four bodies don't equal a massacre." At the deepest level of my being, I was shocked. "So when we are dead, we all look like these broken dolls," I thought. I was young then and all I had seen of death was the closed coffin of my grandmother at a stiff English funeral.

But I summoned enough professional presence of mind to ask the soldier, "Why only four bodies?" Because relatives had already buried some of the others, he said. Many more corpses were still lying out on the mountainside; the Azeris lacked helicopters to retrieve them. The four bodies had not been claimed, perhaps because their relatives had also died.

The next day, a large crowd gathered outside the mosque. Some were survivors from Khojali, others were relatives, and all were desperate because they said the Armenians were shooting at Azeris as they tried to recover their dead. The chief of police, Colonel Rashid Mamedov, said 500 residents of Khojaly had made it to safety in Agdam. Khojaly had a population of 6,000.

The Azeris were calling it genocide. The killings obviously didn't match the scale of the great genocide against the Armenians of the Ottoman Empire during the First World War, but it was certainly starting to look as if something very bad had indeed happened at Khojaly.

The accounts of the slaughter were consistent; these were simple people. They described how the Armenians had surprised them with a heavy attack on their settlement; how they had realised that this was more than routine shooting and they didn't stand a chance of defending themselves; how they had fled at about midnight into the surrounding woods; how a column of refugees had tried to walk down the Askeran Gap to Agdam; and how in the small hours of the morning, Armenian fighters had trapped them and fired indiscriminately on women, children and old men. Many of those who escaped the bullets froze to death on the mountainside, they said.

Ramiz Nasiru, a shoemaker, was hoping his wife and children were still alive, perhaps hiding somewhere. He said he had seen Russians from the former Soviet army supporting the Armenians with armoured personnel carriers. Other survivors also spoke of Russian involvement.

Former Soviet troops were due to pull out from their bases in the area. The new Commonwealth of Independent States had declared itself neutral in the conflict. I thought it was possible that some Russians, facing an uncertain future back home, might be offering their services as mercenaries to the Armenians, who, like them, were Orthodox Christians.

The Armenians said they'd had to flush out Khojaly because it was being used as a base to attack the Nagorno-Karabakh capital, Stepanakert. Azerbaijan claimed that Nagorno-Karabakh had been its territory for centuries. The Armenians said they had lost it as a result of an arbitrary boundary change made by Lenin.

The crowd outside the mosque was swelling by the minute. People from all over Azerbaijan were arriving to arrange funerals for their relatives. Agdam's judge, Adil Gasimov, said 200 bodies had been brought down from the mountain but hundreds more were still up there while other Khojali residents were perhaps being held captive by the Armenians.

Our small group of journalists went next to the Agdam cemetery, where Azeri women were wailing over 75 freshly dug graves. Following tradition, they had scratched their cheeks bloody and were producing a ritual high-pitched howl. Graves decorated with dolls were those of young people due to have been married, we were told.

A middle-aged man stood over the grave of his nephew, Abulfat Aliev, born 1963, died February 1992. "He went back twice into the forest to save women and children. The third time he got killed himself. Write the truth," the man said. This was beginning to look like a massacre, I had to admit.

At the Agdam railway station, a train had been turned into a makeshift hospital, full of women, children and old men with gunshot wounds. Dr Eldar Sirazhev, from the Azeri capital Baku, said 256 people had been treated since the attack on Khojaly. Nubar Duniamalieva, 43, lay on her stomach with bullet wounds in her back. She said she'd been in the forest with her five children and elderly mother. Two of the children had disappeared but the other three had escaped with her. They'd been lucky in that they were shot close to Azeri-held territory and had managed to crawl to soldiers from their own side.

Sayale Zenalova, 60, lifted her skirt to show a bullet wound in her thigh. Her daughter Valide was with her, also wounded in the leg. Sayale said two of her five sons had been shot dead in front of her and the others were missing.

"A terrible tragedy has taken place but the world is silent," said Dr Sirazhev. "The West has always supported the Armenian side because they have a large, eloquent diaspora."

It was time for us journalists to start producing our stories for the next day's newspapers. But the Azeri soldiers accompanying us decided to take a detour on the way back to town. Obviously trying to unnerve us, they drove to another cemetery from where they said they kept an eye on Armenian gunmen in the nearby fields. They kept us there for longer than I would have liked. I can't say we were hostages, exactly, but it was clear we were going to leave that cemetery when the soldiers decided, not when we chose. Seeing that I was ill at ease, one of them said, "Are you scared? Now you know how our women feel."

The Azeris had made their point. I went back to the hotel to write. In the past, in another context, I had written with compassion about the Armenians. I will never forget how, after their earthquake in 1988, I wandered through the town of Spitak. In the rubble of a school where not a single child had survived, I found the perfectly preserved body of a rat in a jar of formaldehyde, obviously from the science lab.

But now I had a different story to write. I pulled no punches and filed a report that on this occasion, the Azeris and not the Armenians were the victims. Other times during the war, it was the other way round. "Six of one and half a dozen of the other," as my mother used to say about playground fights. But the victims of Khojaly were definitely Muslim.

I did my job, went home and unravelled. Some correspondents become war junkies but I had a kind of nervous breakdown about which journalists are not supposed to speak. You may ask why this happened after I'd been through Afghanistan without any problems. But Agdam was different from Afghanistan, which had been basically a happy story because the troops were going home. This time I had seen a lot of death at close quarters and it inevitably concentrated my mind on my own death. At the age of 36,

I became afraid of everything – of flying, of going on the metro. I knew I had to overcome this or risk becoming like an old Reuter colleague who, having survived the Vietnam War, ended up too frightened to leave his own house.

Like many journalists, I drank too much for a while but I knew alcohol wasn't a long-term solution. Meditation was better medicine and in middle age I found the confidence to embrace life once again.

TROPHY ART

At the start of the 1990s, the hunt was on for "trophy art" – paintings and other treasures that Soviet forces looted from Berlin at the end of World War Two and brought back to Russia as "cultural prisoners of war". Had these works all been German, the scandal might not have been great, but many were European masterpieces that the Nazis had grabbed from occupied countries, like Holland. The West hoped that newly independent Russia would come clean about the captured pictures and return them to their rightful owners.

Two art historians, Konstantin Akinsha and Grigory Kozlov, first blew the whistle on Russian museums and churches that were holding the treasures in dark vaults and cellars, sometimes in damp conditions. The art works were being kept not only from Western eyes but even from viewing by the victorious Soviet public, for whom they were supposed to be "compensation for wartime suffering". The authorities flatly denied that thousands of priceless pictures by artists from Durer and Rembrandt to Goya and Manet were rotting in Russia, having been taken from Berlin by Stalin's special confiscation squads, and sometimes by ordinary soldiers helping themselves to "souvenirs".

I got a tip-off that the long-lost Koenigs Collection of Old Master drawings, sold under duress to the Nazis by a Rotterdam museum, was being kept at Glebov's House, home to the Pushkin Museum's Department of Graphics. "Oh yes, they're here; they're definitely here," a young curator told me pleasantly. "I'll just fetch the Dutch expert for you." Two minutes later, the woman returned with a stony face and said, "No, there's nothing here. You misunderstood." I felt the thrill of the chase and the need to find out more.

The confiscation of books, drawings, paintings and sculptures was done mainly by expert commissions sent by Stalin to strip the Germans of their

116

assets. Moscow regarded this as reasonable retribution, as the Nazis had inflicted enormous cultural losses on the Soviet Union, not to mention the deaths of 26 million people. Tsarist palaces outside Leningrad had been pillaged and precious icons taken from ancient Pskov and Novgorod. In revenge, Stalin's squads sent crate after crate of West European works – about two million pieces in all – to Moscow. Also in the boxes was thought to be the famed "gold of King Priam", excavated from the site of Troy by the 19th-century German archaeologist Heinrich Schliemann.

According to Kozlov and Akinsha, these wonders were first shown freely to the Soviet public but at the end of the 1940s, Stalin ordered them to be shut away. "There was a sea of witnesses at the time because so many people had helped to carry the paintings," said Mr Akinsha. "Even now it's an open secret among art teachers and students that the works are here but you need a special pass from the Ministry of Culture to get into the storerooms."

In 1956, the Soviet Union decided to reward East Germany for its "peace-loving" policies by returning art that had belonged to the Dresden Gallery. Great fanfare surrounded this event. A farewell exhibition was held at the Hermitage Museum in Leningrad, after which the works were released and the myth created that the Soviet Union had saved them from destruction by the Nazis. "We were told the Germans had kept the paintings in caves," said Mr Akinsha. "It was a complete lie. In fact the Nazis were planning to build a vast museum for their booty in Hitler's birthplace of Linz and they took better care of the paintings than they did of their human captives."

The return of the Dresden collection still left about one and a half million art works from Western Europe in Russian hands. They were dispersed around the Soviet Union in museums and churches. Some were given to the Ministry of Defence to decorate military sanatoria and colonels' *dachas.*

The hunt for the art took a new twist when a video came to light, showing 17th- and 18th-century French paintings hanging at Uzkoye, a sanatorium on the edge of Moscow enjoyed by scientists from the Academy of Sciences. Some of the pictures were believed to have been taken from Sans Soucis, Frederick the Great's "Prussian Versailles" at Potsdam. I went to the Uzkoye estate, which had once belonged to Prince Trubetskoy, and pretended an

117

interest in the Russian aristocracy. The manager wouldn't let me in, for fear of disturbing the scientists, but she did walk with me in the grounds.

She volunteered the information that the local church of St Anne contained rare books from German libraries. "Oh really," I said. "And I've heard that you also have paintings from Sans Soucis in the main house."

She was aghast. "Where did you get that information from? I don't like the look of this. There's too much interest in those pictures. I won't tell you anything."

It was the pictures that had drawn me to Uzkoye but the story of the books in the locked church turned out to be even more astonishing. Yevgeny Kuzmin, a literary journalist, told me he'd been inside and seen Russian books withdrawn from circulation by Stalin mixed with German books, including rare volumes from Hitler's private library. Hitler's collection contained scores in Wagner's handwriting and it was reasonable to assume that they were there in the church as well.

The books were jammed in so tightly that those at the bottom had been crushed to dust. Rats had nibbled at leather bindings and the books were white with 40 years of pigeon droppings. To make matters worse, the stacks had collapsed and books had fallen into a great heap, needing to be piled up again. The doors were blocked, so Soviet staff entered through the church domes and slithered down on ropes or rode in cradles to put the books back. "This is a kind of cultural Katyn massacre," said Mr Kuzmin, "except that dumped into an unmarked grave are not people but books."

Sensation followed on sensation. After the library revelations, Kozlov and Akinsha came up with documentary proof that Schliemann's gold, which before the war had been exhibited in Berlin's Museum of Pre- and Early History, was indeed among the plundered treasures in Moscow. They gave me access to the inventory that accompanied the crates of gold from Germany and a paper confirming receipt in Moscow, signed by a certain Lapin on 9 July 1945. The inventory referred to "items of women's jewellery" and then explicitly to "treasures from Troy (Schliemann's excavations)".

The gold had been unearthed in 1873. Schliemann thought he had found the jewellery of Helen of Troy, King Priam's daughter-in-law, but in fact the treasure was even older. The centrepiece was a diadem made up of 16,353 intricately worked pieces of gold. Found along with it were a second diadem, necklaces, dozens of bracelets and thousands of rings, all in gold. The inventory said the items were confiscated "from the Zenith tower at the zoo". And indeed the last-known location of the gold had been a concrete bunker at Flakturm Zoo, where the Nazis had stored it for safekeeping.

This was dynamite. And still the authorities in Moscow were denying that they were holding any treasures at all. Irina Antonova, director of the Pushkin Museum in whose vaults the gold was thought to lie, denied all knowledge of it. But then of course she would – since she herself had been a member of the confiscation teams that worked in Berlin at the end of the war.

With all the fuss in the papers about the trophy art, I was desperate to find some small treasure myself. And then it happened. By chance, I attended a wedding. It was a fashionable affair and the bride and groom, film makers with an eye for Soviet *kitsch*, had hired a white, neo-Corinthian palace of culture in the countryside outside Moscow for their reception. The guests mingled among potted palms or played billiards in what was effectively a country club. I wandered into a ground floor sitting room and saw two fine landscapes hanging on the wall.

I didn't recognise the pictures but asked the director, a cheerful old Communist called Vladimir Davidov, where they came from. "Oh, that's trophy art, taken from Germany at the end of the war," he said without batting an eyelid. "I got them from Uzkoye when this club was built in 1954 and we needed something to decorate the walls."

He allowed me back to photograph the paintings, which were later identified by experts as *Vespasian's Temple in Rome* and *The Narni Valley* by Wilhelm Schirmer, a German romantic artist who lived in Italy in the 19th century. Before the war, they had hung in Berlin's Schloss Museum.

The Soviet clubhouse, at the heart of a village built by German prisoners of war, had turned out to be quite a good home for the pictures. True, the over-zealous cleaning ladies had dusted them, which one is not supposed to do to masterpieces, but it could have been worse. The paintings were slightly scratched but otherwise in good condition. "That's how they were when we got them," said Mr Davidov, a seemingly decent chap who could easily have sold them on the black market but who'd resisted that temptation.

With finds like this, it was becoming difficult for the Russian authorities to stonewall any longer. But they had a fair point when they said that a simple exchange of art works would not be possible. For while Russia had something to swap, the looted Russian icons that had found their way to Germany had been sold on the open market and disappeared into thousands of private collections. Art experts said that in a way it didn't matter where in the world all the treasures ended up as long as they were on view to the public.

And so in October 1992, Russian Culture Minister Yevgeny Sidorov bit the bullet and admitted the existence of trophy art. Dutch ambassador Joris Vos was invited to see the Koenigs Collection and pronounced himself stunned at the "unbelievable treasure" of drawings by Rembrandt, Tintoretto, Tiepolo and Veronese, although a hundred sketches appeared to missing.

Next came an official admission that the Schliemann gold was indeed in Moscow. Mr Sidorov told the Russian newspaper *Literaturnaya Gazeta* that he had held it in his hands. "It doesn't look very brilliant," he said, "but it gives out a warmth and energy which just grabs your soul." Ms Antonova of the Pushkin Museum, who'd denied to the last that her institution was holding it, finally crumbled and told the same paper, "Since fate has disposed that the gold should turn up in Russia, I would very much like to give an opportunity to our specialists to study it." As well as Russian academics, the Germans and belatedly the Turks were eager to get their hands on the gold, for ancient Troy was of course on the territory of modern Turkey.

But it took another three years for the Pushkin Museum to put on an exhibition of trophy art, entitled Saved Twice Over. Opening the show, Ms Antonova did an elegant *volte face* and said she was delighted to be able to display the works; she particularly recommended visitors to pay attention to two paintings by Goya. She said the world shouldn't blame Russia for having hid the art for half a century but, on the contrary, be grateful to the confiscation squads who'd "saved" the pictures from the ruins of Berlin, handing them over to museum staff, who "saved" them again through painstaking restoration.

After which, you might think the trophy art went back to Western Europe but the Russians continued to drag their feet. Following the 2004 Orange Revolution, Ukraine, which was holding half of the Koenigs Collection, did return its drawings to The Netherlands. But the rest remained in the Pushkin Museum, their fate still "under consideration" by a very slow-moving Russia.

IRISH INFLUENCE

The Catholic Church of St Louis, glowing in the shadow of the Lubyanka secret police headquarters, was a refuge for Western European people living in Moscow. We would go there on 24 December to remind ourselves that it was Christmas in the West and we brought our sorrows to the church as well. It was here we gathered for the funeral of my close friend Sian Thomas, who was knocked off her bike and killed while on a cycle marathon through Siberia. The church was mock-Gothic, with an organ – something you didn't hear in the onion-domed Russian Orthodox churches. The priest was a Frenchman and the regular congregation was mainly made up of Poles, with a scattering of Africans and a tiny minority of Russian Catholics.

So on a visit to the church in March 1993, I was rather surprised to hear this: *Ar nAthair ata ar neamh, go naofar tAinm, go dtaga do riocht, go ndeantar do thoil ar an dtalamh.* Going to the choir stalls to investigate, I discovered Michael Carey from Tipperary drilling the choristers in the Gaelic version of the Lord's Prayer. They were going to sing at a special Mass to launch Moscow's St Patrick's Day parade, he said. In fact, it was the second year they were holding the event, which expressed the pride and confidence of one of the city's most active foreign communities. For out of all proportion to its size, Ireland was leading the way in doing business with the new capitalist Russia. Interesting: I hadn't realised Ireland was playing that big a role.

Before I met Mr Carey, the only "Celt" I'd known in Moscow was Vladimir Laserson, a Russian Jew who'd dropped out of his flute class at the Moscow Conservatory and taught himself to play a range of Irish and Scottish instruments. His friends called him "Highlander" because he was completely obsessed with everything Celtic. He'd made his own kilt and even a sporran by cutting up his mother's leather handbag and adding strips of sealskin. When I wrote about him in *The Independent*, a kind reader in Scotland sent him a set of real Scottish bagpipes.

Helen, with Highlander, Vladimir Laserson

I used to sing sometimes with Laserson. My repertoire included old Scottish and Irish ballads and we performed at private parties and in schools. We were even on the radio once. In love with his bagpipes, Laserson used to call me his "second bag". Being English also made me a bit sub-standard from his point of view. Needless to say, Laserson was way ahead of me when it came to finding out about the St Patrick's Day parade – he'd already wangled his way onto one of the floats and was going to play with some real Irish fiddlers.

The Irish had come to Moscow to work as managers in the retail trade. Back in Gorbachev's time, Russian officials flying to summits with the Americans had made stopovers at Shannon Airport and noticed the duty free shops there. That was why the Irish were given the contract to develop the duty free business at Moscow's Sheremyetyevo Airport and from there, they branched out into running supermarkets in the city.

Mr Carey worked as a buyer at Irish House, a huge supermarket on the New Arbat, which was jointly owned by Aer Rianta – the operators of Shannon – and a Russian partner. On the other side of town was the Garden Ring supermarket, managed by Colm Fitzsimons for the Irish firm of Coughlan, Flannery and Pratt. "There's a healthy rivalry between us but actually there's loads of room in Russia for everyone," Colm said tolerantly as we chatted over the counter. I used to prefer his shop, simply because it was nearer to my flat.

The supermarkets and other Irish-run shops and bars changed the face of Moscow. Gone were the special hard currency stores for the privileged, and state "produce" shops with lumps of fat and rotten cabbage for the majority of poor Russians. Helped by the Finns, Swiss and Germans, the Irish broke down that Soviet version of apartheid. Now, regardless of nationality, whoever had enough roubles could buy Mr Carey's cornflakes, or fish fingers from Mr Fitzsimmons.

The shops, which employed cheap local labour and sold imported goods at sky-high prices, raked in money but to reap these rewards, the Irish took risks that other businessmen, including the timid British, found too off-putting. In the absence of a legal framework, there was the mafia and the system of "roofs" (protection). The Irish said they left their Russian partners to handle the gangsters for them.

At Garden Ring, most of the customers were the better-off Russians. Some of the Russian staff, who'd worked in the shop when it had been a Soviet food store, couldn't get used to these New Russians. "We had one customer," said Colm, "who got out of a Mercedes with a mobile telephone and a wife in a fur coat. And the old lady who mops the floor for us said to him, 'I hope you've got money to be coming in a place like this.'"

It was a laugh a minute with the pioneering and good-hearted Irish. So naturally it was to Colm I turned when I was looking for sponsorship for a ground-breaking cultural event. I wanted to bring Handel's *Messiah*, with its uplifting Hallelujah chorus, to Russia.

As a child, I'd heard it often because my Uncle Jack was a singer and would take the bass solo part in Christmas performances all over Yorkshire. I loved it when he rumbled dramatically, "I will shake all nations, all nations I'll shaaaake". It came as a huge shock and disappointment to me when I arrived in Russia, with its great musical traditions, to learn that the Russians had never heard of Handel's *Messiah*. This was because in Communist times, atheist ideology prevailed and the oratorio repertoire was not much known.

In the summer of 1993, I was at party where I happened to meet a man called Andrew Sparke, who was then working for the BBC. We got talking about music and he confided to me that his great dream was to conduct a performance of *Messiah*. "And I would love to sing the contralto solo," I said. There and then we cooked up a plan to put on a performance of the oratorio and raise money for charity.

We advertised among the expat community and by early autumn, had gathered a choir of enthusiastic amateurs, mainly from Britain and America, many of whom knew the work pretty well, if not by heart. There were a few Irish faces in the choir as well, including that of Michael Carey.

What were we going to call ourselves? I came up with the idea of "Moscow Oratorio" and the name stuck. We needed a professional choirmaster or mistress, though, so soprano Tatyana Gridneva from the Moscow Philharmonic, from whom I had started taking additional singing advice, stepped into that role and coached the choir until they were note perfect.

Ms Gridneva was going to be the soprano soloist, the bass solo would be sung by a diplomat from the American embassy, and yours truly was going to be the fat contralto in a velvet dress. But we needed money to fly out a student from the London Guildhall who had agreed to sing the tenor part and also to pay the professional string players of the Russian orchestra.

Approaching Colm for the sponsorship cash, I played first on his generosity and good nature. We were planning to raise money for soup kitchens for the homeless, I said. He seemed quite interested but didn't immediately open his till. I realised I was going to have to employ and bit more charm and blarney. Quick as a flash I said, "Well, of course you do realise the *Messiah* had its first ever public performance in Dublin, so there's a big Irish connection." I wasn't quite sure this was true and needed to consult an encyclopedia afterwards to confirm it. But it did the trick. "Will a thousand pounds do you?" Colm asked.

The tickets sold like hot cakes. Over two evenings in St Andrew's Anglican Church, then still used as the state Melodia recording studios, we performed to packed audiences and raised hundreds of dollars for the soup kitchens. The choir gave one hundred per cent. Conductor Sparke took a well-deserved bow. The only thing that jarred slightly was the sight of the Russian orchestra professionals counting their money before the audience had even left the church.

After the event, I forgot all about Moscow Oratorio. More than a decade later, I was astonished to learn that it was still going – indeed the original choir had divided into two groups, one which sang seriously and the other which met more for fun. Both these choirs had expat and Russian members and in both cases Russian conductors, who had widened the repertoire far beyond the *Messiah*. Moscow Oratorio had taken on a life of its own, which I found rather gratifying.

The Irish, however, had a more bitter experience. They were betrayed by their Russian business partners who, having taken advantage of all the investment and know-how from Ireland, suddenly kicked the supermarket managers out and took over their businesses. This was a blow to people like Colm, who had married in Russia and envisaged their futures in the country.

In retrospect, the rough sidelining of the Irish can be seen as the start of "raiding", which continued into the Putin era, when the mafia (or was it the authorities, and was there in fact any difference?) took over successful businesses at gunpoint and threw the managers in jail on trumped-up tax evasion charges.

The Irish had the last laugh, though, according to an Irish journalist colleague of mine. Apparently, they got a tip-off that gunmen were coming and managed to move their money out of the country in time. They lost their businesses but saved their cash to start again somewhere else.

"Back home in Dublin?" I asked.

"No," said my colleague. "I believe most of them went on from Moscow to China."

GENTEEL AND POOR

The vet called one day to give our cat Minky an injection. I hadn't seen Raisa Yevgenyevna for some time, so naturally I asked her how she was getting on. In a barely audible voice, she said, "Oh, don't ask."

She was pathetically grateful to earn the equivalent of 10 quid for treating Minky. She said she hadn't been called out for weeks and was having a hard time making ends meet. All her clients used to be solid Soviet middle class people – scientists, artists, teachers and doctors – but since the drastic cuts in state spending, they had become the new Russian poor. "Just feeding their families is a terrible struggle, so pets are very low on the list of priorities," she said.

The division between rich and poor was widening into a huge chasm. A minority of New Russians, who were getting rich God only knew how, shamelessly flaunted their wealth, spending fortunes on flashy cars, designer clothes and exotic holidays. The new poor, together with the old poor – the working class who had had nothing much in Soviet times and still had nothing – made up the downtrodden majority. Russian society under Boris Yeltsin came increasingly to resemble Latin America, where tiny groups of super-rich enjoyed the good life, protected by high walls and bodyguards from the rest, who lived in poverty. No wonder the most popular soap opera on television was a Mexican serial called *The Rich Also Cry.*

Wild cowboy capitalism created some of the new inequalities but perhaps worse, the process of privatisation entrenched old inequalities from the Soviet system. Probably the national pie couldn't have been cut up any other way without causing anarchy but it was very unfair.

Where housing was concerned, people were allowed to become owners of the flats in which they lived. So if you were a privileged member of the Communist Party elite, with a five-room flat in the city centre, that was what you got to keep. If you were a member of the proletariat, living in a box on the edge of town, that's where you remained. And if you didn't have a flat because, say, you were young and living with your parents or you were divorced, then you got nothing; simple as that. Not surprisingly, many of the new rich were the sons and daughters of top Communists and now they had the power of ownership as well. A division was soon to open up between those who could dispose of million-dollar properties as they liked and those who were forced to become tenants, paying astronomical rents.

I focused a lot in my reporting on the new poor. It wasn't just a question of sympathy or the fact that the genteel were on the whole the most intelligent, articulate and pleasant people to deal with. I knew that in any society, it's the middle class that forms the backbone and provides stability. With an almost non-existent middle class, Russia was dangerously unstable. How the middle class developed would determine the development of Russia as a whole.

In early 1993, I interviewed a teacher called Marina Minayeva, who worked in a state school and was therefore among the most vulnerable. She had a doctorate in history, specialising in the 1920s and 1930s, but this wasn't much use in an ordinary school and what she actually taught was English. Because languages were not her speciality, she was paid only the basic salary of 3,500 roubles a month (then worth £5).

Outside school hours she worked, as she put it, "like a squirrel in a wheel", to supplement this meagre income. On her day off and on Monday evenings, she gave lessons to future teachers at the Pedagogical University, which brought in another 3,500 roubles a month. During the rest of the week, she gave evening coaching to students who were trying to get into university, which earned her 1,600 roubles. And on top of that, she had five private pupils who contributed 9,600 roubles to her budget. That made a grand total of 18,200 roubles, which in those days was worth all of £26. She handed a portion of it over to her parents, with whom she lived, because they were struggling on a pension income that was a quarter of hers.

Marina, 25 and unmarried, remembered a happy childhood. Her father Yevgeny, a professor of history, had earned enough to provide everything the family of three needed. "For special occasions, there was always a good spread, with caviar and tongue on the table," she said. "I had clothes and holidays in Crimea. I went to the cinema and exhibitions and the theatre several times a week. Now I have no strength, no time and I'm not in the mood to relax." She was nevertheless hoping to get to a Matisse exhibition that had just opened at the Pushkin Museum.

Because she worked so hard, Marina did survive but her diet had deteriorated considerably. Never one for meat, she used to like plenty of fruit and vegetables, fish, and milk products such as *kefir* (a kind of yoghurt). Now she made do with fewer fruits and greens and just milk instead of more expensive dairy products; of fish she could only dream. Her parents had a poorer diet still. She said her mother Lyudmila was often "hysterical" with worry about this, and her father had lost weight.

"Mum and Dad used to like meat and sausage but now they live on their stocks of porridge. In wartime, they grew up on bread and potatoes. They have gone back to that. I had a good childhood but I know that if I have any kids, I won't be able to give them what I had."

Marina said she didn't envy the rich, provided they had earned their money honestly, but she felt a great weariness and sense of hopelessness. She had always been sceptical about Yeltsin and was losing faith in him by the day. "I try to keep calm; I try not to think about the situation or I would go mad. But I know things will only get worse. We will not get out of this economic hole while I am still a young woman."

There were millions of people like Marina; millions even poorer, more scared, more dispirited and resentful. They formed a potential constituency for anti-Yeltsin politicians holding out the dubious promise of a return to "order", be it Communist or extreme nationalist.

But the intelligentsia were not fools; by definition they were not fools to be easily manipulated. Neither were they wallowing in self-pity and telling sob stories – at least not the majority of them. I think what I found most compelling about them was the dignity they mustered in difficult circumstances; the triumph of the human spirit.

One woman who particularly impressed me as a battler and free thinker was Natalya Sokolova. In Soviet times, she'd been a minor dissident. A biologist by training, she used to perform experiments on animals at the same institute that pickled and preserved the body of Lenin. That had been her day job. By night, she'd typed out carbon copies of banned books. Her flat had been an underground publishing house. Her own mother had reported her to the KGB but luckily, when they'd come for her she'd been out, so the secret police had filled their quota by arresting someone else.

In the early 1990s, with five children to feed and a husband who was more nuisance than use, Natalya found herself on the street, selling books in 30 degrees of frost or 30 degrees of heat, regardless. But she wasn't complaining of humiliation. She knew there were many more people with higher education who had similarly gone down in the world.

I went to visit her at her home. The walls of the flat were covered with newspaper because she couldn't afford wallpaper. The only food visible in the kitchen was a white loaf on the table and a pan of beans on the hob. But the children were creatively occupied, drawing or listening to music. Sleeping in the corner was a gorgeous black cat, rescued from superstitious neighbours who had kicked it out because they thought it was unlucky. Somehow, Natalya was finding spare scraps to put in its bowl.

We talked about the changes since Soviet times. "Then the issues were black and white," Natalya said. "It was a simple matter of conforming or daring to fight for freedom. Now the situation is murkier. With our corrupt politicians, you can't really say we have democracy. But the people have the leaders they deserve. You cannot achieve democracy by presidential decree. Citizens must learn to take personal responsibility."

"The authorities don't need labour camps any more," she went on. "They control us by keeping us in perpetual uncertainty; by not paying our wages. They do not quite let us die but neither do they let us live. And so people are obsessed with nothing higher than material problems; where the next meal is coming from."

Natalya had turned to the church but she was not an Orthodox Christian of the fanatical, nationalist kind. "I tell all the anti-Semites at church that the Virgin Mary was Jewish too," she joked.

Compared with other Russians who couldn't or wouldn't squarely confront the mistakes of the past, she took the concept of personal responsibility to an extreme degree. Not only did she pray for forgiveness of her own sins but she also believed she must answer for the crimes and stupidities of past generations, including the misplaced political zeal of her own mother.

As for her children, Natalya said she tried to teach them that man does not live by bread alone.

"It is not easy when they see wealth around them," she said. "Naturally, they want things too. But most gains in Russia these days are ill-gotten. It is almost impossible to make big money by honest means. When they see shiny black jeeps, I tell them to look not at the cars but at the thugs driving them. I say, 'those people are poorer than we are.'"

MOSCOW TEA PARTY

Russian politics became extremely tedious in 1993. President Boris Yeltsin was bogged down in seemingly endless arguments with parliamentary deputies, many of them old Communists, who were carping, criticising and resisting his economic reforms every step of the way. This was the nitty-gritty of democracy and it became a real challenge for me to make it interesting for my readers. If I yawned every time Speaker Ruslan Khasbulatov opened his mouth, how much more frustrated must Mr Yeltsin have been, for he was essentially a man of action, at his best leaping onto a tank in a crisis (and then going off for a quiet vodka or two afterwards).

Market reforms were starting to cause real pain to the population. The deputies were so disgruntled they were planning to impeach Mr Yeltsin. In September, the President's patience snapped and he dissolved the whingeing assembly. Russia was more of a parliamentary democracy in those days and the constitution didn't give the President the tsar-like powers that Vladimir Putin was later to have. Parliament responded by declaring Yeltsin's presidency unconstitutional. We newshounds started to take a bit more interest.

In open revolt, parliament appointed Vice-President Alexander Rutskoi as acting President. An uprising started and Russia came close to civil war. The deputies barricaded themselves inside the White House where, if Interior Ministry figures were to be believed, they were joined by about 600 armed men. From the balcony, Rutskoi, an Afghan war veteran, urged crowds to seize the television centre at Ostankino. In the street fighting that ensued, dozens of people were killed, including my colleague, cameraman Rory Peck.

Yeltsin declared a state of emergency; he was fighting now for his political survival. On 4 October, he ordered tanks to shell the White House.

They fired into the building, which soon became a charred wreck. Troops went in to flush out the resistance, floor by floor. Rutskoi and Khasbulatov were arrested. Police said afterwards that 187 people had died and 437 been wounded in the crushing of the "second October revolution". It had been the worst street fighting since the Bolshevik Revolution of 1917.

Yeltsin won this war but only thanks to the army and former KGB, in whose debt he now found himself. From this point on, the balance of power between President and parliament shifted in favour of the one man at the top. The West unthinkingly applauded, believing that the main thing was to root out the weeds of Communism and get the free market growing as rapidly and lushly as possible. As a Western reporter, it never crossed my mind that there might be any other way of seeing events but as a struggle between the foot-dragging "baddies" in parliament and the forward-marching hero Yeltsin.

Which was why I was stunned when, during a singing lesson with Tatyana Gridneva, she suddenly burst into bitter tears. It turned out she had a very different view of what had happened at the White House. If I called myself a journalist, I felt I had to listen to her. I suggested she organise a tea party with other like-minded Russians and I would come, with an open mind, to hear their take on the situation.

The party took place early in the evening, so we could all get home before curfew. We met in the antique-furnished

Tatyana Gridneva

flat of Tatyana's son, Kirill Vyatkin, a specialist on Germany, and his wife Dasha, a schoolteacher. The other participants were Tatyana's husband Sergei Vyatkin, a retired military lawyer, and Pavel Podlesny, an academic from the Institute of Europe. They were the cultural intelligentsia, who had not done too badly for themselves in Soviet times.

The table was spread with ham and cheese sandwiches, biscuits and a kind of chocolate mousse known as "bird's milk", with vodka for the men and rum for the women. The conversation began with the group exchanging accounts of how they had spent the past week at home to avoid the violence. "Most of the day, I spent lying on the floor for fear of bullets coming through my window," said Pavel, who lived right beside the White House. "At one point, I thought the army might take over my flat to use as a base for their attacks."

Our talk was accompanied by the low hum of Russian Orthodox Church music from the television, as the evening news reported on the funerals of some of the victims. "This has been a terrible national tragedy," said Sergei. "It is a giant step back for Russia."

"It was the worst battle here since the Second World War," said Pavel. "What possible joy can anyone find in it? And do you believe we can have free elections after this? Thank God, when he spoke, the President at least had the decency not to claim a victory."

"That speech really churned me up," said Tatyana. "He was giving his condolences to the families of the dead. But he gave the order to storm the White House, so he must have known there would be victims. He might as well have sent his condolences in advance."

I ventured the view that Yeltsin had had no choice but to use force after his opponents had rejected all his initiatives, and especially after their armed attack on the Ostankino television centre.

"But he caged those deputies in parliament," said Tatyana, "and he put them under such psychological pressure that they lashed out like tormented animals."

"You'd never accept such violence in England or America," said Sergei. "That would be unthinkable. But it's all right for Russia."

What about Mr Yeltsin's claim that he had saved Russia from fascism? (In those days, the extreme left met the extreme right in what the Western-leaning democrats called the "red-brown" threat.)

Now it was the turn of Kirill, the expert on Germany, to become heated. "That's nonsense. I don't see a risk of fascism here at all. Of course, there are extremist groups but they are a minority. The fascist movement in Russia is no worse than in other European countries. This slogan of fascism is used here only to blacken the likes of Communists and socialists." Tatyana, whose father had been a singer in the Red Army Ensemble and whose other relatives had fought to defend the Soviet Union from the Nazis, said she became very upset every time she heard Yeltsin lumping Communists and fascists together. "This rhetoric is infuriating," she said. "He should get a new speech writer. When he talks about the red-brown threat, he means *me*!"

Sergei, a former Communist Party member who regarded himself as a social democrat and wanted to see support for the state as well as the private sector, said the President was alienating a whole section of society who recognised that Communism had had its faults but who didn't want to throw the baby out with the bath water.

"Of course Stalin was a tyrant; of course there was the law on anti-Soviet agitation and propaganda. But if I'm honest, I'd have to say that I didn't experience the Soviet Union as a huge labour camp. It wasn't like that for me."

"Yes," said Tatyana, "we were freer then, under Brezhnev. We saw the weaknesses of our leaders but we laughed at them and got on with our professional and private lives."

"And now you believe you *aren't* free?" I asked with some surprise.

"No, because I don't know where I belong. There is no order in society."

"You mean the rising crime?"

"Not just that. There is complete anarchy here. We are completely bewildered."

The Russian intelligentsia always preferred talking about art or poetry to "dirty politics" and at this point Sergei tried to turn the conversation round to "eternal things". But I persisted. I wanted to know how they were faring in the new enterprise culture that left once-respectable middle class people impoverished and disregarded.

Kirill and Dasha said they had enough money to feed themselves and their

136

little girl Masha but luxuries, such as a boat ride down the Moscow River, were beyond their means. Tatyana remembered that as a music student, she had earned enough from a single performance to go out afterwards and buy a kilo of cheese, a litre of milk, 10 eggs and a loaf. Now, as a grade-one singer with 20 years' experience, she could afford little more than a kilo of sausage after giving a concert. Whereas once she'd had to appear on stage 10 times to buy a pair of good shoes – "lacquered, with bows and high heels" – now she had to sing 20 times. She hadn't bought new clothes or shoes in years.

Tatyana and Sergei and Kirill and Dasha had privatised their apartments, so at least they weren't paying rent. But they hadn't made use of vouchers that the government had given out to help people buy shares in former state companies. "Mine are still lying at the bottom of a drawer," said Tatyana. More economically savvy people were scooping up these vouchers like little boys collecting battle cards from cereal packets.

The way privatisation had been conducted was one of the main complaints of the group. "In the past, Soviet people lived quite poorly," said Tatyana, "but everything we had was in a common kitty. Now rascals are coming along and saying 'that's mine'. But what about me? It's mine too because I contributed to the state's wealth with my taxes and by accepting low wages for all those years."

She accused politicians in Mr Yeltsin's entourage of bullying and corruption. Specifically, she was angry with state secretary Gennady Burbulis, who had evicted her from a small mansion that the Moscow City Council had previously said she could turn into a music school. I knew this to be true because I'd been with her when Burbulis's heavies had turned her out and grabbed this rather attractive piece of real estate.

"I understand how you feel," I said. "But it's easy to criticise. What would you do if you were President?"

Sergei dodged the question, saying jokingly that he would rather be in the House of Lords. But Pavel was prepared to give me an answer.

"Perhaps Yeltsin has taken us out of the political cul-de-sac we were in," he conceded, "but we're still in an economic cul-de-sac. Now the people don't have a parliament to complain to, so they will focus all their anger on the government. If Yeltsin doesn't achieve something very quickly, people will say Rutskoi was right. So now he needs to concentrate on bringing down price inflation, correcting the privatisation programme and bolstering social welfare. Otherwise there will be unrest."

I asked him, since he had such concrete ideas, why he didn't consider standing in coming elections for a new parliament.

"Ah," replied Pavel. "I'm 53. I'm a man between two epochs. What Russia needs is a new generation."

MINIGARCHS

I never knew any super-rich Russians or oligarchs as they came to be called. But as President Yeltsin's economic reforms progressed, I started to meet Russians who were considerably richer than me – minor tycoons or minigarchs, if you like. This came as a relief because I'd found it tiring always to be wealthier than my Russian acquaintances, like the Queen of England in relation to everyone I met.

I had a cleaning lady. And here I would I like to stress that this was not because I was Lady Muck, incapable of vacuuming my own carpets, but because I never had a choice in the matter. In Soviet times, when I'd had to live in the special foreigners' compound, I was allotted a domestic servant. Nadia used to iron my clothes, make soup and dumplings for me and, when I was out, read my letters on behalf of the KGB. She was a nice woman; she was just doing her job.

When it became possible for Costya and me to rent in the private sector, I thought I would do without a home help but it was not to be. Our latest flat had some antique furniture. When we took it, the rather fussy landlord insisted we continued to employ Nina Veniaminovna, whose job it was to come once a week and polish the precious cabinets. (In the end, our cat Minky knocked over one of the landlord's "priceless" icons and smashed it but that's another story.)

Nina duly arrived and in fact we got on with her like a house on fire. She was a retired opera singer. She must have had quite a career because she had once performed for Soviet leader Nikita Khrushchev. But she happily descended to our level and not only cleaned but made some delicious meals for us. When she first came, I think there was no doubt that she needed the money. But as time went on, I began to wonder.

She took to arriving in a chauffeur-driven car. Then I noticed that she had got a new fur coat. One day she came in, gave the flat a quick flick with a feather duster, and plonked herself down to show me snaps of her holiday in Sri Lanka. "Andrei paid for me," she said.

It turned out that her son, Andrei Zaborsky, was doing rather well. He'd started a company called A-Z, which supplied all the fiddly little necessities of life. "From acorns mighty oaks do grow" could have been the motto of his firm, which according to Nina had a turnover of four million pounds from trading in the humble battery. She arranged for me to meet him.

Andrei was very friendly and easy-going. We soon got chatting about modern times and old times. Like me, he well remembered the queues and shortages of the Soviet era, when shopping had been a hit-and-miss affair. Small but essential items like soap and matches had often been the hardest to find. Andrei had regularly found himself short of a battery for his cassette player and been unable to listen to his beloved rock and roll. "Batteries are like bread. You need them every day," he said, explaining why he had started out by selling this particular item.

He was 34 when I met him. He'd studied French and worked for the Soviet travel agency Intourist before going into business on his own. Now he employed a hundred people. The batteries he imported were on sale in kiosks and his advertising was plastered all over Moscow.

Andrei admitted he broke the law when starting out. He bought batteries that were past their sell-by date and passed them off as fresh ones. "They were cheap. I had no choice. I broke the law from poverty," he said. "But not any more. Now I am determined to work within the framework of the law."

Like many Russian entrepreneurs trying to make their fortunes in those days, Andrei worked punishingly long hours and had little time to enjoy his wealth. He lived in a three-room flat in an ordinary suburb and his black BMW, he said, was too old to be called flash or fancy.

His one luxury was travelling with his wife Olga. "For years, I worked for Intourist but I was never allowed to go anywhere. Before that, I was a translator in Cambodia but you can't call that travelling. It was more like military service. Now I have a real thirst to see the world."

"So where have you been?" I asked.

He said he'd spent New Year in Denmark and recently visited France, Italy and Greece. He'd stayed in Greece a little longer than he'd intended because he was being threatened by petty racketeers back in Moscow and took fright. "I was inexperienced. I got scared," he said.

On his return to Moscow, he got himself some security guards and instantly felt better. He didn't carry a weapon himself, he said. "I am against that on principle."

Andrei was optimistic that Russian economic life would normalise until the country came to resemble the West. He saw no danger of a return to Communism or the rise of fascism, and was committed to living and investing in his homeland.

In fact, he was planning to sow another acorn. The battery business had taken off and he was going to sell a slice of it to partners in Hong Kong. Then he was going to turn his attention to another small but very necessary item – the light bulb.

"Did you know," he said, "that in Communist times there was a black market in dead light bulbs? If you needed a light bulb at home, you would steal a good one from work and replace it with a dead one. Now things will be much simpler. People need only look out for the A-Z sign."

MARRIED LIFE

Costya building dachas

If Costya and I were grateful to Mikahail Gorbachev for enabling us to marry in the first place, then I guess we had Boris Yeltsin to thank for giving us a normal married life.

In 1993, I was finally able to visit Costya's home town of Kirovsk in Leningrad Region, which had been strictly closed to foreigners because of its top-secret factory producing submarine parts. Unfortunately, I was too late to see his father Policarp Ivanovich in Kirovsk (although I had, of course, seen him in other places including Leningrad or St Petersburg as it was renamed, Moscow and even London and Yorkshire). In Kirovsk, I saw his grave among the pine trees in the cemetery.

Costya's mother, Lyubov Andreyevna, had moved in widowhood from the family house on the banks of the Neva River to a flat on a squalid estate, which she seemed to find more convenient although she missed the garden where Policarp had grown roses. She was living on a pension of 6,400 roubles (just over £9) a month and had benefitted not at all from Yeltsin's reforms. But I admired her enormously because despite her age and the routines of a lifetime – she had taught Marxist theory – she found the mental flexibility and courage to deal with change. In that year's political crisis, she supported Yeltsin. "He has his faults but he is Russia's best hope," she said. "I will not live to see any positive change here but maybe the next generation will."

Costya took me walking round the town. Despite the collapse of Communism, Lenin still stood on the central square, pointing the way forward to the people who lived in the wooden shacks and concrete apartment blocks. Children chased stray cats among the mounds of litter. After dark, yobs would come out, making the streets unsafe. Kiosks were selling beer and sweets but there didn't seem to be much edible food.

During the Second World War, Kirovsk had been right on the front line and every square inch of earth had been riddled with bullets. Costya's older brother, Sergei, had lost his hand at the age of 11, playing with a grenade. Now he had a drink problem. "Shall we go and see him?" I asked. "No, we won't bother," said Costya.

We passed the Ladoga factory, the reason why I had not been allowed to see Kirovsk for so long. Apparently it was now trying to produce electronic goods to compete with Japanese imports. I couldn't really see why the authorities had kept Kirovsk closed for so long, unless they didn't want foreigners to know how dreary the place was.

"Come on, let's get back to St P," said Costya, and we got into the Volvo. That evening, we were meeting Little Kostya in St Petersburg, which was his hometown.

The two Kostyas, who had grown up together, had realised their dream of going into business together. Costya Gagarin (who spelt his name with a c, although k is the usual way) had moved to Moscow first because he'd met

143

me. Kostya Vasiliev, previously a railway worker, had moved a little later from Leningrad and lived out of a suitcase until he could afford to bring Ira and their daughter Katya to the capital.

Costya and Kostya were running a small painting and decorating business, employing a handful of people and working for a range of clients, including some dollar-paying Westerners I put their way. Except for loans given by friends and relatives, they'd had no start-up capital but they were beginning to make money. In this sense, they represented a genuinely new class, succeeding without the Communist Party connections that gave an unfair advantage to many of the so-called New Russians. And thankfully, they were small fish, of little interest to the mafia, or so I thought.

Costya and mates in the renovation business

The old joke goes that if you want a cupboard built don't marry a carpenter. But over the years, Costya was to prove excellent at providing me with nice accommodation. His trick was to rent a cheap flat in poor condition and do it up to West European standards. We then ensconced ourselves until the landlord decided the so-called "Euro remont" justified a hike in the rent, when we would move on and the whole process would start again somewhere else. The moving was tiresome, true, but between moves we lived in comfort at prices we could afford.

When we first came back to the Soviet Union, we'd lived with friends and then had a series of shocking rented flats, some with cockroaches and some with medieval plumbing and lethal electrical wiring. The flat with the antiques had been an improvement but our cat Minky's smashing of the landlord's heirloom, an icon in a glass and silver case, had rather spoilt matters. In disgrace, we moved to an apartment with frog-green wallpaper and a brown floral sofa. The loyal Nina Veniaminovna came and cleaned for us there too, when she could fit us in between trips to Cyprus and Egypt.

I was dying for something light and elegant. Finally, in September 1993, we moved into the first of Costya's renovated flats, an apartment on Taneyev Street behind the Old Arbat, which was a very prestigious area. We hoped this might be our home for some time to come.

Costya and his workers had painted the walls a tasteful fawn brown and pale blue. We coordinated the colours with cream, turquoise and orange curtains from a shop in York, no less. I sensed that the time had come to spend a furniture allowance of £3,000 that *The Independent* had given us back in 1990 but which had lain in the bank because of our long search for decent housing. The priority, of course, was a bed.

In Soviet times, we would probably have done what the diplomats did and reached for a catalogue to order from Scandinavia. But I reckoned in the new free market we would easily find a nice, simple bed locally and save ourselves the trouble of having one shipped in. How wrong I was, for this was the era before IKEA gave everyone in Moscow plenty of fresh ideas.

There were beds in the Dom Mebeli (House of Furniture) on Leninsky Prospekt but none Costya and I would have been seen dead in. The water beds, the king-size beds with mock tiger-skin quilts and the white and orchid-mauve bridal beds, imported from Italy and Turkey, were clearly for a clientele for whom a show of wealth was all-important. The ghastliest was a bed the size of an average Russian's entire flat, with a shiny black headboard like one of the ostentatious headstones in the VIP section of the Novodevichy Cemetery. Buy the bed and for *The Godfather* effect, supply the silk sheets and severed horse's head yourself.

Perhaps I should not have been surprised, for the main topic of conversation at foreigners' dinner parties had become the vulgarity of the Russian nouveaux riches. I had assumed this was sour grapes on the part of Westerners, miffed that they were no longer the wealthiest people in town. But no, it was true, the Russian mafia were not only ruthless but also completely lacking in taste.

It was the same story of monstrous furniture at other stores we visited and I began to lose hope that we would ever find a modest bed, let alone a sofa to go in our new peach living room. One shop had an enormous fake marble Jacuzzi at a price of £5,000 which, since this was eight times the average annual income, few but criminals could afford.

Another store had desks with embroidered thrones, obviously intended to appeal to power-obsessed godfathers. Here too were plastic palm trees.

"Oh, we must get Daddy a palm," I heard a young woman in high heels and jewellery say. It was the sort of remark anyone might have made jokingly but this woman was deadly serious and she bought one.

In the end, persistence paid off and we found a no-nonsense bed and a neat sofa in brick-coloured leather in another branch of Dom Mebeli on the outskirts of the city. The shop couldn't provide transport, so Costya flagged down a passing lorry to carry our precious load home.

As we followed in the car, I reflected that all the seemingly empty lorries that careered round Moscow probably had similar private cargoes hidden under their grubby tarpaulins. Then the thought struck me that there was nothing to stop the lorry driver from zooming off and stealing our furniture.

But he delivered it and soon it was safe behind our new metal door, which we'd thought prudent to install to protect ourselves against the kind of people who bought plastic palm trees and water beds.

8 MARCH

Costya and I had a deal: he could give me flowers on any day of the year except 8 March, International Women's Day. I was determined not to become the kind of woman who slaved away in the kitchen for 364 days in exchange for a bunch of limp mimosa once a year; a woman who would regard it as a special treat to go to the sort of *estrada* (variety) show I attended for purely professional reasons on 8 March 1994.

"Dear ladies," cooed the host in the glittering Kremlin concert hall, "what better present could you have for Women's Day than Philipp Kirkorov?" What better indeed?

Down the illuminated staircase to sing for an audience mostly plump, middle-aged, overburdened in their daily lives and not entirely fulfilled by marriage came the most gorgeous toy boy with long, black wavy hair, enormous dark, almond-shaped eyes, and a hairy chest showing under his diaphanous shirt.

"I'm not an artist," he crooned. "But I'll paint you a picture of lurv. I'm not an artist; I'm not Raphael..." Well, you could have fooled us, chuck, I thought to myself.

Philipp was then one of the rising stars of *estrada*, still a very popular form of entertainment in Russia. Western singers such as Sandy Shaw, Cilla Black, Lulu and Tom Jones had practised something similar in the 1960s and 1970s before their caramel-sweet music had been swept away by the more aggressive beat of hard rock.

But the Russians never lost their ability to wallow in sentiment. Indeed Philipp dedicated the first part of his show to the greatest hits of Tom Jones and Englebert Humperdinck, which he sang in passable English before launching into Russian songs with lyrics such as "If you stop loving me, the same day I die" and "I don't smoke, I don't drink, dear lady, I just lurv".

The excitement in the hall was palpable. Some of the women were accompanied by their awkward, grey-suited husbands, who had bought bunches of red tulips and ice creams to complete the payment of their one-off debt for the women's year-round drudgery. But many of the women, dressed in their best frilly blouses and sequined hairbands, had come with their mothers, sisters and daughters for a real hen night out. After all, who needed a balding spouse when there was Philipp?

Oksana, a bakery worker, was in rapture. "I can't afford to go out often," she said. "This is a real treat for me. I love Philipp, the way he holds himself on stage and belts out the songs. He's got a great voice. And he's very romantic. That's what women want."

Part of the attraction of Philipp was that he seemed so wholesome, unlike Western punk and heavy metal artists whose music was starting to gain a following among the Russian young. He dedicated the show to his parents and even brought his ageing dad, also a singer of *shlyaga* ((romantic songs), up on stage to perform one of his old hits. The mothers in the audience approved of this show of respect.

But more to the point, Philipp was a young man who evidently preferred the older woman. The proof was that he had just become engaged to Alla Pugacheva, the red-haired veteran of Russian pop (or dinosaur, if you listened to the young). And Pugacheva must have been twice Kirkorov's age.

When Russian women had read in the papers that Philipp had showered Alla with roses for weeks before she'd accepted him, they were on the one hand beside themselves with jealousy. On the other hand, the mere fact that he had courted one middle-aged·woman seemed to raise the chances for all the rest. After all, the showbiz marriage was unlikely to last, they reasoned.

I actually had the good fortune of getting an interview with the happy couple. *The Independent's* Moscow office manager, Olga Podolskaya, who set up most of my meetings very efficiently but normally showed little interest in attending them, trusting me to cope on my own, suddenly decided that I couldn't possibly see Pugacheva and Kirkorov without her being present to translate for me. Could it be lurv?

Unfortunately for any hopeful women attending the concert, Alla was also there in the Kremlin hall. We all saw her arriving in her white stretch limo and afterwards taking her seat in a box overlooking the stage. She never took her eyes off Philipp, as he kept appearing in different costumes, first velvet, then gauze and finally feathers. When he sang "I raise my glass to you", he turned in her direction and the spotlight fell on her. Like the true professional she was, she made a good play of seeming embarrassed, then beamed at him and tossed him a huge bunch of white lilies.

After that, what was left for the women in the audience? Only to queue for a poster of Philipp and trudge home to do the piles of washing-up left after their Women's Day family parties.

For music lovers seeking something more contemporary, it would be a while before Linda, a new singer who was a little like Madonna and a bit like Bjork, with a little-girl voice and subtly erotic themes, broke onto the Russian scene. Linda would challenge not only Alla Pugacheva's aesthetic but also her domination of the music business. But we had to wait until 1996 before we could buy Linda's hypnotic CD *Songs and Dances of the Tibetan Lama*, which wove ethnic music into tapestries of sound and teased us with lyrics like "Play with me, tenderly as you want".

As for the condition of Russian women, the 8 March concert convinced me that feminism had still to make as much as a dent.

CAREER CHOICES

When Boris Yeltsin first came to power, he urged the regions of his vast country to take as much autonomy as they could handle. The Chechens, a proud Muslim people living in the mountains of the north Caucasus, took this at face value, moved in the direction of independence and received a shock in 1994 when Russia launched the first of two wars against them. Yeltsin was to say later that his war in Chechnya, which lasted from 1994 to 1996, had been his biggest mistake.

Chechnya became Russia's internal Afghanistan. It caused terrible loss of life on both sides. It undid plans Yeltsin had had to put the army on a professional footing, and required the urgent press-ganging of conscripts to send to the meat grinder. It brutalised a generation of young Russians, who survived in body but not in mind. It also created a generation of Chechen hostage takers and terrorists, who in due course would bring the war back to Moscow's civilian population.

I did write about Chechnya, although only from the safety of Moscow. Once I got called in by the FSB and had to spend an afternoon in Lefortovo prison, explaining my coverage of Chechnya. Olga Podolskaya from the office went with me again and on this occasion, I was very grateful to have her at my side, translating just to be on the safe side.

The FSB waved one of my articles in my face. "Why is this so one-sided?" they demanded to know. I took a look at it and recognised it as a piece I had written, except that the quotes I had carefully put in from the Russian Defence Ministry to balance the quotes from Chechen rebel sources had been cut out. It turned out that a Russian journalist, acting without my permission, had taken the story, translated it into Russian and dropped the balancing quotes, either because he didn't have enough space in his paper or, more likely, because he had an axe to grind. As soon as

I was able to show the FSB the original version of my story, they let me go with their apologies.

And that was the extent of my involvement with Chechnya. Other colleagues went down to Grozny and performed feats of courage and heroism. For my part, I had no appetite to go to a place where the rebels beheaded people and displayed their severed heads on tablecloths by the roadside, as had happened to four hapless engineers from Britain and New Zealand. It was partly cowardice, I admit, but not only that. I'd come to feel that war, while terrible and frightening, of course, was more than anything boring, with the claims and counter-claims of the clashing sides and the inevitable destruction. I'd run out of words to describe it. Or rather, I couldn't engage with it any more because I'd started to see the recurring patterns of human stupidity.

It made more sense to me in the tough and turbulent mid-1990s to concentrate on social and economic affairs in Russia. I also thought it was important to cover culture and to record instances of unexpected beauty. I wrote about the man who tended the Zanzibar water lilies in the Moscow botanical gardens, the ornithologist who specialised in the song repertoire and migration patterns of nightingales, and the team that cared for the national lilac collection. To me it was news that Russia *had* a national lilac collection.

This was not some attempt to focus only on the positive, as Vladimir Putin was to do when he came to power and strangled the free media. I never shied away from confronting troubling issues. But I also thought that if life was a rainbow of emotional states, ranging from ecstasy through normal contentment to dissatisfaction and sorrow – and not forgetting humour – then it was actually *inaccurate* to write about the bleak, grim and grisly all the time.

At this point, I took the plunge and went freelance in my career. *The Independent* remained my main client but I also started to write for *The Moscow Times* and *The Irish Times*, and to broadcast occasionally on the BBC. As an "expert" on Russia, I would go on to see my byline in all the major British broadsheets and Sundays, some of the tabloids, and foreign papers including *The Washington Post*, *The Sydney Morning Herald* and *The Age* of Melbourne.

I never regretted giving up my staff job and becoming my own manager. I remembered what my old friend and colleague from Reuters, Les Dowd, told me about his brother Eric in Canada. Les played safe and made his whole career at Reuters, by luck avoiding redundancy and retiring to Thailand with a good pension. Eric went freelance and always asserted that he was the one with the more secure job. "I'm never going to sack myself, am I?" was Eric's way of thinking. It became mine too. It's true there were many days when I wasn't sure what work I would get next and how I would pay the bills. But in a void, I always trusted that something would be around the next corner. If God clothed the lilies of the field and fed his sparrows, surely I would be supported in the risk I was taking.

At about this time, Vitaly Matveyev also made an important career decision. He'd been having trouble feeding his large family on the money he earned as a musician, so for a while he'd had a go at being an estate agent. In Russia in 1994, that profession was a shark pool, if ever there was one.

Vitaly had tricked two old ladies into selling their flat in Moscow at a price far below market value and found them instead a "nice little country cottage", in fact a derelict shack miles from anywhere. He was returning from the country with a wad of cash in his pocket from the deal when, at the railway station, he was hit over the head by a mugger and robbed of all the money he'd made. At that point, he woke up and realised that real estate was not for him. He would go back to playing the piano, even if it meant living on crumbs.

I asked him if, when he had time from his music, he would like to work for me as a driver-assistant, and he jumped at the chance (although first I had to teach him to drive). We decided that our motto would be "pleasant and useful"; we would make earning a living a pleasure. As it happened, I had just won a contract to write a weekly column for *The Moscow Times* called Faces and Voices, in which I would paint the portraits of ordinary Russians and give them a voice. It soon became popular and if I'm honest, I should acknowledge that many of the best ideas for Faces and Voices came from Vitaly.

FACES AND VOICES

The Moscow Times was an innovative, English-language newspaper whose first editor was my American colleague Meg Bortin. Although it reported local news, the Russian story was so important and in Meg's hands covered so sharply that the paper quickly gained an international reputation. I used to write music reviews for the arts pages.

When I went freelance, I naturally wanted *The Moscow Times* among my clients. Meg left and Marc Champion took over as editor but the quality of the paper remained high. I suggested to Marc the idea of a column about the lives of ordinary Russians. "Isn't there a danger it will just become a litany of Russian complaints?" he asked. I said it was more likely to be a story of triumph over adversity, and he warmed to the idea.

The target audience for Faces and Voices was the growing community of expat foreigners, who didn't speak much Russian but who wanted to understand the country to which they had come to do business. It never occurred to me that soon my column would be being used in Russian schools as an example of English writing (probably they were just short of text books).

It turned out that as many of my readers were Russians as expats. The locals were no doubt following the column to see what the daft foreign lady was saying about them each week. This created a challenge for me because I was conscious of having to address two very different audiences simultaneously. But the portrait gallery of Everyman celebrities took off. A Nigerian wrote to me from prison somewhere in central Russia to thank me for the column, saying that it was helping him to get through his sentence. A Western businessman wrote to thank me for "meeting Russian people, thereby saving me the trouble of having to do so myself".

One of the early columns, dated 10 May 1995, marked the 50th anniversary of the end of World War Two, or Victory in the Great Patriotic War, as the Russians call and celebrate it. That year, they were celebrating in Moscow while pursuing another war in not so distant mountains.

Although 50 years have passed since Alexander Tikhonov served as an army lieutenant at the front near Vitebsk in Belarus, he still finds it emotionally draining to remember the war. He saw too much death; he lost too many friends.

A music student from Vologda, he was only 17 when he was called up in 1943 and hurled into the terrible chaos of war. He survived there for a year, a relatively long time at the front. Many men were killed or wounded within days of arriving.

Tikhonov remembers how a Siberian friend named Ivan died. Two soldiers had been playing cards in their trench. Suddenly Ivan stood up to stretch his legs. He was hit by a shell and fell back into the trench.

"I shouted for a doctor," said Tikhonov. "But when the medics arrived, they said it was hopeless. A minute before, he had been playing cards, and then he was dead."

Not all Tikhonov's memories are so grim. One intense scene runs repeatedly through his mind and would make a stunning episode in a film. It took place when he and a group of fellow soldiers entered an empty house in Lithuania and found a white grand piano standing on a spotless parquet floor in the main room.

"I couldn't resist it," he said. "In my filthy boots, I tramped across the floor and with my dirty, black hands began playing on the white keyboard. I played Beethoven for the lads. Suddenly I became aware of someone standing at my back. It was the owner, an elderly Lithuanian who stood with his arms folded. I thought he might be angry; that he might regard me as a dirty occupier. But he just stood and listened. Music knows no frontiers."

Tikhonov's war ended in October 1944 when a German

154

shell hit him, severing his leg. His life was saved by a fellow soldier named Konstantin, who was less visibly but, as it turned out, more seriously wounded.

"Konstantin had been hit in the lung. He did not realise how badly hurt he was. He saw the dramatic fountain of blood from my leg and began dragging me to a quiet place. He pulled and pulled until he collapsed and died."

Tikhonov underwent several operations. He came out of hospital in May 1945, just in time to celebrate Victory Day. At last, he was free to resume his life as a musician. He went to the Moscow Conservatory for voice training. Because he limped on an artificial limb, a career in opera was out of the question but his voice got him work as a radio singer.

Now nearly 70, he lives in a one-room flat in Vykhino with his wife Vera, a "veteran of labour" who was forced to forego an education when war pushed her into work in a munitions factory at the age of 15. The couple survives on a pension equal to £30 a month – enough for basics such as kasha (porridge) but leaving them too poor for "luxuries" such as fruit and vegetables.

To this day, Tikhonov suffers excruciating "phantom pain" in the leg that no longer exists. When the pain strikes, he cannot wear his artificial limb and must manage on crutches. In the old days of the planned economy, factories turned out rubber ends for crutches. "I expect you can get them in the West as well," he said. But now, for some reason, they are impossible to find.

Tikhonov's wish-list for Victory Day is modest. All he wants is a set of new rubber tips for his crutches. "But I expect the state will be too busy with pomp and circumstance to get round to the little things," he said.

Readers asked me where I found the subjects for Faces and Voices. It wasn't difficult. If I didn't have a contact to someone interesting, then I could always find a colourful character on the streets. In the height of summer 1995, the street markets of Moscow were like a gallery of Dutch oil paintings – with fruit and faces everywhere.

Describing a stroll through a luscious garden, the 17th-century English poet Andrew Marvell speaks rather comically of "stumbling on melons". This is precisely what happens to one in Moscow at this time of year. The arbuzy (watermelons) and dyni (melons) come up from Central Asia and wherever you go in the city, you are literally tripping over them.

In Soviet times, they were brought in from collective farms and sold on the streets from wire cages. The idea was that the cages could be locked up at night so that the traders, after finishing their statutory eight-hour shifts, could go off and rest. But the cages always seemed to me symbolic, as did the melons with their overtones of sexuality. So repressed as well as repressive was the old Communist system that it had to imprison fruit.

The free market liberated the melons but made life harder for the traders. Now the fruit just lies in permissive mounds on the pavement while the sellers have to sit nearby until every last melon is sold.

A particularly fruitful place, if you're looking for a nice, juicy melon, is the road leading out to Minsk, the route many Muscovites take to their dachas on the Moscow River. Here, every few metres, are piles of melons, presided over by traders who do not have licences to sell in the city.

The traders come from Central Asia but they are mostly ethnic Koreans. I always knew the Koreans were big in the onion business because once, visiting the traditional Cossack lands in southern Russia, I found them growing onions on the banks of the quietly flowing Don. But I didn't know that they were also melon kings.

Alla Lee, who sits at the roadside on a little folding stool, shading herself from the sun with a red umbrella, explains, "Koreans have been here since the 1940s. Stalin brought us over to work in agriculture. Some went to Russia, some to Central Asia. We kept our culture. We are hardworking, enterprising people. In Central Asia, we concentrate on melons."

Alla is selling yellow dyni at 8,000 roubles a kilo (just under a pound at 1995 rates). They were grown on a family allotment in Tashkent. Alla, who is a hairdresser in the Uzbek capital, sacrificed her summer holiday to help her brother bring a truckload of melons to Moscow. She has been sitting here for a week and has sold about half the consignment.

It is dirty and uncomfortable by the roadside, although Alla, a pretty woman in her early thirties, manages to look immaculate. At night she stays in a flat rented by the Korean community. She accepts the loss of her holiday because the trip will help her to make ends meet when she goes home.

"Life is hard for everyone these days," she says. "It's hard for me, and it's hard for Muscovites too. So I am glad to be able to bring them a little sweetness from the south."

She slices off a sample of melon for a customer from a BMW. A ragged Russian boy approaches. "Got any rotten melons?" he asks. He claims to be hungry but I suspect he is running his own little sideline in spoilt fruit.

I turn to the question of profit. How much will Alla make from her venture and will she have to pay any "tax" to the mafia? At this point, a man comes up. Perhaps it is Alla's brother.

"Hello, who are you?" I ask brightly. "Chelovek (a person)," he says through the side of his mouth. The Koreans smile a lot but evidently there are some questions one should not ask.

157

THE FACTORY

If the cultural intelligentsia were doing badly under President Yeltsin, the traditional working class was faring, if anything, even worse. In many state factories across the vast country, wages were not being paid at all. In early 1995, official unemployment stood at just over one million – not excessive, you might think, for a country of 148 million, but millions more were in effect idle, on extended unpaid holidays or short-time working. Instead of receiving money, some people were being paid in kind – in anything from lampshades to pots and pans – and you saw these unfortunate workers by the roadsides, desperately trying to hawk their unwanted wares for cash so they could eat.

Promising state enterprises were being privatised but the outlook wasn't good for the Soviet industrial dinosaurs, many with technology dating back to the early 20th century. It seemed they were lumbering to their extinction. Bankruptcy laws had recently come in and a handful of small factories had been allowed to go to the wall. It was expected that these laws would soon extend to the obsolete giants, and submerged unemployment would break to the surface and give the authorities nightmares of social upheaval.

Optimists said there was nothing to worry about – the private and service sectors would grow to absorb the redundant and everything would balance out in the end. Pessimists thought that would only happen in Moscow and St Petersburg, which were islands of relative success, effectively separate states within the state, while disaster awaited whole provincial communities that had grown up around single industries. (Hindsight allows us to conclude that the pessimists were right in many ways. The revolution the authorities feared didn't materialise. Rather, depressed Russians stopped having babies or simply lay down and died, as falling population figures would eventually show.)

Having seen the decline of mining communities in my native Yorkshire, I had some sympathy for these workers who found themselves cast on the scrapheap, and I wanted to visit a one-factory town. "Well, why don't we go to Kolomna?" suggested Vitaly. "Both my parents worked in the factory there."

Vitaly's mother Yelena Zaitseva had been dead for several years, having been knocked off her bike by a careless lorry driver. But his father Mikhail Matveyev was still alive at the age of 63 and going through the motions of clocking on at the Kolomna Heavy Machine-Building Plant, where he had worked all his life as a lathe operator.

It wasn't far to Kolomna – only a 60-mile drive south of Moscow – but it was another world. The factory, which employed 30,000 to produce conveyor belts and heavy machine tools for similarly immense enterprises in other cities, dominated the skyline as we approached. In Soviet times, Kolomna was a closed city and as a foreign journalist, I wouldn't have been allowed to walk unsupervised among the golden-domed churches in the old town, let alone visit the factory. But nobody cared any more. I was able to wander around the cavernous plant without showing any identification. Young workers were conspicuous by their absence; I was told they had left to try and make a living elsewhere. The older ones still reported for duty and I saw them lounging around, playing dominoes.

Old Mr Matveyev was sitting with them, of course. He had given his best years to the factory and should have been enjoying his retirement but his monthly pension of 72,000 roubles (by this time worth £24) was inadequate, so he continued to go into work every morning for a further 82,000 roubles (£27.30). At least in Kolomna, some wages were still being paid, it seemed.

"In the old days, you knew you could pay for your funeral if you had 5,000 roubles saved up but now, with inflation, you need millions to get buried," he said.

From the factory, he took us across the tram tracks, home to a flat that had once been communal but which the Matveyev family now had all to themselves. It was still far from spacious or palatial but it was homely. Mr Matveyev's daughter Natalia put the kettle on.

The Matveyev family in Kolomna

Like both her parents, Natalia had worked at the machine building plant but since the collapse of Communism she had become dependent on her husband Anatoly, who was struggling to support her and their two children by doing odd jobs on top of what remained of his factory work. Eventually, Anatoly would go on to have a small business, selling tools on the market in all weathers. Natalia was thinking of going into business as a dressmaker. She had artistic tendencies, of which the Communists had made use.

Natalia had had an unusual and now utterly redundant job – she used to paint Communist Party slogans on the walls of the factory to encourage the workers. Her slogans still decorated the vast halls of the plant. "There is only one way for the party and people," read one. "With Lenin, we will grow and strengthen year by year," was another one. "My favourite," said Natalia, "was 'The successful completion of the 12ᵗʰ five-year plan is a secure guarantee of workers' living standards', because with that one, all I had to do was paint in a new number every five years."

Even as a child, Vitaly had found this nonsense revolting. He remembered being brought to the factory and told by his father that he could press the buttons on a machine if he wanted to. "Not for anything was I going to press those buttons," he said. Shortly afterwards, the boy who first expressed his musical talent by banging spoons on a metal washing rack, was given an accordion and his path was set to a career in music.

But Mikhail Matveyev believed the slogans his daughter painted. He worked conscientiously and paid his dues to the Communist Party right up to 1991, the year of the coup against Gorbachev.

"I was deceived," he said of the Communists.

It looked like he was being deceived (or deceiving himself) again because he believed his factory had a future. In fact it was drifting, neither privatised nor yet declared bankrupt but failing to find clients and clearly going down the tubes.

Meanwhile, the enterprising but not entirely honest were having a field day. The plant's production had plunged but for some strange reason, the use of its electricity had soared. Like ants crawling over a dead carcass, some of the workers were tapping into the energy supply and helping themselves to raw materials to run private ventures on which they paid no tax. One of Anatoly's friends was doing this.

"He makes tools and sells them to people in Moscow who make metal doors for the houses of the new rich," he said. "Of course, he's stealing materials and not paying tax but can you blame him when the bosses are carting off lorry loads of state property?"

Another worker at the factory, an old man called Vladimir Mikhailovich, said it had been months since the management, which used to meet the workers regularly, had consulted them about anything. "It's in their interests for this anarchy to go on as long as possible," he said. All of which old Mr Matveyev found very distressing. "It's not right; it's not proper," he said. "But it has always been like this in Russia. We have a saying: 'Honest work won't build you a stone castle.' "

Perhaps it was a good thing Vitaly's father hadn't been to visit him in Moscow for quite a while, as the capital was turning into a garish boom town that would have given him a heart attack. But he must have suspected something of the sort because at parliamentary elections in December 1993, he had registered a protest vote against President Yeltsin by choosing the party of the rabid nationalist Vladimir Zhirinovsky, not that the kind old man was in any way a fascist.

The one compensation that Mr Matveyev had for the three decades he'd spent building a "bright Communist future" was an allotment on a little piece of land among woods and fields just outside Kolomna. When his wife Yelena had still been alive, they'd built a one-up, one-down wooden house with a traditional *pechka* (wood burning stove), where they spent their holidays, digging the garden.

This was the secret to survival for many Russians. In the short growing season, they produced their own potatoes, tomatoes, cucumbers and fruit. The tomatoes and cucumbers were pickled while the raspberries, cherries and blackcurrants were turned into jam and wine to last them through the winter. There were never many flowers in Russian gardens in those days.

Life at the *dacha* was hardly relaxing – basically it was a second shift of farm labour for those who had already worked hard at the factory – but at least it brought Russians close to nature. "The house is at a place called Druzhba (Friendship)," said Mr Matveyev. "It's beautiful in summer. Why don't you get Vitaly to bring you down there sometime?"

DRUZHBA

The sun was scorching in the inner-city but the pavements of Moscow were covered with "snow". Actually, it was *pukh*, a cotton-wool-like substance released by poplars that Stalin had planted with the aim of beautifying the city, failing to realise that the trees reproduced in such a way that Muscovites would end up with allergies. The fluff was also a fire hazard. One summer, a hundred cars in corrugated iron garages were burnt out after a boy put a match to *pukh*.

When the heat and the fluff became unbearable, a mass exodus would begin and Moscow would be abandoned to mad dogs and inexperienced foreigners. The Russians went, as they had since Chekhov captured the delight and ennui of rural life, to their *dachas* in the country. The old elite had elegant wooden mansions. New Russians had brick ranches with tennis courts. But for most Russians, the *dacha* was really just a wooden hut on an allotment, rather like the place where my granddad grew rhubarb in Yorkshire in the 1950s.

Costya and I didn't have a *dacha* of our own but with another Russian-English couple we shared the rent on a rather splendid old-style mansion in the village of Lutsino. These grand wooden houses had been given by Stalin to atomic physicists to reward them for their work for the Fatherland. The children of the scientists were struggling to get by and supplemented their incomes by renting out the houses in summer. Lutsino was idyllic. We swam in the river and had barbecues in the garden. Nearby was an observatory, where one year we went with the young astronomers' club to look at the stars. Inside the house was a huge German billiard table, which I discovered had been brought back from Berlin, along with all the trophy art.

But for some reason, in the summer of 1995, Costya and I couldn't get out to Lutsino and I was stuck in the sweltering city. This was when Vitaly suggested we take up his father Mikhail Matveyev's invitation and visit him at his *dacha* outside Kolomna. The trip in my new car, a Russian-made Niva jeep that was well suited to rutted rural roads, proved to be the first of many and I spent lots of happy times among the fields, birch woods and froggy ponds of the Druzhba (Friendship) settlement.

Vitaly at Druzhba

When I'd been to a *dacha* before with Vitaly, that had been his in-laws' place at Valdai, deep in the countryside of northern Russia. Druzhba was closer to town and really just a working class gardening community.

The *dacha* itself was very modest, as I had been warned it would be. There was no running water and the toilet was outside. The surprise inside was that Mikhail Alexeyevich (to give him his patronymic) had covered the whole of one sitting room wall with a "fresco" of an Alpine scene. "I copied it from a calendar," he said. Elsewhere in the little house were his wood carvings, some being put to use to hang coats on but others giving a decorative, pagan feel to the place. On the table were bunches of wild flowers. "He's like the Green Man," I thought to myself.

I learnt that old Mikhail had been born in the same year as Mikhail Gorbachev. He'd kept a diary of all his summers in Druzhba, with entries such as: "Weather hot, watered the cucumbers, that cretin in the Kremlin is still ruining the country". He said he wrote poetry too. He was lonely, of course, since he'd become a widower.

He went out into the garden and came back with dandelion leaves and other fresh herbs to make a healthy salad for our tea. After that, I was thinking of making a move back to Moscow but the Matveyevs assured me I could have the best bed upstairs, so I ended up staying the night. The evening turned into a gently boozy affair. Mikhail Alexeyevich was resisting the idea that, like millions of his fellow countrymen, he was an alcoholic.

"Of course you are, Dad," said Vitaly. "You have vodka for breakfast."

"Ah, but I don't fall asleep in flower urns in the park like our neighbour."

The table was covered with a goodly selection of bottles, since Vitaly had just received his musicians' pay for the whole summer – in a lump sum. For Mikhail Alexeyevich, there was vodka, made in the city of Ryazan. For Vitaly, there was German red wine and, for a special treat, there was also a bottle of Greek brandy.

Mikhail Alexeyevich pronounced the vodka drinkable. "You have to be careful with vodka because there are so many fakes on sale these days," he said. "Laqueur, not liquor." The German wine proved fit only for washing windows. The small print on the label said it was "produced from grapes from various European Community countries".

This got us talking about drink in the good old days. "I remember the day Brezhnev died," said Vitaly, "because it was my birthday. The whole country was in mourning but I was having a great time. I was mixing Caucasian wine, champagne and cognac. I knew a hole had been punched in the totalitarian system." (What he didn't know was that the teetotal Gorbachev's rise to power would prove to be a mixed blessing from the drinker's point of view.)

Mikhail Alexeyevich's memories of drink and Kremlin leaders went back even further, to the years immediately after the war. At the expense of the rural population who starved, Muscovites enjoyed a "horn of plenty" provided by Stalin to make the capital a Communist showcase.

"In Moscow," said the old man, "you could get aniseed and coriander and mountain ash vodka. There was Spotykach and 777 port, very good quality. There was Northern Lights liqueur, Crimean wines... you mention it. And the funny thing was, in those days you never saw anyone rolling round drunk in the streets."

I had quite a bad hangover when I left Druzhba the following morning. But it wasn't long before I was going out there again to join Vitaly and his children too, as they were spending some time with their grandfather. That year there was a bumper crop of cherries and we all had to work hard to make sure none was wasted. As well as picking the fruit in Mikhail Alexeyevich's garden, we also went over to Aunt Dusya's cherry orchard and helped her.

Dusya, who was the sister of Vitaly's late mother, was a real character. Stalin had taken their father away as an "enemy of the people" and the sisters never saw him again. They grew up in the country, helping their mother on a smallholding. "Everything we produced had to be handed over to the state. We were hungry all the time," she told me.

In later years, she'd gone on to manage a bread factory and even worked in Vietnam, helping the rice-eating Vietnamese to produce bread. When she returned from Hanoi, she brought a porcelain tea service, which was the pride of the family, and retired back to the land, where she kept ducks and goats. Ironically, she was self-sufficient in everything except for the bread she once taught the Vietnamese to bake. When we'd finished gathering the cherries for her, she was going to take them in great baskets to Izmailovo market in Moscow and sell them to raise money for winter stocks of bread and macaroni.

But at Mikhail Alexeyevich's, Vitaly was going to show the kids how to turn the cherries into jam. In Gorbachev's time, with vodka scarce, jam-making housewives had had to compete with home brewers for stocks of sugar and there had been a shortage. Under Yeltsin, the arrival of imported drinks lessened the need for *samogon* or moonshine, and sugar became available again. We easily got a sack from the local market but there was a drawback. The sack was hairy, so before we could start to make the jam we had to pick all the hairs out of the sugar. But we didn't stone the cherries. "Part of the joy of cherry jam is spitting out the stones," Vitaly said.

166

Then we had a crisis. We realised we had no large pans. Foolishly, I had driven past Ukrainian factory workers sitting by the roadside and selling exactly the pans we needed back in the spring. Now it was too late. Every pan in the Moscow region was bought up. Instead, we got a bucket and an enamel basin of the kind used for rinsing yourself off in the *banya* (steam bath).

My inclination was just to pour the cherries and sugar into the vats and start boiling but Vitaly said if we did that, we would get what he contemptuously called "squash". He meant Western-style, spreadable jam in which the berries are all mushed up together. He wanted syrup, in which the individual cherries would be suspended evenly from the top to the bottom of the jar. This was a complicated process – and I confess I went out for a walk while it was going on – but the end result was 30 litres of aesthetically perfect jam that would also provide the children with vitamins through the long winter.

After that, I went back to work in Moscow but late August saw me out in Druzhba again to check on progress at the *dacha*. On this occasion, Vitaly and his second son, Kirill, were staying with Granddad.

Mikhail Alexeyevich had been working like a squirrel to fill his larder for winter. His tomatoes had done well and the potatoes were ready for harvesting. When I arrived, I found him wearing his distinctive battered trilby hat, on a ladder up his *oblepikha* (sea buckthorn) tree.

This bright orange berry, which grows wild in Siberia (and also in coastal places in England), is cultivated in European Russia because the vitamin-rich fruit makes good jam and wine and the seeds, when crushed, produce oil that heals burns. In Siberia, the early frost brings the berries down so that they can be gathered with ease from the ground but around Kolomna, where fields of maize and sunflowers give a more southern feel, the berries have to be picked by hand from very prickly branches.

But there wasn't going to be any jam-making with this season's *oblepikha*. Rather, Mikhail Alexeyevich was planning to go into competition with Coca Cola for the favour of his visiting grandson by crushing the berries to produce an orange juice he called "Fanta". Kirill guzzled it down with approval.

Kirill was a precocious lad. He asked me to spell his name the American way, so from then on he became Cyril. A fanatical, self-taught astronomer, he had brought to the *dacha* a laboratory-sized telescope that his mother Marina had given him as a present when it was still possible to buy sophisticated optical instruments very cheaply in Soviet shops. When darkness fell and the moon came up over the *oblepikha*, he set it up on the veranda and delivered a lecture on the night sky in August in pretty impressive English for a kid of his age (he was about 12 at the time).

I was hard-pushed to identify much more than Orion and the Plough but I quickly became infected by Cyril's enthusiasm as he pointed out Jupiter with its four satellites, the Cygnus constellation and a foggy spot that he said was the nearest galaxy beyond our own star system.

Cyril was absorbed by the mysteries of infinity but Mikhail Alexeyevich was worried lest he catch a chill. "Put something on your head," he said and managed to get the lad to don his trilby hat.

Then Cyril was focusing on the skies again. "Look at this; look at this, Granddad," he shouted as he swivelled the telescope towards Saturn.

"Lord," sighed the old man, "I shall be seeing Heaven soon enough."

Meanwhile Mikhail Alexeyevich's concerns were very much down to earth. Because he couldn't survive on his pension, he'd agreed to spend winter at the allotments, guarding his neighbours' *dachas* from burglars who often broke into empty summer cottages. It was going to be a cold, dangerous and lonely job for him. He needed to get the rest of his crops in and stock up on firewood. A ginger collie, abandoned by people who had already gone back to town for the winter, was wandering round the allotments, whimpering. Mikhail Alexeyevich said he didn't want a pet but soon Ginger would be his only companion.

And so the *dacha* season ended for another year. My enduring memory of Mikhail Alexeyevich was waving him goodbye at the main road to Moscow, as Vitaly, Cyril and I set off on our journey back to our busy lives in the metropolis. The old man had a heavy rucksack of potatoes on his back. He waved once and then set off on his trek across the autumn fields to Druzhba. He didn't turn to watch us go or wave a second time as he walked off into the gathering darkness.

THE FLAME

Imagine this. You are kept alone in a narrow, windowless cell that you never leave, not even for a short walk in the prison yard. Every time you hear a footfall in the corridor, you think the guards are coming to execute you. Your mother visits you once a month and every time, you have a tearful farewell. And this recurring nightmare goes on for six years.

Such was the hellish existence of Nikolai "the Flame" Pozhedayev, who I visited on death row in the town of Yelets in 1995. I'd been called out there by a local reporter called Igor Chichinov, who thought the wider world ought to know about the case. The drive down to Yelets, through golden autumn countryside, was very pleasant but the job was one of the grimmest and most upsetting I ever had to do.

Getting into a Russian jail was not normally easy but Igor made the arrangements and accompanied me on the visit. We were met at Yelets prison by the acting governor, Yuri Frolov. "Don't get the wrong idea," Frolov said of Prisoner Pozhedayev. "This guy is no national hero. He is a real killer."

Pozhedayev had earned his nickname for taking the leading part in a brutal gang murder of three men travelling in a lorry. The killers had committed robbery before setting the vehicle alight with the victims trapped inside. For this, in 1989, "the Flame" had been sentenced to death. His appeal to then President Mikhail Gorbachev had been turned down and so he'd prepared himself, as best he could, to take a bullet in the back of the neck.

And then he'd been given the cruellest thing of all: hope. President Boris Yeltsin had come to power and Pozhedayev had been encouraged to apply to have his sentence commuted to life imprisonment. Yeltsin, it seemed, had lost this application somewhere in an overstuffed drawer or down the back of a radiator and the convicted man was left in a dreadful limbo of uncertainty, waiting for a clear answer, yes or no.

169

Even the prison authorities had started to feel that this was a form of torture, which was why they gave me access to him. What can you ask a man on death row? "How do you feel?" I felt very unsure of myself.

As I was taken into his cell, I remembered that Pozhedayev had seen no woman except his mother for six years. Pale-faced and dressed in the regulation navy and grey striped uniform of a *smertnik* (death row prisoner), he stood to attention as we entered. The guards hovered in the doorway.

But there was no threat. He was infinitely more afraid of me than I was of him. Perhaps I had come to announce his death.

Timidly, I asked for an interview. He begged an hour to marshal his thoughts. I just had time to notice the tight mesh over the window, blocking out all natural light, and the narrow bed and toilet hole in the bleak cell.

The guards organised a tour of the prison to pass the time until Pozhedayev was ready. They told me they were "strict but humane"; that they welcomed the government's drive against corruption; that they had not been paid for five months. They even offered me the chance of a drink and a sauna with them when they finished their shifts but I declined that hospitality.

Yelets Prison

170

We tramped the corridors of the fortress-like jail, built in 1830. In one cell, I saw muscle-bound former bodyguards, reduced to assembling chandeliers. The pain in their eyes was unspeakable.

My own ideas of Russian prisons came from Alexander Solzhenitsyn – icy cells, guard dogs and watchtowers. But what made Yelets prison unsettling was its attempt at cosiness.

The cells had black and white televisions and the prisoners were allowed to put posters on the walls. The library was perhaps a little overstocked with the works of Lenin but soft pornography was available too. In the kitchen, young men peeled potatoes into bathtubs under the motherly eye of a former factory canteen manager, who said that meat was on the menu every day. Daily exercise was also guaranteed.

The privileges of the ordinary prisoners were not for Pozhedayev. Thirty-one years old, he had been in and out of custody since he was 11. His father was also a convicted murderer.

Igor had warned me that "the Flame" had developed animal instincts. "He smelt me through the metal door. He said he recognised my aftershave. He'll smell you too."

But in the interview, Pozhedayev was all too human. Handcuffed, he spoke softly, haltingly, obviously overwhelmed by the space of the conference room where he had been brought for our 10-minute talk. The time was short but enough for him to convey his agony.

"I thought it would be quick," he said, "but it has dragged on. Each time I hear a sound in the corridor, I think the moment has come. When you came, it was strange. I thought, 'Maybe this is it.' My mum visits me once a month and every time we say goodbye."

Pozhedayev said he passed the time like a caged beast, "pacing to and fro". His cell light was always switched on but he said he had control over the radio switch and sometimes listened to pop music. He once gave up smoking for two weeks but then thought, "What's the point?"

He said he was hoping for a life sentence because "while there's life there's hope". His other requests were modest. "Tell the civilised world I need medicines for my stomach ulcers. And say I want magazines – magazines with coloured pictures."

Igor and I left the jail and walked back out into the fresh, vibrant world. Yelets was a pretty town with 19th-century merchants' houses and an imposing cathedral set against the rolling landscape of the "black earth" farming country. True, the shops were a little musty, full of buckwheat porridge, outsized bras in one shade of beige, and precious little else. It seemed that private enterprise had yet to make much of a mark. But Igor and I came upon a restaurant with an Arab name, run by a thoroughly Russian woman who said she was trying to introduce something "a bit exotic" to the town, and that was fun.

Over dinner, Igor and I discussed the Pozhedayev case. If we thought at all, we assumed that our intervention would secure a life sentence for the prisoner. Russia was about to accede to the Council of Europe and one of the conditions was that it should abolish the death penalty.

But in January 1996, Pozhedayev was executed. This came as quite a shock to us.

Yeltsin, it turned out, had urged parliament to ratify the Council's conventions on different aspects of human rights but said Russia could not implement all the clauses immediately. In particular, it was "absolutely unprepared" to give life sentences to murderers, as in the rest of Europe.

Part of the problem was that Russia lacked the accommodation to keep dangerous criminals locked up for life. It had a few prisons, mostly built before the Bolshevik Revolution, but generally used the Soviet network or *archipelago* of labour camps, which gave prisoners fresh air and occasionally the chance to escape. If a court decided a convict deserved worse than the maximum labour camp term of 20 years, the only alternative was death by shooting.

The other problem was public opinion. Since the collapse of Communism, violent crime had overwhelmed the country and most Russians wanted the authorities to be tough. Presidential elections were looming and Mr Yeltsin couldn't afford to appear softer than opponents such as the nationalist Vladimir Zhirinovsky, who was calling for the summary execution of gangsters.

It was in this atmosphere that a decision about "the Flame" was taken. Three months after our visit, he was transferred to a special prison in Novocherkassk, southern Russia, with what the authorities called "facilities for carrying out the sentence" and his problem was solved once and for all.

The prison service refused to comment but it looked as if our intervention had sealed Pozhedayev's fate. An official at the courthouse in Yelets wrote to Igor, saying, "We received so many letters and phone calls as a result of your articles that we thought it time to decide the matter of Pozhedayev. Thank you for your useful work."

"You can imagine how I feel," said Igor when he phoned to tell me the news.

You can imagine how I felt too.

I went on to receive a commendation from Amnesty International for drawing the world's attention to this unusual human rights case but it didn't make me feel any better. Occasionally my writing had a positive effect, for example when readers sent teddy bears to Russian children dying of AIDS. More often, I was accustomed to my work in the newspaper being used the next day to wrap up fish and chips. In this instance, I had to conclude that my article had contributed to killing a man.

With the Flame in Yelets Prison

OLD AND DESPERATE

British retirees planning Mediterranean cruises or round-the-world "trips of a lifetime" would have found it hard to believe how deeply their contemporaries in Russia were plunged into poverty in the 1990s. It was distressingly common to see old people, who should, if not travelling, at least have been sitting comfortably at home, instead rooting through rubbish bins, looking for scraps of food.

Many tried to top up their pathetic pensions by working well beyond retirement age and that usually meant street selling. The desperate pensioners carved out a niche (or were allotted by the mafia) the trade in small items, such as cigarettes and nylon stockings. At the lower end of every market were the headscarved beggars (for they were mostly women), kneeling with icons and holding out their hands for coins to buy bread.

But the old people loitering outside Chemist's Shop Number One in the city centre just seemed to be hanging out like teenagers. For a long time, I couldn't work out what they were doing.

It defied belief but they were pushing drugs. These respectable grandmothers and grandfathers were supplementing their meagre pensions by selling medicines obtained on their doctors' prescriptions to teenagers, who were mixing them into potentially lethal cocktails. The sordid trade was going on right under the windows of the Lubyanka, the headquarters of the former KGB, but it barely aroused the interest of the ordinary police, let alone the security police. It was just part of the anarchy of post-Communist Russia.

The problem was first revealed by *The Moscow Times*, which quoted doctors at a special drug addiction centre as saying there was virtually nothing they could do to treat kids as young as 12 who'd become dependent on substances sold to them by pensioners. They were going down into cellars and injecting themselves with ketamine, an anaesthetic, or mixtures brewed by experienced addicts called *varilshiki* (boilers). Popular cocktails included *vint* (screw) and *moulka*, whose main ingredient was ephedrine, obtained from nose drops.

Learning of this, my colleague, the photographer Igor Gavrilov, and I went down to the chemists to see if we could catch the drug pushers in action. While Igor took pictures from an upper window of the army recruitment office opposite the chemist's, I walked along the street, observing. Almost immediately, I saw that the newspaper's report was right.

An old man in a fur hat was deep in conversation with a girl in red leather trousers. When she ran off, I asked him if we could have a quiet chat. He told me he was a retired military officer but wouldn't give his name. He said he had come to the chemist's for cough mixture. "I don't trade myself," he said, "but I know it's going on. I've seen people doing it."

Red Trousers joined a group of youths, who approached a woman in her sixties. "Have you got any ketamine?" they asked openly. She said she hadn't. The pensioner then turned to me and asked if I had any iodine. I said no but suggested we take a walk together.

She identified herself as Lydia and said she'd been an engineer in the Arctic mining town of Vorkuta, where in Communist times the hardship bonuses on top of regular wages would have been good. But now she was struggling on an inadequate pension and couldn't make ends meet.

"I have three children but they have their own lives to lead," she said. "I must manage on my own. You know what the Communists used to say – 'Those who don't work don't eat.' "

So sometimes she sold ketamine?

"Oh no, love, not ketamine. Vitamins," she said with an embarrassed laugh.

And why did she want iodine?

"For technical reasons," was all she would say.

Perhaps iodine was an ingredient in the drug cocktails or perhaps it was a codeword for some other substance. The youths were more open. "Talk to this woman from London," said Red Trousers, and the lads obliged.

"We're buying ketamine from them [the pensioners]," said Alexei, a 15-year-old schoolboy with greasy, shoulder-length hair. "It's *kaif* [a thrill]; you fly."

Zhenya, 21, said he would give me an interview or anything else I wanted if I would supply him with ketamine. It cost 12,000 roubles (£4) a shot. How could he afford it? "I'm a racketeer," he grinned.

Inside the chemist's, a pre-revolution confection with chandeliers hanging from the pink-plastered ceiling, youths were laughing at the sanitary towels and annoying customers. They weren't bothering the shop manager, Tamara Maximovna, though. "Drug problem? What drug problem?" she said. "What happens out on the street has nothing to do with us. Go and talk to the police."

As it happened, a policeman was passing on his beat. "I hear there's an interesting trade going on here," I said.

"There are lots of interesting things here," said the cop. "The Kremlin's just down the road. Go and take a look at that."

Of course there were laws against the trafficking of hard drugs, such as heroin and cocaine, and the police, despite being overwhelmed by violent organised crime, did try to enforce them. But Soviet legislators had failed to foresee a time when pensioners might be reduced to trading in medicines, and the most the police could do was move on the drug-pushing grannies and their adolescent clients.

Beyond saying that they experienced *kaif*, the teenagers were mostly unable to articulate their feelings about drug taking. But a guy in his twenties called Viktor recounted how he had narrowly missed addiction to *moulka*.

He said he'd been offered the drug by one of the doctors whose job it was to treat addicts. As well as pensioners, corrupt doctors were sometimes a source of narcotics. His young wife was already hopelessly hooked.

Viktor had tried the cocktail while out in the countryside. "I felt an enormous surge of energy," he said. "I felt I could do anything; that I was a god. Clouds were covering the moon. I wanted to see it. I lifted my arm and punched a hole in the clouds so the moon shone through. It was a wonderful feeling. But afterwards, when I realised my human weakness, I was more miserable than I have ever been in my life. My first thought was that I must immediately take the drug again. But then I realised this was a trap. Desperately depressed, I walked out onto the frozen lake and came to my senses again. Thank God I was in the countryside and not in Moscow. The beauty of nature saved me."

ROAD TO RUIN

Russia's main road from Moscow to St Petersburg told me a lot about the state of the country. It was the equivalent of the M1 but only a few miles beyond the city limits at both ends, it narrowed to a mere two lanes, one in each direction, and became potholed and bumpy. It was lined with villages that may have looked as if they came out of a fairy tale, especially on a summer day, but life in the little wooden houses was anything but magical.

As I passed small hamlets, with curious names like Bolshaya Kiselyonka (Big Jelly) and Malenkaya Kiselyonka (Little Jelly), I would look to see what the peasants were selling by the roadside. If it was radishes, the first vegetables to appear in gardens, I knew it was May. If it was buckets of bilberries and mushrooms gathered from the forests, it must have been August. In the absence of motorway service stations and cafes, the women in one place had set up *samovars* (tea urns) and sold hot pies from prams; yes, empty children's prams. But that was not the strangest roadside trade.

On a summer evening in 1996, I was spooked to see ghostly figures looming out of the twilight, holding up crystal goblets, as if in some piece of theatre. They were workers from the Krasnoe Mai (Red May) glass factory, unpaid in cash for more than a year and trying to realise their production by marketing it themselves. I'd heard about people like this before and now I had a good chance to talk to some of them.

Cars were zooming by, ignoring them. When I pulled up, dozens of the crystal sellers surrounded me, hoping to make a sale. They were disappointed and wary when I said what I really wanted was an interview. "Oh, come on, guys," said a middle-aged woman called Svetlana. "Our cops are hardly going to read a London newspaper." At which they relaxed a bit but they let her do most of the talking.

Svetlana said she and her fellows worked only every other week at the 130-year-old factory because its financial difficulties were such that electricity was rationed. In theory, they should have received wages of one million roubles (by then £150) a month but instead they were paid in the cut-glass vases and wine glasses they had made and which they then had to sell in the rest of their working and leisure time. The trade itself was legal but the traffic police moved them on and fined them, saying they caused road accidents.

"In fact, we have not caused a single accident," said Svetlana indignantly. "We just stand at the side, waiting for the motorists to stop. Sometimes tourists pull up and buy a vase for 100,000 roubles (£15) but we can stand here from morning to night and go home without making a sale."

The standard of living of workers in this position depended very much on whether the goods their factories happened to produce were in demand or not. The workers of the Yaroslavl tyre factory, being paid in tyres, had no problem because there was a lively demand for car parts. Likewise, Siberian workers paid in tampons always found women in need of them. But crystal was another matter. "You can live without it, can't you?" said Svetlana philosophically.

She was married to a man who also worked at the glass factory, and somehow they had to feed their two children. "Can your readers in the West imagine what it would be like if they had not only to work but also to market whatever they made? In your case," she joked, "you'd be selling newspapers on the street."

I bought a set of crystal champagne glasses from her, not from charity but because, as it happened, I really needed them to give as a wedding present. I suppose I made her day.

But there wasn't much I could do to help another group of road workers I'd heard about and was keen to meet. I found them on another occasion when I drove up the main Moscow–St Petersburg highway.

"Look out for the war memorial just after Torzhok," I'd been told. Where the road turned off to Vydraspusk (Otters' Chute), there was an overgrown garden with a white plaster statue of Mother Russia, beckoning with one hand, with the other protecting a child. Could that be it?

On closer inspection, I noticed that the lips of Mother Russia and of the child had been painted a bright, carmine red. That was all; the monument was not defaced in any other way. It was hard to be sure. Kids might have done it for a joke.

But when I drove into the village of Domoslavl, there could be no mistake. A teenage girl, dressed in white like the statue and with lips painted the same shade of red, was sitting on a bench. Down the whole length of the village, outside the gingerbread cottages, other girls were sitting in the dusk. It was as my source had said. Here, on the edge of the Valdai lake district, one of the most beautiful national parks in Russia, the population was reduced to such poverty that young women were selling themselves as prostitutes to passing drivers. The war memorial marked the start of the sex zone.

How do you start a conversation with a prostitute? In Domoslavl, it was all so obvious that the conversation happened naturally. "Yes, it's true," the pretty girl in the white dress said simply. She introduced herself as Katya. Soon she was joined by a fat lass in a white blouse, also called Katya. And a woman with straggly blonde hair called Ira. And a giggly girl in velvet called Vika.

They were working; they were ready to serve clients, to be sure. But consciously or unconsciously, they were also making a statement. By the identification with the statue, they were saying, "We and our country have come to this."

Back in Moscow, I'd interviewed a prostitute – an educated young woman from Siberia, supporting an elderly mother who had no idea of her daughter's profession – and she'd told me that call girls, making more than 300 dollars a month, were among the top 4.5 per cent of wage earners in the country. That really said something about the poverty of the other 95.5.

I doubted the girls of Domoslavl were earning Moscow rates. With a pimp hovering in a nearby shop doorway – he made a note of my car registration number – our conversation was necessarily terse. Pretty Katya gave direct, practical answers but was not inclined to chat.

The girls earned the equivalent of a quid for oral sex and double that for intercourse during daylight hours, she said. The rate went up at night. The mafia controlled the business and the police took their cut. "Sure, it's dangerous and frightening for us," said Katya. "The clients take us off the road and we do it in their cars. So far, none of the girls has been hurt."

Katya, who was 21, said she'd trained as a hairdresser but there was no work in the area. Fat Katya, 18, said that her qualification as a seamstress was equally useless as jobs were unobtainable. Ira, older and married with children, said that since her husband was unemployed, she had to go on the game to feed the family.

The area north of the industrial city of Tver was indeed an economic wasteland. Apart from the Red May glass factory, there were textile factories in Vyshny Volochok but they were dying and private agriculture had not developed to replace the collapsed collective farms. The region, with its pine forests and lakes, had great tourist potential but the infrastructure wasn't there to attract visitors, who could get the same beauty with more comfort and service in Scandinavia. Young women who might have made hotel receptionists or waitresses had no choice but to turn to the oldest profession.

"If there is nothing for the older generation, then it is even harder for the youngsters to find a place in life," said Valya, a retired teacher, tending her goat on the grass verge. "It's common knowledge that this [the prostitution] is going on. Of course we don't like it. We find it painful and embarrassing. But we all turn a blind eye to it."

"Never happened in my day," said Nina Vladimirovna, a pensioner. Suddenly she had to dash for the bus, as this was a public transport desert and there wouldn't be another one along that evening.

The next day I went to Vyshny Volochok, the nearest administrative centre. The police station there looked like a jailhouse in the Wild West. On the pavement outside, a middle-aged man in a shell suit stood smoking with a swaggering youth in a cowboy hat, shoelace tie and square-cut black boots.

"Have you got permission from the chief?" asked the junior detective inside the station. I answered in the affirmative, although I'd only seen the chief through a crack in the door to his office. The junior agreed to speak on condition I didn't name him.

"What can I tell you about the situation on the road?" he said. "We know who all the pimps are. And the ex-prostitutes, who are now the madams. We know that something stands above them. The mafia, Russian in this case, not Caucasian. The girls are mostly local. They get transported from village to village by minibus. Both soliciting and exploiting prostitutes are illegal in Russia. Of course, the girls are only to be pitied really. We would like to help them but it is a hard struggle. They simply won't give evidence against the people using them."On the street outside again, I saw the shell suit and the cowboy in conversation with the police chief. Laughing, they all got into a car and zoomed out onto the highway.

Returning to Moscow, I passed through Domoslavl once more. At a motel outside the village, some women "hitchhikers" I had seen before were still flagging down cars in the same place for the second day running. In the village, five lorries were parked. "Broken down," said one of the drivers. "I know about the girls, poor things. Would never use one. Happily married man with kids; hurrying home to the wife."

Five lorries, all broken down in one village. As I drove away, I saw in my mirror a couple of girls approach the cabs. Waifs in white dresses. It was one of the most haunting sights of my years in Russia.

DRIVING LESSONS

Vitaly was working for me as a "driver-assistant" but in fact he couldn't drive and I had to teach him before he could do the job fully. I used to take him up and down country lanes where the only traffic was the occasional tractor or local car. Vitaly loved my red Niva jeep, which he called "Lastochka" (Swallow). When we'd been out at his father's *dacha*, old Mr Matveyev had stuck learner plates on the back of the car, using mashed potato because he didn't have any glue. All of which may have been charming and amusing but sooner or later Vitaly was going to have to drive in the highly aggressive conditions of Moscow.

There was an old Soviet joke about a man in the back of a taxi. He's alarmed when the driver speeds through a red light. "Relax," says the driver, "you've got a master at the wheel here." The taxi whizzes through another red light. "Relax," says the driver again, "I told you, I'm a master." At a green light, the taxi stops. "Why have you stopped?" demands the passenger. "Ah," says the driver, "there could be a master coming the other way."

This anecdote didn't begin to describe the anarchy of post-Soviet Russia's far busier roads, where might was right, the Mercedes always trumped the Lada or pedestrian, disputes were sometimes settled at gunpoint, and all the traffic police were interested in were bribes.

Many drivers bought their licences and drove powerful vehicles without any instruction. Passing the driving test the official way was not easy but bribing an official at the equivalent of the DVLC couldn't have been simpler. The received wisdom was that only poor fools went through driving school. Perhaps in the end, we would be reduced to obtaining a licence for Vitaly by means of an under-the-counter brown envelope but I wanted him to try and pass the test the official way. I went with him when he joined the poor idiots at Moscow's Extern Driving School.

The school, which was down by the Moscow River, had been a closed naval college and it still offered courses in navigation and deep sea diving. If you had the money, you could learn to sail your yacht there. But most of the students were ordinary people, wanting to learn to drive cars.

Tired after a day's work, they came for long lectures on road theory. We sat staring at a huge screen with cartoons of cars improperly parked and lorries and horse-drawn hay carts bearing down on each other at crossroads. "Here we see the hay cart has right of way," droned the instructor. Most of the students were asleep. Vitaly and I were nearly choking with laughter.

To complete the theory course, the students had to memorise scores of signs and study 700 road situations. They had to answer 9 out of 10 questions correctly to move on to practical instruction and the test itself. If they failed the theory, they could repeat the lectures as many times as they liked without paying extra. Indeed, they could spend the rest of their lives in the theory lectures, if they liked.

They also had to appear before a medical commission and bring a certificate from a psychiatrist declaring them mentally sound. "It's really to weed out drug addicts and alcoholics," said the deputy director, Vladimir Trofimov, "because we are all mad, aren't we?" Any young men who had feigned mental illness to avoid army conscription would find themselves unable to get a driving licence the official way.

Women had to bring a certificate from a gynaecologist.

"What?" I said.

"You'd better ask the doctors about that," he said. "It's got something to do with some women being prone to a disease that can make them lose consciousness."

With so many hurdles, was it any wonder that lazy or busy Russians preferred to give a quick bribe, even in the knowledge that they risked jail if they had an accident and were found to have documents not registered in the central computer?

Mr Trofimov was horrified. "Corrupt police officers are literally sending killers out onto the roads by providing such papers," he said. He insisted an honest person could succeed; almost all his students passed sooner or later. "Be honest and you will be safe too. That is our credo."

Among the students, there were probably fewer idealists. A man in an orange T-shirt, who looked a bit like a traffic light himself, made it clear he wouldn't be doing the lessons if he could afford to avoid them. A professional skier called Natasha said, "I want to learn properly and then I am going to go fast in my dad's car. Show me a Russian who doesn't like fast driving!"

I found the driving school interesting as a model of society as a whole. After so many decades of Communism, when Russians sought loopholes through restrictive laws and bought the favours of arbitrary bureaucrats, could they adapt to becoming law-abiding citizens? After years of believing the opposite of what they'd been told officially, could they accept that red was red and green was green?

As for Vitaly, he got his driving licence somehow, eventually. With me, he continued to pootle mainly on country roads because I used the metro when I was working in Moscow. But an important colleague was coming out from London and needed a driver. I recommended Vitaly. This was a serious job, requiring him to meet visitors at the airport and move efficiently from interview to interview. Vitaly was very nervous because the vehicle he drove best was a grand piano. The colleague was less than gracious, saying after his visit that Vitaly had driven "like a maiden aunt" and he'd nearly missed the plane home to England. But he survived his trip to Russia and with Vitaly's help found offbeat material for his article. I reckoned he should have been grateful.

CHANGED BEYOND RECOGNITION

On my regular trips home to England, I used to find the old country reassuringly familiar. Nothing much changed in the West Yorkshire town of Ilkley, where the shops were almost all the same as the ones I'd known as a teenager. This was the surest sign of economic and social stability. But each time I returned to Moscow after a short break, I hardly recognised the place. If it wasn't a street being renamed to remove some Communist connotation, then it was a shop that had disappeared to be replaced by a casino, or a new shop where before there had been a kiosk.

It was really quite unsettling and I started to understand why Russians clung to small things that stayed the same, for example the famous *tot sami chai* (the very same tea) that was frankly nothing to write home about, being a crude brew a bit like PG Tips. But the yellow packet with a picture of an elephant had remained unchanged since Soviet times, and Russians loved it.

On an outing to the old Orthodox monastery of New Jerusalem, I was astonished to see the transformation of the Russian countryside in the space of a single year. The gentle hills around the town of Istra were still dotted with tumbledown wooden cottages and peasant women in headscarves still sold pork fat, jars of home-made jam and flowers at the roadside. But the landscape bristled with red-brick mansions, many of them with towers and turrets.

The golden dome of the monastery, returned to the Church and being restored, used to be the biggest landmark for miles around, but no longer. The country homes being built by the nouveaux riches hit you in the eye. Like the *dachas* of the elite in Communist times, these palaces, coyly called *cottagi*, were surrounded by high fences. But from the road you could see the huge bay windows, tennis courts and triple garages.

"That's nothing," said Vitaly when I told him. Apparently, up in Valdai, where he and Marina took their holidays, a rich man had built a huge house that took up half the territory of the village. Having corruptly bought planning permission from the local council, he'd fenced off the whole of the lakeside for himself, and the locals no longer had access to the beach, except through prickly bushes at one end.

Another shock was in store for me when I returned from a day trip to the country down the Volokolamsk highway. It had been a perfect summer day – Eternal Russia with her lovely birch forests, mushroom hunting: bliss. Suddenly I was in a rude new reality. It seemed that all the *dacha* dwellers had decided at the same moment that it was time to go back to Moscow, and we found ourselves stuck for three hours (no exaggeration) in a poisonous-smelling, loud-honking traffic jam.

Soviet traffic had consisted of state lorries (almost always empty), taxis, the limousines of bureaucrats and the dinky little Zhiguli (Lada) and Moskvitch cars driven by a small number of private owners. Russians had been used to queuing placidly for everything from bread to shoes but they'd never queued on their roads.

Suddenly, private car ownership was shooting up and you could feel it. On some days, Moscow was as choked as Mexico City or LA and you had to allow hours for journeys that had previously taken minutes.

On the Volokolamsk highway, engines boiled and tempers flared. The air grew thick with fumes and unprintable words as cars became inextricably tangled after impatient drivers tried to zoom off on the wrong side of the road. This was the first time I experienced a monster Moscow traffic jam of the kind that was to become routine and turn the city into one of the most polluted, least liveable places on the planet (according to official world rankings).

I didn't have to go out in the car to see dramatic changes. They were happening right under my windows on the Arbat. The Old Arbat was a historic street that had been turned into a pedestrian precinct. The New Arbat was a broad avenue whose shops had included the ill-fated Irish supermarket. They ran parallel to each other and I tended to walk on the Old Arbat to avoid the noise and traffic on the New.

But for some reason I was walking down the New Arbat one day in 1996 when I had the sudden feeling that I was in an American city, not Moscow at all. The street was only a few steps from my flat but you know how it is – if you live in Paris, you never notice the Eiffel Tower. Somehow it had slipped my attention that the New Arbat now had two huge shopping malls in addition to its flashing casinos and gaudy nightclubs.

When economic reform first began, Moscow had been covered with two things: kiosks that were prototype shops; and banana skins, which reflected a Russian passion for the once-unobtainable fruit. But Mayor Yuri Luzhkov, a human dynamo in a leather flat cap, hated untidiness and by the mid-1990s he was trying to sweep away the messy street trade and put shopkeepers behind shiny glass counters. (In the opinion of conservationists, he would go on to destroy much of the old architecture of central Moscow.)

Believe it or not but an indoor shopping centre was even being built under Manezh Square, right by the Kremlin walls. It was the equivalent of an Asda going up by Buckingham Palace. Archaeologists were working furiously to remove whatever medieval treasures might have been buried in the ground before the whole area was covered in concrete.

Together with the new shops, equipped with beeping cash registers instead of the old abacuses, Mayor Luzhkov was trying to introduce the concept of customer service. An instruction went out that shop assistants had to be polite. If a housewife wanted her salami sliced, then the assistant should do it with a smile. And if, near tea break time, a customer had chosen an item but not managed to pay for it, the assistant should complete the transaction before slamming down the closed sign and starting to paint her nails. A Russian revolution indeed.

Consumers were responding and coming out to spend. True, the prices were still very high – Moscow had joined Tokyo and London as being among the most expensive cities in the world – but more and more Russians did have at least some money in their pockets and the new shops attracted them as an experience. They could go to the West without having to go to the West. (The imaginative owner of the Arbat Prestige perfume chain understood this very well when he decorated his shops – giving women affordable luxuries like bubble bath and lipstick – with paintings from his own private art collection. Sadly, under Putin, his shop was seized from him and he was unjustly jailed.)

Shopping was to become a leisure activity for Russians, as it is for many people in the West. They didn't have a word for it – just the verb *delat pokupki* (to make purchases) – so they called it *shopping*, pronounced with a heavy Russian accent.

But in 1996, not enough Russians were shopping. Not enough were benefiting from the changes and too many were traumatised by the sudden transformations. It was no wonder that people were starting to feel a bit nostalgic. Along with outright disgust and desperation, the sense that Russia had lost its way, nostalgia seeped into the political mix. That year there was a very real chance that Boris Yeltsin would be defeated in the presidential elections by the Communist candidate, Gennady Zyuganov.

Fearing a return to Communism, the West supported Yeltsin. Despite all the hardships I'd witnessed, my private sympathies lay on balance with the reformers. But I was assigned to cover the Zyuganov campaign and did my best to be objective.

It was unfortunate that on the eve of Zyuganov's big press conference, I got food poisoning from some yoghurt that I'd bought on the street. I was sitting in the front row at the press conference, feeling most unwell. "Ladies and gentlemen, may I introduce Gennady Zyuganov?" said the moderator and at that precise moment, I knew I was going to vomit. I was carried out and rushed to the American Medical Centre, where I was diagnosed with salmonella and put on an intravenous drip. Unfortunately, in the TV coverage, Zyuganov's entrance coincided with my dramatic exit, which didn't do much for either of our images.

Yeltsin went on to win re-election for a second term. Although I like to think that my throwing up over Zyuganov played its role, the main difference was made by the oligarchs, who got together and financed Yeltsin's campaign in exchange for being given rights to Russia's oil, gas and precious metals resources. They got the old man to twist at a disco like a dancing bear and nobody had the least suspicion of the heart problems that would soon strike him down.

Communism was stopped in its dastardly tracks. The *quid pro quo* was that Russia now belonged to a tiny, secretive clique who would go on to buy yachts, villas in the south of France and even Chelsea Football Club; a brat pack who would think nothing of filling Swiss ski resorts with their prostitutes or spending five million pounds on a single New Year party in the Caribbean.

THE MERC

The nearest I came to meeting an oligarch was when I went to interview Rustam Tariko, a vodka baron who lived out on the famous avenue of the super-rich: Rublyovskoe Shosse. He wasn't in the league of Boris Berezovsky, Roman Abramovich or Mikhail Khodorkovsky but he was big enough; big enough to say to me casually, as if he'd just bought a second-hand car, "I've bought a bank".

I was making a programme for a BBC World Service radio series on cars in different countries. America was covered, obviously, and I think Nigeria was in it too. Russia was represented by the Mercedes – symbol of success under the new capitalism but also symbol of post-Soviet social division. The job took me to limousine showrooms, fancy restaurants and casinos. I didn't imagine, though, that I was actually going to get to drive a Merc in Moscow.

I'd been asking Mr Tariko about his cars. To my astonishment, he said I could borrow his Mercedes for a day.

"I couldn't possibly. What if I crash it?" I said.

"It's OK," he replied, "I've got five of them." And with that, he ambled off for a game of tennis in the back garden of his villa, just down a wooded lane from where President Yeltsin and his wife lived. (I couldn't help thinking of the joke about the rich Russian who buys a new Mercedes every month. Asked why, he says, "Because the ashtrays keep filling up.")

Mr Tariko's car came complete with a driver. His name was Sergei and he was as calm as Baikal, the deep-water lake in his native Siberia. He may have begun his career driving buses but he had risen to become a chauffeur for the Russian Foreign Ministry and had even driven in the convoy that accompanied President Bill Clinton when he visited Moscow.

The neighbours stared when Sergei came to pick me up at my flat. I'd recently been having a conversation with one of them about my Niva jeep. He'd called it an old rust bucket and told me he'd be doing me a favour if he bought it from me for the equivalent of 500 quid. We'd had a laugh about it. The neighbours liked me, I think. I might have been a batty foreigner but they saw that I lived more or less the same low life as they did.

But the neighbour's jaw dropped when he saw the Mercedes waiting for me, and he hung back shyly. Suddenly I was another person, leading the high life, driving in the fast lane. The chauffeur drove me off, sparing me the embarrassment of having to try and find first gear in the unfamiliar limousine while numerous pairs of eyes watched me from behind twitching curtains.

I was still feeling very apprehensive about handling the powerful car. So aggressive was the Moscow driving culture that cars sped up at zebra crossings to scatter pedestrians while among themselves drivers were merciless. As in many spheres of Russian life, power was what counted; to be considerate and courteous was seen as a sign of weakness.

In the Niva, I knew my place. I trundled along in the slow lane and gave way to almost everyone. I'd developed a trick to cope with traffic police bullies, who stood on every corner, their grey uniforms helping them to merge into the asphalt, just waiting for drivers to make a mistake so they could pounce. When, picking on some minor fault, they tried to extract a bribe, I would say I had no cash on me and offer them a credit card, which I knew they couldn't take. But there were still times when they reduced me to a trembling jelly.

But in the Mercedes, I was going to have to change my psychology and become the Queen of the Road. I would have to go a lot faster or other drivers would immediately start honking and flashing their lights at me. What if I lost control and pranged the precious Merc? How would I explain to the traffic police that I wasn't driving my own vehicle? Visions of me doing a 12-part BBC series from inside a Russian prison sprang to mind.

But in the event, everything turned out marvellously. Sergei was of course the living proof that I had permission to be driving the car. We agreed that he would drive for a while first, giving me a few tips as we went, and then hand me the wheel but remain at my side like a solicitous driving instructor.

Throughout, I would also be recording a running commentary for the radio.

We settled ourselves in. The leather seats were so soft and all enveloping that I felt as if I was back in the womb. The purr of the engine made my cat sound noisy. We set off on a quiet road down by the Moscow River. Bringing up the rear in the Niva was Vitaly who, as a joke, we cast in the role of bodyguard, like the shaven-headed heavies who drove American jeeps behind their bosses in their limos. The rich thought this precaution was necessary because quite a few businessmen had been assassinated in the wild transition to capitalism.

"Don't go too fast or I won't be able to keep up," said Vitaly, who kept seeing his job description changing alarmingly.

At first, I drove like a pensioner on a Sunday outing in the countryside, risking no more than 40 km an hour. Other drivers could stare at me open-mouthed or fly into apoplectic rages but that was their problem. Gradually, I began to pick up speed. At 60, I went over a double white line right under the nose of a traffic police inspector but he didn't even bat an eyelid at this outrageous violation of the Highway Code.

I began to enjoy myself. At 80, I was cursing some stupid woman for pushing her pram into the road and at 90, I was screaming at a rickety Lada to get out of my way. Having completed one lap of what was, I realised, a circular road, I whizzed at 100 over the double white line in front of the same traffic cop who, again, didn't turn a hair. He was afraid of me. I might be someone important. Instead, he would harass the next little nobody to come driving by.

Power was going to my head. The Russians have a saying: "You quickly get used to the good life." It was true. I could have got to like driving a Merc. But just as the fairground controller says, "Come in, number seven; your time is up", Sergei was telling me it was time to park. I got back in the Niva and found myself sitting with my feet in a pool of water, leaking from somewhere. When Vitaly dropped me off at home, I heard the neighbour say, "Back in the rust bucket, are we? I've told you. I'll give you 500 for it. The offer still stands."

NAKED TRUTH

Listening to politicians lying is always tiring; in a heatwave it becomes unbearable. After the sweaty presidential elections of summer 1996, I was ready to cool off and find a bit of honesty.

"Why don't you try the nudist beach?" said a friend.

"The what?"

Yes, it was true; Moscow by this time had a legal nudist beach. It was at Serebryany Bor (Silver Forest), a beauty spot of pines and sand dunes down by the Moscow River. The area had always attracted the occasional naturist – along with diplomats, elegantly dressed of course. I remembered having attended a garden party at the British Embassy *dacha* there. A string quartet of Japanese schoolgirls had played on the lawn.

But since the authorities had decided to stop harassing nudists – police used to "pat" them with their truncheons, I was told – the parkland was on the map for people who liked to shed their clothes and worship the sun. It was popular with Russian gays, who were just starting to come out, as homosexuality was no longer a crime punishable by imprisonment. These were among President Yeltsin's lesser known gifts of freedom, and worth recording.

"You'll enjoy it. There's nothing sleazy about it," said my friend, so I decided to give it a go. At the nudist beach, surely, I would meet people comfortable with the naked truth.

The nudists were at the farthest edge of the park. You walked past groups of dressed families picnicking and people swimming in bathing costumes until you came to a no man's land in the sand. There was no fence or sign. People just knew that beyond a certain spot lay the Garden of Eden.

I ventured in, undressed and lay down under a willow near the water. There was an atmosphere of tangible calm. In the section where people

193

still adorned themselves, however scantily, radios blared and adolescents strutted. But here were only the sounds of nature and, it seemed, sincerity and goodwill among men.

It was mostly men, of course. Russian women never really became nudists in large numbers, although they enjoyed whacking each other with birch branches in the *banya* (steam bath). I peeped at the pot bellies and bobbing penises, the odd pair of boobs here and there; it would be a lie to say that I didn't look.

Faced with all this naked flesh, it took me a while to summon enough confidence to go out interviewing, with only my sunglasses and a notebook behind which to hide. (Many years later, when I taught journalism and had a student who was too shy to go out on the street and do *vox pop* interviews, I told her about the nudist beach and it helped her to take the first step into the brash world of reporting.)

The nudist beach would eventually become a less than innocent place, with pants and socks flung over the tree branches, broken glass crunching underfoot, furtive sex going on in the bushes, and other disturbing undercurrents. But in those early days, what you saw was what you got. Most of the people seemed to be gentle, hippy types.

"I want to be at one with the Earth," said a thin, bald, guru-like figure. "If people can take their clothes off, it means they are relaxed and open and have started to understand themselves as they really are."

"I've been coming here for a long time, even before it was legal," said another man, happily exposing his rolls of fat. "I just like to blow the cobwebs off after winter and I can't be bothered to keep getting in and out of my trunks when I go swimming. There's no deeper meaning in it than that for me."

A third man spoke earnestly of merging with nature. He was naked except for a little triangle of paper covering his nose, which was fair enough because the sun was brutal. But it got me thinking about all the other ways in which people were naked except for…

Quite a few were naked except for their cigarettes; they revealed their inner tensions by chain-smoking even as they strolled in their birthday suits. Others had kept their watches on and glanced at them nervously. Those with crucifixes on chains proclaimed their religion. A bodybuilder pranced and preened as if he was modelling designer clothes. He was naked except for his muscles.

Yuri and Yuri, two young friends sunbathing together, called me over and invited me to share a beer with them. In the world of clothes, they laughed, they wore green uniforms. They were soldiers. They had become nudists because they had forgotten their swimming trunks. It was as simple as that.

"There's nothing sexual about nudism," said Yuri One.

"Oh no," said Yuri Two. "Women are more erotic when they are dressed. Naked, they are not interesting at all."

Afterwards, I overheard the lads dismissing me, as I was obviously pushing 40. It didn't take them long to find a couple of bouncy girls half my age and off they went, in high spirits.

I gathered up my things, dressed and set off back to town. I'd had a break from the news and benefited from some fresh air. All in all, it had been an amusing experience. Paradoxical really – the patently naked politicians trying, like the emperor in the fairy tale, to persuade the people they were wearing new clothes; the people, trying to kid themselves they were naked, while all the time wearing their old complexes, principles and vanities.

SAMOTECHNY LANE

Costya and I had moved house again. Our beautiful flat near the Arbat, where we had hoped to settle, had proved not so permanent, as the landlady's son had turned up from somewhere – abroad, or prison more like – and laid a claim to it. So we were back to renting a place in poor condition and doing it up to our standards. "Don't worry," said Costya, "we'll soon have it looking nice." I didn't want subtle shades of grey, all the rage among the sophisticated rich, because the Moscow skies did shades of grey very well. So Costya and his workers painted the flat pink and orange and I was happy.

The address was 18/15 Samotechny Peryulok (Lane) and that became the title of a column I started to write for *The Independent*. Life in Russia had often reminded me of my post-war childhood in working class West Yorkshire, with its back-to-back community life that was at once cosy and stifling. Russia was a veritable Coronation Street with Slavic accents, and it cried out for the soap opera treatment.

Our own flat might have had a Euro *remont* (refitting) but the neighbours still lived on top of each other in communal conditions. The residents immediately below us kept forgetting their front door key, so they would knock on our door and ask if they could climb down from our balcony onto their own. In this way, I got to know them quite well and hatched the idea of turning them into the stars of Samotechny Lane.

Unlike the one-off sketched portraits in Faces and Voices, the neighbours appeared more than once in the stories so that the readers got to know them and see how they were progressing. Each column turned around a small drama intended to reveal volumes about the Russian way of life. The stories were all true and the people were real.

There was no equivalent of the Rovers Return in Samotechny Lane because the Russians didn't really do pubs. I'd convinced myself of that when I'd visited a new "English-style" pub called the John Bull, where the barman pulled me half a bitter, served me a pile of crisps on a gold-edged dinner plate and charged me a tenth of the average monthly salary. But there were backyards and corner shops – plenty of places to meet and catch up on local news.

The main characters were the balcony-hopping people from downstairs – Tanya, a frowzy but good-hearted single mother, her tearaway son Lyosha and their lodgers, who were Azeri guest workers. There was also Oleg the handyman, Raisa Yevgenyevna the vet, and Timur Gagua, a Georgian former astro-physicist who ran the pet shop where I went to buy cat food.

Astro-physicist Timur Gagua selling pet food at Samotechny

What happened to the neighbours in Samotechny Lane happened to millions of other Russians in the 1990s. What stayed the same for them also stayed the same for the whole country. I think I used them to explain to the West – and even more to myself – what was really changing in Russia and what was a case of *plus ca change.*

197

Local Car Thief Aids Foreigner in Distress

The doorbell rang. I looked through the spyhole. A policeman was standing in the corridor outside. I opened up and he came in, stamping the snow off his boots. It was Constable Bocharev, wanting to know how he could get hold of my landlady's grandson. I told him and he was about to go when he thought to say, "You shouldn't have done that, you know."

"What?" I asked.

"Open the door to a stranger."

"But you're a policeman," I told him.

He replied, "You should never open the door. Not even to the police. This area is full of bandits. They could dress up as the police. Those neighbours of yours at number 13, they're bad lads."

I knew he meant Lyosha, the cheerful local car thief, and his mates. They had never done me any harm but perhaps Constable Bocharev was right and I should be more careful.

The doorbell rang again. "Who's there?" I demanded through the metal door. In the spyhole, I could see an unsavoury-looking fellow in a ginger fur hat.

"Phari," he bellowed through the door.

Having already given myself away, I pretended not to be in. I saw him make a dismissive gesture and lope away. I went back to my reading.

About two hours later, the meaning of phari suddenly hit me. It had not been Comrade Phari, wanting to rob me because I was a rich Westerner living among poor Russians. It had been a neighbour, trying to do me a good turn.

Phari is the Russian word for "headlamps" and the man had been trying to tell me that I had parked my car and left mine switched on. I rushed downstairs to find the battery in my Niva as flat as a pancake without any caviar on it. That same night the winter started and the temperature plunged to minus 16 degrees.

If you are warm and well fed, the legendary Russian winter can have its positive sides. Most Russians love it, in fact, drawing their strength and identity from the idea that frosts beat Napoleon and Hitler but never beat them. It's also magical and a good excuse to wear fur coats.

My local pond, called Andropov's Puddle, looks as delightful as a Breughel painting. Children skate, fruit traders sell mandarins from glass cases and women walk dogs in little coats that match their own.

But winter is the bane of drivers. Most of my neighbours have put their precious cars away in rakushki (shells), pavement-side metal garages that open and close like concertinas. They will not get them out again until spring, when they will be needed for the economically vital trip to the dacha to plant potatoes.

Only Lyosha and the bad lads are still tinkering around with their various cars. And another neighbour, the highly respectable handyman Oleg, whose winter work includes clambering onto roofs and breaking off the icicles, lest they drop like swords and kill unsuspecting passers-by.

When morning came, I fell on their mercy. In his battered, ex-army four-wheel drive, Oleg dragged me up and down the road on a rope, trying to get my car started. He would never allow his wife to drive. Russian women should be at the stove, boiling up pelmeni (dumplings). But as a foreign woman, I am a creature from another planet.

"It's no use," said Lyosha, fag in mouth. "You'll have to get a new battery. I'll drive you down to Yuzhny Port." And so we went to the enormous car parts market near the Moscow River's Southern Port, a mecca for muzhiki (real Russian men) who, in the absence of a proper system of service stations, all fix their own cars.

In Soviet times, when free enterprise was illegal, there was a black market in car parts. Drivers would go to appointed road junctions and meet in huddles to be told the latest venue for the moving market. Then, always keeping one step ahead of the police, they would continue on to some lay-by or side road for a surreptitious exchange of cash and windscreen wipers.

Yuzhny Port, though out in the open, is still a black market in a way, since the mafia which runs it almost certainly under-declares to the tax man. It is not a place in which to linger. I bought a battery and an air freshener and we left.

Later, as Lyosha and the bad lads were helping me to install the battery, Constable Bocharev plodded by. (He doesn't have a patrol car.) We nodded to each other. I am grateful for his security advice. I am sure he is right about crime. And I hope he hasn't got the wrong idea about the Englishwoman at number 15.

If You Want to Make Friends, Get a Flamingo-Coloured Cat

The surest way to make friends in Russia – better even than being a ready drinking partner – is to keep a pet. The Russians are as daft as the English when it comes to animals, perhaps more so if you consider the number of bemedalled pedigree hounds kept in cramped apartments where there is barely room to swing a cat. So, whether you own a dog, a cat or a canary, you are quickly accepted as a member of the community.

My neighbours in Samotechy Lane know me as Yelena, or more often just Lena, but the entire Novoslobodsky district knows me as "the English cat woman". Likewise, I recognise members of the dog-walking fraternity as the "Alsatian man" or the "Airedale terrier bloke" and know the cat owners as the "Siamese woman", the "tortoiseshell fellow" and so on.

It all started when I lost Minky. Once, he had been a sweet, flamingo-coloured kitten but after he became a castrato in the opera of the cats and ate the food the advertisements said he would have bought himself, he turned into a finicky and bloated beast. Still, I was upset when he went AWOL, and put up signs offering a small reward to anyone who found him.

The response was astonishing and not, I'm sure, because of the reward. Every five minutes, the phone would ring. "We have found a ginger cat. Is it him?"

I would go and look and of course it wasn't Minky, who was an indescribable shade of pale ginger, more apricot really. Ginger cats would be brought to my door. It was amazing how many ginger cats there were that weren't Minky. We never did find the runaway.

This only increased the concern of the neighbours, who began searching for a replacement cat. A 14-year-old boy called Stas gave me quite a good match for Minky – a marmalade kitten whom we christened Scooter. He liked bath time; he was an aquatic cat. But after a few weeks, he jumped over the balcony and disappeared. True to his name, he scooted off.

A cat-crazy pensioner, who had 12 at home, gave me one of them, a mushroom-coloured thing that turned out to be riddled with fleas, so I politely returned it. I was of a mind to try and live without a cat.

But then one night, I saw with absolute clarity – I was not half asleep or drunk – a rat emerge from the hole under the bath and scuttle across the kitchen floor. Naturally, the neighbours had plenty of advice.

Lyuba upstairs said I should call in the rat man, who would poison her "using coloured grains like Indian rice". Her husband said this was a terrible idea as the rat would just crawl away to die somewhere and stink for months under the floorboards.

"Broken glass is the answer," said Tanya at number 13. "Just spread broken glass around your flat and the rat will go away because she will not want to cut her little feet."

Fortunately, before it came to that, a new cat danced into my life, black as the ace of spades and promising to be lucky. Costya had picked him out from a litter born in a shoe factory and his fur smelt of glue. I called him Blackjack. He did quite an efficient

201

job, patrolling the passage between bathroom and kitchen and I didn't see the rat again.

Since it looked as if he was going to become a permanent fixture, I decided we should call our old friend Raisa Yevgenyevna, the vet, to give him a health check. I knew she didn't remember names very well. I'd first been introduced to her as "a friend of the blue Persian". So when I called, I said, "It's the English cat woman. We've got a new one we'd like you to take a look at."

Raisa Yevgenyevna arrived, neatly dressed like Miss Marple. She examined Blackjack, pronounced him in good condition and advised me not to spoil him with too much tinned meat. As I paid her ridiculously modest fee, I asked her how business was going. "A bit better, thanks," she said, "but I could do with a few more rich or foreign clients like you."

I assured her, if anybody asked, I would certainly recommend her. I would tell them to say they got the contact from the black cat in Samotechny Lane.

They Gave a Residents' Working Party – but Nobody Came

"Respected Muscovites! You are invited to help clean up your local backyards. Please come to GREP on Saturday morning and we will find a job for you."

"You're not thinking of volunteering for that, are you?" asked my neighbour Tanya, lazily. She was sunning herself on the pavement at Samotechny Lane, sitting not in a deckchair but in an old car seat from the wreck her son, Lyosha the tearaway, was cannibalising.

"Well," I said, "I thought I might. After all, it's not like the old subbotnik. It's just to improve the environment, isn't it?"

In Communist times, Russians were made to celebrate Lenin's birthday by doing unpaid overtime on the nearest Saturday to 22 April – hence subbotnik, from the word for Saturday. Usually they washed windows or did other spring cleaning at their factories and offices. The work was supposed to be voluntary but they earned black marks if they refused to join the collective effort. The sign on the wall at Samotechny Lane was a polite invitation. There was no sense of coercion any more. After winter, the yards were filthy. And I was curious, so I decided to join the cleaning party.

On Saturday morning, there was a deadly hush in the yard, as on a public holiday. I looked out of the window but could see nobody at all. Undeterred, I went to GREP, the council office responsible for repairs and maintenance in those flats still owned by the state and for the upkeep of communal facilities such as roofs, lifts and staircases.

The door was flung open by a man in goggles, with an overpowering smell of vodka on his breath. I had encountered this flying ace before.

I had woken up a few mornings earlier to see his face at my third-floor window. He was riding in the basket of a crane. Our balconies had been disintegrating, dropping brick fragments onto passers-by below. For some reason, I thought he was going to fix my balcony. But what he actually did was to bash the bricks with a metal pole so that all the loose ones fell down. Then he rode away, leaving me with a balcony riddled with holes onto on to which I would have been mad to step out.

Now here was this Biggles again.

"There's a volunteer for you!" he shouted and lumbered off down the GREP corridor. The manager, Galina Mikhailovna, invited me into her control room. "There's no one else here yet," she said, "so we might as well put the kettle on."

Over tea, she told me about her work. Like a Star Wars commander, she sat at a huge panel of buttons, knobs and flashing lights. "People call in, complaining that their toilets are blocked or the light bulbs need changing in the stairwell. We send out plumbers and joiners and electricians."

Jobs that in the West are mostly done on a private basis are carried out here by the council workmen. Galina Mikhailovna admitted that while Russians are often house-proud inside their flats, they take little care of the areas that belong to everybody and therefore to nobody.

We had another cup of tea. Galina Mikhailovna answered an emergency call from someone stuck in a lift. I was still the only volunteer for the yard clean-up. Biggles, really an Azeri called Vagif, and a couple of other handymen, being GREP employees, were obliged to be present but they had arrived with hangovers and were already resorting to the hair of the dog.

"You could go out into the yard on your own and pick up a few twigs," said Galina Mikhailovna. I looked out of the window at the potholed yard, needing proper asphalt, turf and saplings to renew it in any meaningful way, and was overwhelmed with a sense of futility. Instead, I went home and swept up the cigarette butts that had been dropped in the immediate area outside my own front door.

Then, because I could no longer sit on my balcony, I took a book out into the nearby Children's Park. It was about Africa – cruelty, absurdity, heat and dust – but it only made me think about Russia – cruelty, absurdity, cold and mud.

Tanya strolled past me and gave me a wink. An old man sat on a bench, playing an accordion. Life is short and Russia is eternal. Just enjoy it while the summer lasts.

FINLAND

During the Yeltsin years, more and more Russians started to go abroad. Travel not only broadened but blew their minds. They had lived, like children in a kindergarten, in a closed society that told them their country was the best in the world. Seeing the wealth, development, freedom and order of the West, many started to suspect their country was in fact the worst in the world. It would be a while before a new generation came along, free of superiority and inferiority complexes, understanding that they were neither better nor worse but simply a part of the world.

For every Russian who went abroad, a small change occurred. The traveller got a new outlook and brought back to Russia the "infection" of foreign ways. You could tell the Russians who had travelled – and not just from the souvenirs they carried in their suitcases. They stopped their cars at pedestrian crossings; they politely held the heavy doors of the metro open for the next person coming through. A few hated what they'd seen overseas and became more nationalistic as a consequence, but most fell in love with the world and dreamed of the chance to travel again. They'd had life's greatest gift – experience – and nobody could take that away from them.

Vitaly was 38 years old and he'd hardly been anywhere. A Dutch couple who had helped his family had invited him and Marina for a short holiday in Holland, so he had seen a little of their life as a guest in the Netherlands. But he felt you couldn't really compare Russia and Holland, as their histories were so different. Through long experience of travelling, I knew that you shouldn't compare any countries but just accept when you're abroad that it's going to be different from home. But if you had to compare Russia with any country, then the comparison with Finland was perhaps meaningful.

Finland had been part of the Russian Empire before the Bolshevik Revolution. Its geography and climate were like Russia's. "I think Finland could show me better than any other Western country what Russia might have been like if we hadn't had Communism," said Vitaly, "and what Russia might be like in the future. It might help me to understand myself."

As luck would have it, a travel magazine wanted me to examine whether Russia was about to become the "new Scandinavia" for Western tourists. I'd been to Finland many times, as Helsinki had been a popular place of RnR (rest and relaxation) for Western correspondents based in the old Soviet Union. I suggested to the editors a piece on Russia and Finland and asked Vitaly if he would like to do the driving. He was thrilled at the prospect of his first job abroad but the adventure would turn out to be as painful for him as it was exciting.

Before we set off on the journey that was to take us over 3,000 km, we checked the Niva into a garage, where mechanics Slava and Oleg worked from early morning until late at night in a den of grease and girly calendars. They advised us to carry spare parts with us in case the old rust bucket broke down on the road. Knowing that service stations would be few and far between until we reached the Finnish border, we took canisters of petrol. Also pot noodles and toilet paper, for we knew not to expect much comfort in Russian hotels.

Setting off at dawn the next morning, Vitaly was distracted by the sight of a drunk hanging by his collar from a bush, and he drove straight into a deep pothole that nearly took the right front wheel off the car. Fortunately that was to be the only mishap on a road where far worse could happen. The Russian roads were not free of bandits and there had been cases of Finnish and other Western lorry drivers being hijacked as they tried to deliver goods to Moscow.

For us, Russia was smiling as we drove north. Caucasian traders lined the highway, presiding over piles of watermelons. Yellow signs advertised small roadside cafes, which were fledgling service stations. Patches of fresh asphalt had been laid in places – Russia was after all celebrating the 250th anniversary of its roads in 1997 – but just as you gathered speed, the new surface ended abruptly and you were back with a lurch on the cratered track. Every few kilometres were the booths of the traffic police. At one, the cops were exhibiting the wrecks of crashed cars on podiums, as the heads of criminals used to be displayed on stakes in the Middle Ages.

We passed through Tchaikovsky's hometown of Klin, which reeked of rubber from a factory, and through Tver, where an advert for a bank that had collapsed amid scandal still welcomed careful drivers to the city. We were heading for the town of Valdai, where we intended to spend the first night.

We got in at the old Intourist hotel, which maintained the discriminatory Soviet-era system of allocating rooms according to the colour of the visitor's passport. Vitaly, being a Russian citizen, got a room at the back with a smelly toilet for the equivalent of six quid. It must have been a bit strange for him to stay there when the village of Terekhovo, where he and his family had their holidays, was just up the road. With my foreign status, I got a room with a view of the lake for twice the price of Vitaly's. The chambermaid was lying full-length on the bed. "I'm exhausted," she said. "Don't mind me, Dear. Go and have a nice walk."

For the magazine, I wrote that Valdai was beautiful but to any Westerner contemplating a holiday there, the most I could say was that the area had "potential". St Petersburg was a better bet, with its palaces, museums and Scandinavian-renovated hotels. You could spend your entire holiday in the city and still not do the former imperial capital justice.

Vitaly and I didn't even try to do St Petersburg in a couple of hours but bypassed it completely and pressed straight on to Vyborg, the last Russian town before the border. Already there was a strong flavour of Finland, in the architecture and the neatness of the parks and streets. It was hardly surprising as Vyborg, or Viipuri in Finnish, had only been lost to the USSR at the end of World War Two. Its medieval castle had been built by the Swedes, who ruled Finland before Russia did.

The Hotel Druzhba (Friendship) was overrun by the worst kind of Finns, who only came to Russia to get drunk on cheap vodka and sleep with prostitutes. With their hard currency, they had turned Vyborg into a relative boom town. "We are obliged to smile and be polite," said the receptionist at the hotel.

The Finns could enter Russia without visas but the compliment was not returned to the Russians (although later that was to change). Finland's desire to protect itself was understandable at the time. The economic difference between the two neighbouring states was greater than that between the US and Mexico. For most poor Russians in Vyborg, Finland was as far as ever it had been in Soviet times.

Vitaly and I crossed the border on a bright morning, the start of a heatwave that was to make Finland seem like Greece. The Niva was starting to grumble but we trusted it would keep going until we reached a Finnish garage.

After the first Russian checkpoint, we entered a 70-km-wide zone where, in the Communist era, only guards had patrolled and a few trusted farmers had lived. Totalitarianism had helped to preserve nature here. Russian grandmothers supplemented their pensions by selling cloudberries, the rare northern berries that look like yellow raspberries. The old women sold them by the bucketful for the equivalent of pennies while on the market in Helsinki we were to find them on sale in tiny pots for the same price as caviar.

At the border itself, we passed three more stern and suspicious Russian checks but the Finnish frontier guards were so laid back that we accidentally drove past them and had to return to show our passports.

Vitaly was now beside himself with excitement. "I can't believe that I, a little guy from Cockroachville, am actually driving in Finland." The smooth roads were what impressed him immediately.

We stayed in Helsinki in the flat of a Finnish friend. Riikka lived modestly in two rooms in the city centre. "She doesn't even have a bath, just a shower," noticed Vitaly.

The general material standard of living in Helsinki was, of course, much higher than in Moscow, although there were super-rich Russians who lived beyond the wildest dreams of most Westerners. Vitaly was not surprised by or much interested in the cornucopia in the shops. He was trying to understand the behaviour of Western people.

He appreciated the lack of aggression, the civility strangers showed each other, the respect for privacy, the service, the can-do attitude, the cleanliness and the care for the environment. "The Finns live in their country as if it was their home," he said.

"Don't Russians feel Russia is their home?" I asked.

"How can we? We have been slaves. We have owned nothing. We have no pride, no self-respect. We are filled with resentment."

We wandered down Bulevardi to the market by the harbour. The presidential palace, a small, lightly-guarded pastel building, looked out onto the stalls of strawberries and onions. President Martti Ahtisaari was away visiting Boris Yeltsin, who was on holiday in the part of Karelia incorporated into the Soviet Union in 1945. The Russian press said a whole lake had been closed to the public and filled with fish for Mr Yeltsin to catch, as deer used to be drugged for the Soviet leader Leonid Brezhnev to shoot. "We still have a Tsar," said Vitaly. "How can you compare Yeltsin to modest Mr Ahtisaari, who only has to look out of his window to know the prices his people are paying?"

Moody Russian that he was, Vitaly only had eyes for the positive in Finland and felt bleak despair about his own country. He did not register the middle-aged Finnish woman from whom I asked directions, dead drunk in the middle of the afternoon, wailing, "I am empty, I am empty".

For the magazine article, I noted that to some extent Finland had Russia to thank for becoming a flourishing country. Under the Swedes, it hadn't had its own capital but the Russian Tsars, less absolute in Finland than they were at home, developed the fishing port of Helsinki into a major city in two generations. The Winter War, when Stalin attacked Finland, and the difficulty of living next to the Soviet Union had made the Finns wary of Russia. But they were sufficiently faithful to history not to have torn down the statue of Tsar Alexander II on Senate Square – the only statue of a Russian Tsar in the world, as Russia preferred to cover itself with Lenins.

A few New Russians were to be seen in the shops in Helsinki but more, we were aware of the presence of Old Russians. In the Orthodox cemetery, red squirrels played on the grave of Sinebrychoff, 19th-century founder of the famous brewing business. On Suomenlinna, the garrison island across the harbour, Vitaly found Cyrillic graffiti on the rocks. "Ivan" must have been a bored soldier of the Tsarist empire because he'd spelt his name with the hard sign, which went out with the Bolshevik Revolution.

We also found Russian restaurants in Helsinki. The Alexander Nevsky, horrendously expensive with Georgian rabbit in lime sauce and *blini* (pancakes) with black caviar on the menu, had been there for years, but Babushka Ira's was a post-perestroika addition. "Can't we go to a Chinese?" moaned Vitaly, as I insisted on sampling the *borsch* in the cheap and cheerful little café run by two lads who'd recently emigrated from St Petersburg.

Having reached Finland, Vitaly wanted to forget Russia. "The last thing a Russian abroad wants to do is to meet other Russians," he said. He wanted to see the "true Finland", so we drove up to Joensuu in the part of Karelia that had remained Finnish territory after the war. With its architectural dullness, it reminded me of small-town America but Vitaly loved it. The welcoming receptionist at the Hotelli Atrium gave us each a room with our own personal mini-sauna. By day, we swam in the crystal-clear lake and, it being July in the far north, the daylight seemed to go on for ever.

But we had to start thinking about fixing the car for the long journey back to Moscow. We headed for Lappeenranta, the Finnish border town that was saved from economic depression by an influx of New Russians buying cars and materials for home improvement. Costya and Little Kostya used to buy wood for their renovation business here.

At Konela-Auto Oy, a cool blonde Russian woman paid 3,000 US dollars in cash to complete the purchase of a brand-new Volvo. Our wretched banger was repaired with the same care the Finns showed their richer clients. When we went to pick it up, mechanic Mika Simanainen was patiently explaining in schoolboy English the use of a Ford valve to a businessman from St Petersburg.

"What do you think of Finland?" I asked the New Russian.

"It's OK but home's better," he said. "We have culture; the Hermitage. You can hardly call this culture, can you?" Fortunately, Mika didn't understand.

"They make me sick, my fellow countrymen," hissed Vitaly. "They come abroad and learn nothing. When will they understand the difference between East and West is not about material things but attitudes, ethics, relations between people?"

Inevitably for Vitaly, the re-entry to his homeland was difficult, although I was happy to see the wonderful irrationality of Mother Russia again. The bouffant-haired female border guard got difficult because of a mistake on my visa, which identified me as male. I think she would have preferred me to have a sex-change operation rather than correct the paperwork and, Heaven forbid, smile.

Arriving in Novgorod without a booking, we had no choice but to pay 160 dollars each for rooms in the new, Western-built Beresta Palace Hotel, an island of luxury in a sea of poverty. I told the readers of the travel magazine that while they might like to see the icons in Novgorod, they should be aware that Russia was effectively a Third World country and a visit could be a guilt-inducing as well as fascinating experience. The city was in darkness when we entered, as there was no money for street lighting. "You will find the hotel easily," said a ragged boy. "It's the only building with lights." The receptionist asked us if we would like to make a booking for the tennis court after breakfast.

By this time, Vitaly just wanted to go home. He needed to retreat to contemplate all he had seen on his travels that had delighted him, pained him and given him food for thought about his own country.

HOMELESS

The old couple walked in stately fashion up and down the grassed strip that separated the lanes of traffic on Leningradsky Prospekt. It was late at night when I first saw them but the air was warm, so I thought perhaps they were out for a stroll. But I started to see them in less clement weather, although always at night, walking back and forth like a deposed king and queen. The line from King Lear came into my mind: "Poor naked wretches, whereso'er ye be." They were homeless, of course.

Costya had just had his birthday, so I packed some of the sandwiches left over from his party and went out looking for King Lear, who in this case had a wife. Vitaly went with me because he didn't think it was a good idea for me to try and approach the couple on my own in the dark. It was raining tempestuously and at first we didn't see them. They must have had some hole in which to shelter from the elements. But as the rain eased off, we spotted them, promenading again.

I ran after them. "I've brought you some sandwiches. Can we talk?" I asked.

The man, wolf face under a fur cap, body bundled up in a dark, wool overcoat, hesitated but his sharp-eyed wife, swathed in plastic, pulled him on. "Only the food," he growled, grabbing the bag, and they were gone.

With his close-cropped hair and leather jacket, Vitaly looked *krutoi* (tough). "Perhaps I reminded them of the guys who robbed them," he said. For we had concluded that the likeliest explanation for their desperate situation was that they had fallen victim to the sharks of the real estate business, who tricked old people out of their expensive Moscow flats with the promise of help to downsize to the suburbs or the country. Sometimes alternative accommodation was provided and the sharks just made a whacking profit but often the promised new place existed only on paper

212

and once the owners had signed away their rights, they found themselves homeless, if they were lucky. The unlucky ones were murdered.

Something similar must have happened to Lydia Ivanovna. I first saw her trying on old shoes that had been left in a neat line by some rubbish bins in case a poor person like her could make use of them. The bag lady was totally absorbed in her selection of footwear for the new season. Just as if she was in an elegant shop, she slipped into some high heels and tottered a few paces to see if they were right before settling for some more sensible sandals and boots.

Later she told me, "The bins are like an oriental bazaar. You can find everything in them if you're not too fussy – not only bread but jam and meat, not to mention clothes and shoes."

My friendship with Lydia developed gradually. I often found her sitting in the Hermitage Gardens behind the splendid New Opera, which had just been finished as an alternative to the Bolshoi Theatre. To me, she was a victim of the times and a symbol of Mother Russia herself.

Russians believe in *sudba* or fate. It's at once their greatest strength and biggest weakness. Because they often mistake human stupidity for the will of God, they tolerate discomforts and abuses that could be changed. And yet, when faced with real disaster, they show an awe-inspiring ability to endure and overcome.

With remarkable lack of bitterness, Lydia told me the tricks fortune had played on her. In Soviet times, she'd worked as a physiotherapist at a health spa by the Sea of Azov, where patients went for mudbaths and to be healed with the stings of jellyfish. "I was a rich woman then," she said. "I had a two-room flat with carpets, crystal and gold."

When I met her, she was a bundle of rags with an oddly enlarged head (she wore a hat under her headscarf even in good weather). Lydia had lost everything seven years earlier when she'd tried to swap her flat to be near relatives in Moldova and found herself tricked by the property sharks.

"I ran away from the bandits in the nick of time," she said. "I applied to the Russian immigration service and came to Moscow as a refugee. I had a box with my few remaining possessions but I was robbed again at Paveletsky railway station and ended up living there for nine months with other homeless people. The police beat me up twice and put me in the hospital."

There, doctors told Lydia, who was in her mid-fifties, that her only hope of shelter was to go into an old people's home. "I didn't want to be with senile geriatrics, so I chose the streets instead," she said.

Lydia learnt to live outdoors in conditions that would have sent other people insane. She said she'd spent the previous winter, when the temperature dropped to minus 30°C, huddling under a plastic sheet on the building site of the New Opera. "The worst was when I had to crawl out into the freezing cold to relieve myself. I tried not to drink any liquid but a human being can't survive without water. I cursed God but I never stopped believing in Him."

She survived. Kind waiters from the restaurant La Vie de Paris gave her scraps. The officers at Petrovka 38, Moscow's police headquarters, came to know and respect her, as did other tramps. "I keep myself to myself and nobody bothers me. It would be a lie to say I do not drink alcohol but I'm not an alcoholic. It's vodka that kills the homeless. I saw three young men die before my eyes this winter."

Lydia didn't belong to the army of beggars who, according to some reports, had to pay most of the money they collected to the mafia. She was proud of the fact that she earned her living by washing cars parked outside banks. And for the first time since she'd left hospital, she even had a roof over her head. The Yugoslav guest workers on the New Opera site gave her one of their huts when they finished the job. It stood up a side street across from the police headquarters on a patch of land she had cleaned up and was turning into a garden.

The hut was windowless and had no cooking facilities. Also, Lydia kept several savage dogs inside to guard her, so when she entertained guests, she invited them to sit on her "lawn". When I had a picnic with her, I took a small bag of provisions but her table was already covered with dried fish, cucumbers and vodka.

Miraculously, in the summer of 1998, the fragile hut survived a hurricane that brought down trees and damaged cars all over Moscow. But Lydia had no chance against the whirlwind that was coming from City Hall, as

Mayor Luzhkov began a sweep to clean up the city ahead of the World Youth Games.

Everything happened according to a predictable old script written way back in Soviet times. The Asian and Caucasian street traders had already been put on trains back to their republics so they wouldn't make Moscow look "dirty" while the foreign athletes were in town. Lydia thought her good relations with the cops would protect her but hours before the junior Olympics opened with pomp and circumstance in a completely different district of the city, this respectable lady was dragged from her home and caged like an animal because she upset the Mayor's notions of "tidiness".

All countries have homeless people, of course, but only Russia has the concept of *pokazukha* (putting on a show for the benefit of outsiders). Acting on this principle, Mayor Luzhkov swept all "social undesirables" out of sight for the duration of the games.

After her arrest, Lydia rang me and begged me to help her. She was being held at Police Station Number 64, where I found her sitting quietly in a cage, dressed in her best red skirt and made up with matching lipstick.

"Why are you holding her?" I asked the duty sergeant.

He replied with his eyes. "We both know this is absurd and cruel but I have a job to do."

All over the world, those carrying out orders will say it's more than their job's worth to use their initiative but fear of authority makes it especially hard for Russians, however fair-minded they normally are, to be reasonable once they have received a stupid order from on high. Lydia's only hope was that the station chief, Lieutenant Colonel Konstantin Golyshev, might have the authority to show a bit more flexibility.

I waited in the corridor to speak to him and finally he received me. Lydia Ivanovna had been arrested, he said, because there was a "danger" her dogs might bite children. "You mean the young athletes?" I asked, and he smiled but persisted. Lydia "ought to live like a decent human being in a flat". Since she "failed" to do this, she would be taken away to a special reception centre, where "competent organs" would sort out her problem.

Off the record, he admitted this was nonsense and once the games were over, all the homeless would be on the streets again.

Lydia had said she didn't mind leaving Moscow temporarily. "If the Mayor thinks I lower the tone, I will go. I am willing to work on a collective farm. But what about my hut and my things?"

On Lydia's behalf, I asked Lt. Col. Golyshev if he could at least make sure she had something to go back to after the games. And here he made the only concession in his limited power. He gave permission for her to return briefly to the hut and pack up her most valuable belongings.

I went with her and watched her choose a large Communist victory sign that had decorated her garden. She also took two suitcases. The police could give no guarantee that her hut would be safe in her absence (and indeed, weeks later, I saw that it had been razed to the ground). Her four dogs, companions who had never bitten anyone, were released onto the street.

"My babies, my babies," she cried at the loss of the dogs. "It would be easier for me now if I was alone, with nothing in the world." Lydia's home-making instinct, which had made her a bourgeois among tramps, only increased her pain, when what she needed was to be the classic wanderer, free from possessions and responsibilities.

She howled as she was put back into the police station cage to await transportation to the "reception centre", whatever that was. The only way I could have saved her would have been to offer her a room in my own home but I lacked the saintliness to do that. Instead, I observed dispassionately to the last and she no doubt came to see me, the journalist, as just another cog in the repressive machine that was bearing down on her. I'm afraid I can't tell you what happened to Lydia, as I never saw her again.

CAT THEATRE

My Blackjack was a pretty talented cat, or so I reckoned. Like a well-trained dog, he would run and fetch slices of cucumber that I tossed for him across the kitchen. So when cat choreographer Yuri Kuklachov told me that Jack should stick to his day job of wolfing down meat chunks and sleeping on the sofa for 16 hours at a stretch, I felt like a doting parent whose ugly duckling had been turned down for ballet school.

The Kuklachev Cat Theatre in Moscow took only the most gifted felines. Cats like the poster celebrity Ginger, who could stand on his hind legs and push a miniature poodle in a pram across the stage; or the black and white Sosiskin (Little Sausage), who could climb an eight-metre pole and, to the roll of drums, jump "without parachute or gas mask" into the arms of his master.

I was fortunate to see this famous theatre in the company of my friend and driver Vitaly and his two youngest boys, Danil and Fedya. We sometimes had outings together, to the funfair or cinema. One time we'd all been swimming with the dolphins in the Utrishsky Dolphinarium, which was a blast. It was the reaction of the kids that I enjoyed as much as the entertainment.

Danil was an easy-going child but Fedya, it seemed to me, was pretty cynical for his 11 years. I always remembered the time when I'd told Vitaly and Marina's kids that if they wanted Santa Claus to visit them, they had to leave a glass of juice and a mince pie on the table for him on Christmas Eve, to which Fedya had said, "He can manage without". As we took our seats for the cat show, I sensed that Fedya was not going to be very receptive. "I bet the cats fall and splat like mincemeat," he whispered.

Actually, I was rather sceptical myself. As a cat owner, I knew the truth of the old joke where the dog says to himself, "He feeds me, he strokes me;

217

he must be God." And the cat says, "He feeds me, he strokes, me; I must be God." You could never really make a cat do what it didn't want to do.

Of course Kuklachov, who had been working with cats for 25 years, knew that perfectly well and went with rather than against the instincts of his animals. The show opened with a clown setting out a picnic and the cats stealing titbits. It was nature, only choreographed.

When Ginger entered, pushing the pram containing the tiny dog, Fedya said, "You can see the wires."

"That's because the pram's heavy," I said. "But could you make your cat stand up on its back legs and strut across the stage like that?"

Fedya grunted.

The acts became increasingly spectacular, as cats walked the high wire and flew out over the audience on swings. Interspersed with the feline feats were routines by promising child circus performers and at the end, Kuklachov threw giant plastic balls out for the audience to punch back. Forgetting his street cred, Fedya leapt from his seat to join in.

After the show, I went backstage to talk to Kuklachov who was, in his field, as great as Rudolf Nureyev had been in ballet. The smell coming from the cats' clipper cages was rather overpowering but I suppose that was all part of animal show business.

"Love is the key," said Kuklachov, as he peeled off his false red nose. "I hate the circus because everything there is achieved by force. What I do is not circus; it's theatre. The cats are playing for pleasure." He told me that he developed new routines for his stars at night, the time when cats are naturally most active. Altogether, he had 120 performers and they roamed freely at the theatre base, only being packed up in baskets when they went on tour.

Because of his humane approach, Kuklachov's cat theatre was more acceptable to Western audiences than other Russian animal displays, such as bear-dancing. I'd seen things at the Russian circus that were impressive in their way but would not have been allowed in the West, for example an act in which glamorous women came on stage with live Arctic foxes draped around their necks like collars.

Kuklachov had had no problem, when the Iron Curtain had first been lifted, in moving to England and putting on his show in Blackpool. Britain's then strict quarantine laws prevented him from taking his own cats, which were reared from kittens, but he managed with a temporary troupe adopted from the RSPCA. "I can communicate with any cat," he said.

The attraction went down well in Blackpool but Kuklachov was homesick and returned to Russia, where his own home audiences had missed his much-loved show. Unfortunately state funding, which had been generous in Communist times, dried up but a Western pet food firm stepped in to sponsor Kuklachov and donated 120 tins of meat per day – one for each cat.

It was at this point that I asked about Blackjack's chances of a theatre career but Kuklachov only laughed and gave me a book of tricks that I could do with my pet at home. "Keep him active," Kuklachov advised. "Cats need to move and play or they age, like us humans."

I emerged from the theatre, carrying an armful of posters signed by the kindly clown. Vitaly and the boys were waiting for me on the pavement.

"Can I have one of those, can I?" begged Fedya.

"You liked the show, then?"

"It wasn't bad," he said, and from an 11-year-old boy who'd seen it all, I knew that was praise indeed.

MAD ENOUGH

Russia is rich in wacky stories. You could write a whole book about its great eccentrics. Over the years, I met quite a few of them – the inland submarine builders, the people who kept wild animals in their apartments. Some were plain bonkers; some were original and inventive and, who knew, perhaps their far-sighted ideas might make a mark in the world? All were fired with an enthusiasm that distinguished them from the complacent masses, and made them attractive subjects for my tongue-in-cheek articles.

Take Alexander Golod for example. He believed in the healing energy that came from pyramids and was spending a small fortune building a circle of these structures around Moscow. I met him after seeing a feature about him in *Rabotnitsa* (Working Girl), a Soviet-era women's magazine that reinvented itself as a publication of New Age ideas.

Mr Golod, whose name means "hunger" in Russian, sent a white limousine to pick me up. I was taken through a maze of Moscow back streets and an unmarked blue gate into a defence factory that produced meteorological equipment for aerodromes, ships and spacecraft. "I'm the director," said Mr Golod, "but since the Defence Ministry hasn't paid us for months, I am working on my private pyramid project."

A small white pyramid stood on his desk, with a map of Russia, scattered with crystals, amethysts and other semi-precious stones. He reached into a drawer and gave me a handful of similar stones. "Take those," he said, "and I'll explain."

He told me to imagine the room we were in was made up of cubes. "There's a distorting mirror on the wall. The cubes become twisted and deformed. The space in which we live now is like that. Adam lived for 900 years but we live for only 70 because our space has become distorted. This leads to war, economic problems, earthquakes, holes in the ozone layer and other ills. But pyramids correct the distortion and restore harmony."

It was as clear as mud to me. Equally unclear was how Mr Golod had amassed his fortune but he said he had spent the equivalent of 1.2 million pounds on building pyramids around Moscow, and planned to erect more. He showed me a video of the biggest, towering 22 metres above Lake Seliger, 400 km north of the capital. There was another, 11 metres high, at Ramensky in the Moscow region, and a complex of five-metre-high pyramids in the republic of Bashkortostan to the east. I myself had seen one of the structures while driving on the highway going out of Moscow towards Riga.

Mr Golod's pyramids were made of glass fibre rather than stone blocks and were more elongated than the tombs of the Egyptian pharaohs or the pyramids used by the Mayas to observe the stars. Indeed, they served a different purpose.

"My pyramids are protecting Moscow from flu, cancer and AIDS," said Mr Golod. "Soon these diseases will disappear. Some people speak of the apocalypse. I say we can live as long as we want. It depends on the harmony we create around us."

"I see," I said. "And where do the stones come in?"

"I buy bags of them and put them inside the pyramids. They become charged with the special energy there. Then I drive round Moscow, scattering them on the roadsides. Sometimes the snow shifters sweep them away and I have to scatter more. The stones are resonators, spreading the energy of the pyramids."

He said he had dropped some stones around a prison near Tver, north of Moscow, and the restive inmates had calmed down. He also gave stones to the sick to put around their beds. "I do not charge money for this service. It is an act of charity."

"Is it white magic, then," I asked, "you know, positive psychological suggestion?"

"No," said Mr Golod, who was a mathematician. "It's science. The stones work for you whether you know they are there or not. Of course, the effect is stronger if you know."

He claimed that since he had built his pyramid at Seliger, the lake water had become purer, harvests had improved, rare wild flowers had appeared in the forests and storks had returned. Mr Golod had persuaded a cosmonaut to carry some of his pyramid-charged stones and they were on the space station *Mir*, orbiting around the Earth and emitting harmonious waves. If only he could build some pyramids in Yugoslavia, he sighed, the Kosovo crisis would be resolved.

And since great shafts of energy rose up from the tops of pyramids, such structures could help to close the ozone hole over Australia, he said. "I have written twice to the Australian embassy about this but they do not seem interested."

Perhaps the Aussies might have been more taken with a woman I met who had started Russia's first ostrich farm in the rolling hills of the Vladimir region. It happened to be International Women's Day when I visited her, and numerous guests were sitting around expectantly at the farmhouse kitchen table. To feed them all, Valentina Mikhailina had cracked open an ostrich egg the size of a melon and made a giant omelette. The equivalent of 25 hens' eggs, it tasted much like an ordinary omelette but our hostess declared that it was cholesterol-free and packed with vitamin-E, "the vitamin of eternal youth".

Valentina and her husband Igor said they had chosen a future in ostriches as a healthy way of investing in their country. The magazine *Ogonyok* had run an article about the strangeness and beauty of the "ostriches in the snow", which was how I found out about the farm in the village of Banevo. The local people all knew the way.

"It's up there on the hill," they said, pointing to what looked like another New Russian red brick "cottage". But instead of a black Mercedes parked in the drive there was a tractor and, behind a wire fence, the ostriches.

"We're refugees from Moscow," said Valentina, who in her city days had bred dogs while her husband ran a car servicing business. "Every person has a piece of the countryside in them. We have settled here very well."

First they built the house and then, since there was no infrastructure in the place, a road to go with it. They also drilled down to a water source and set up a transformer, providing electricity for the whole village, which had been in darkness. "Some locals were grateful but others resented what they saw as our interference," said Valentina.

Next, the couple bought up a local farm where they saw the cattle were neglected. They turned eventually to ostriches after seeing a television report about a new craze for the African bird meat in Finland.

"My zodiac sign is Aquarius, which means I'm an adventurer," said Valentina. "I reckoned if I could breed dogs, why not ostriches?" There was method in her madness. "Ostriches are far more profitable than cattle. Apart from the eggs, they provide excellent, health-giving meat, feathers for boas and dusters, skin for leather and grease for cosmetics."

Her husband Igor chipped in, "Ostrich products might be expensive now because the market is undeveloped. But look what happened to bananas [which used to be rare in Russia]. They became as common and cheap as potatoes."

The couple had a vision that one day the vast lands of Russia would be covered with ostrich farms. They travelled to Finland during the summer to acquire their birds – seven of the Black African variety at a cost of £1,280 each. That was the easy part. When they arrived at the Russian border in their trailer, customs officers baulked at the cargo. Eventually, the customs let the ostriches through, having classified them as "large-horned cattle". Valentina said, "They demanded to see certificates proving they were free of cattle diseases. Obviously, we could not provide this. Paperwork of another kind did the trick."

All seven of the original birds survived, despite the harsh Russian winter. The Mikhailins bought incubators to hatch the eggs of the first ostriches and bring on a new generation. Valentina took me out to see them in their pen. It being March, there was still some snow on the ground. The ostriches were elegant, with their long necks and extraordinarily large eyes. The black and white male, Feofan, batted his blue eyelids at the grey-brown females. In the snow, they performed a feathery, exotic dance.

"Ostriches never bury their heads in the sand, or in the snow, for that matter," said Valentina. "Only unimaginative human beings do that." Of the many eccentric ideas I saw, I reckoned the ostrich project was just mad enough to stand a chance of success.

SUZDAL

I always used to set out with high hopes on the roads of Russia. The country was so vast that a lifetime would not suffice to discover it all, I thought. Never mind that every past journey had been tinged with *toska* (a melancholy yearning or sense of hopelessness). Next time I was sure to come to the Promised Land.

So, full of optimism in the summer of 1998, I set off on the M7 to Vladimir, 120 miles east of Moscow. In the 19th century, when shackled prisoners walked for months down this road to exile in Siberia, begging for alms as they went, it was the highway to Hell, effectively a sentence of death. But times had changed.

My cherry red Niva bounced merrily over the potholes as I passed fields of sunflowers and settlements with quaint Communist names like Red Electrician. Impatient Mercedes drivers, hurrying to their "cottages", overtook me on the inside. The narrow road became the slow lane and the ditch became the overtaking lane. Suddenly we were all driving on the left, like in England. It was anarchy.

By and by, I came to Petushki, immortalised in Veniamin Yerofeyev's comic novel of the Brezhnev era, *Moskva–Petushki*. It is about a boozer from Petushki, who travels to the capital to see the sights but ends up in the buffet of Kursky railway station, drunk again. He never does get to see Red Square and goes home none the wiser. It is a symbol of the hopelessness of Russian life.

By the side of the road in the real Petushki, some drivers were having a picnic. Vodka bottles were arranged on the bonnet of the car. They were drinking the vodka from plastic cups. They were going to drink it all and then get back into their vehicles. Corrupt as they were, there were times when one should give thanks to the traffic police, I thought.

I decided to rest too. I didn't fancy the *kvas* (cola-like drink made from fermented black bread) from the fetid roadside barrels or the delights of the Café Kormilitsa (breast-feeding woman). Instead, I plunged into the forest, dry as tinder after a heatwave, and picked a handful of wild raspberries, in exchange for which I must have donated a pint of my blood to the mosquitoes.

Further down the road, I was able to buy some more of these raspberries from an old woman, who had spent all day in the infested forest, picking them. She was selling them for pennies. I bought five cups and still only spent about 50p. She cried with gratitude, saying that at last she could afford bread.

Along its length, the road was lined with traders, desperate as ever to make a sale. This time the villagers were selling towels printed with the face of Marilyn Monroe, giant toy tigers, popcorn, electric fans and rubber boats, although there was no expanse of water in sight. Suddenly the skies opened and the locals rushed to cover their goods, imported from China and delivered to the villages by the Moscow mafia. When the Russians had brought down Communism, they had carried placards speaking of "70 years on the road to nowhere". After the experiment with the free market, I could see they were still on the road, seeking a turn-off to somewhere.

My car lurched. The strip of asphalt on which I had felt confident to raise my speed came to an abrupt end, and without warning I was back on lunar craters. Ahead were the wrecks of a BMW and a Lada that had been in a head-on collision. The BMW driver was alive but I didn't give much for the chances of those in the more vulnerable car. The ambulance would come, I supposed.

I drove on through Pokrov (the Virgin's Veil), with its sleazy motel, and the towns of Noginsk and Lakinsk. All over Russia, these shabby, inconsequential places were indistinguishable, with their war memorials, their chicken-coop apartment blocks, their rusty garages, their gardens with cabbage and phlox. Irreverent Muscovites called them *Perdyulinsk* (Fartville) or *Mukhasransk* (Flyshitville).

I was leaving them behind. The belching lorries and buzzing motorcycles thinned out and I emerged onto a plain of golden cornfields, lined with silver birch trees in bright green leaf. On the horizon I could see my destination, the ancient city of Suzdal. My hopes could not have been higher.

Suzdal is one of so-called "Golden Ring" religious centres of old Russia. An architectural jewel, it is perhaps comparable to somewhere like Oxford. The sun was setting as I came over the plain, giving me a prospect not of dreaming spires but of dreaming onion domes.

"Need somewhere to stay?" A private hotelier leapt out into the road just as I entered the city, trying to attract me to his new bed-and-breakfast. Unfortunately, I already had a room booked in the concrete Tourist Centre, a former state Intourist hotel. I promised the private man I would dine at his guesthouse instead.

The renovated but rather soulless hotel turned out to be fine. It was good value for money at the equivalent of £12 a night and there was soap and toilet paper in the bathroom. I couldn't really have asked for more.

"Having a lovely time. Wish you were here," I wrote on my postcards from Suzdal which, knowing the Russian post, were probably never delivered. Actually, it would have been reassuring if anybody had been there in Suzdal. At the height of the tourist season, the place was deserted.

Undeterred, I set off to explore the city. It had a kremlin (fortress), a convent, two monasteries, dozens of churches dating from the 12th to the 18th centuries, and a nearly-200-year-old shopping arcade with wrought iron signs for the cobbler, the milliner and the wine merchant. Little wooden bridges took me back and forth across the River Kamenka, meandering and thick with water lilies.

I was looking for the world famous Church of the Intercession on the Nerl. It featured in lots of postcards and calendars I had seen. Simple, white and standing alone on the bank of the River Nerl, it looked as perfect as a pearl.

But I discovered the church, built in 1165, was not in Suzdal itself. I had to drive through the nearby city of Vladimir, grim and industrial despite its historic centre, to a place called Bogolyubovo.

When I arrived, I found the church was smaller than I'd expected, not that size mattered. What spoilt it were the electricity pylons, cars and other modern trappings all around the little chapel. It was a let-down in the same way that Stonehenge disappoints. A raucous wedding party was just coming out of the church, so I slipped away.

Returning to Suzdal felt like going home. There were no high-rise buildings; the city was an extended village of wooden houses with lace curtains and geraniums in the windows. Goats and geese stood at the bus stops. It was delightful.

The locals were clearly poor. A sign in the supermarket listed the times when the hospital would be open to pay blood donors. At night, the streetlamps were not lit; the council evidently lacked the necessary funds. But there was a feeling of quiet dignity about the place. The statue of Lenin in the central square was not overpowering. Neither had wild capitalism marred Suzdal's charms. Absent were the kiosks that made other Russian cities sleazy. This was a town that had kept its character through the centuries.

If only there had been a few more road signs to guide and encourage visitors. If only at the private Kuchkova guest house, where I kept my promise and went to dine, they could have done something about the flies that tried to settle on my meat cutlets. Then Suzdal would indeed have been a five-star tourist destination, up there with York or Bath.

Why were there so few visitors, I asked the locals. Because rich Russians went abroad while poor Russians didn't have holidays and Westerners were put off by the difficulties of "Russian reality", they told me. If foreigners came at all, they came in shepherded groups. There were almost no individual foreign travellers like me, who just jumped in the car and went to Suzdal.

It seemed a pity. Suzdal was distinctive, an island of beauty in a sea of mediocrity and modernity. Yet, linked as it was to the rest of Russia by the unreconstructed M7, it was dragged down to the common level. It couldn't develop in splendid isolation but would only prosper if and when Mother Russia herself finally made some progress. Well, that was my Western opinion, anyway. I know many Russians thought their country was just fine as it was.

MIDDLE C

With child pianist Fedya Veselov

The vacuum cleaner was droning as I hoovered the apartment. "That's middle C, isn't it?" piped up young Fedya. I was nonplussed. "You know, the note middle C," he said. The lad had perfect pitch, so I'm sure he must have been right. Having Fedya Veselov to stay was a fascinating experience. He was a promising pianist, just 12 years old, and as well as being able to identify the notes emitted by my domestic appliances, he could also play Chopin like the Devil.

Fedya had come down from St Petersburg to take part in a competition for young pianists at the Moscow Conservatory. He'd brought with him a keyboard drawn on paper, which he planned to "play" silently to exercise his fingers and jog his memory of the music. But as soon as he saw my upright piano, he began playing furious scales. "Don't worry that you haven't had it tuned," he assured me. "I can make the adjustments in my head."

It was fun – and a great revenge on my pop-music-loving neighbours – to have him hammering out exercises by Czerny for hours on end. I must admit he disturbed me a little by refusing to break off for ice cream when he still had an hour's practice to do. But he showed a healthy interest in my video collection; a normal lad's reluctance to take a bath; and great excitement when, on an outing into town, we saw some criminals in handcuffs.

Then came the day of the competition and I went to watch him perform. That morning, he'd risen at seven and trotted nervously between keyboard and lavatory before it was time to set off. He'd put on thick wool gloves to keep his fingers warm. In the event, some of the other competitors outdid him in virtuoso skills but Fedya played his Chopin with soul and when the results were announced, he received a commendation. His mother Lena, who was with him on the trip, was satisfied and said his father would be proud of him.

Lena was an amazing woman. Not only was she a devoted mum but she was also a fantastically talented designer of costumes for the theatre. How she found time for all her creativity was a wonder to me. One summer at the *dacha*, for example, she'd "knocked out" a set of intricate, quilted wall hangings, using scraps of material left over from costumes and velvet from old theatre curtains. Her "lone wolf in the forest" had pride of place on our living room wall. The wolf had a tear in his eye, sewn in silver thread.

Lena's husband Sasha had also worked in the theatre, as a director. The Veselovs (the name means "jolly" in Russian) were a theatrical couple, with two musical sons. Along with Fedya, they had a second son called Misha, who played the cello.

"Children are our future," you often hear the Russians say. The world over, people want the best for their children but the Russians in particular seem to invest their hopes in the next generation. They accept that their own lives are going to be hard in the hope that their children will live better. The Veselov family provided the clearest example I knew of parents sacrificing everything for their children.

Sasha Veselov, who originally came from Siberia, had loved his work as a director and been very good at it. The theatre had been his life. But in the early 1990s, he'd decided he couldn't indulge himself in an airy-fairy profession, however rewarding it might be for him personally, if it wasn't going to provide adequately for his family.

Sasha was fortunate in that he did have another string to his bow – he was excellent at mathematics. And so he'd gritted his teeth and retrained to become an accountant. Eventually, he rose to be chief bean counter at a company that provided services for the Russian national railways and started to bring him home a solid middle class salary. The only sign he ever gave that his soul was perhaps quietly crying was that he smoked like a chimney.

When I next saw the Veselov family, they were renovating their small flat on Tuchkov Lane in central St Petersburg. They were lucky, I suppose, because by chance they had inherited a piece of prime real estate, within walking distance of the world famous Hermitage art gallery, but the flat needed a lot of improvement.

Lena had painted the kitchen an arty shade of red and preserved the old tiled stove, while adding a modern oven and microwave. They were going to lay some tasteful wood flooring. But they couldn't do anything about the view from the window – a yard so grim that the BBC chose it as a location when filming *Crime and Punishment*.

The neighbours, it seemed, still lived and thought like characters from a novel by Dostoyevsky. "Some of them resent our success," Lena said, as she drew the curtains in the middle of the afternoon and put on the shiny new machine for coffee.

I knew that whatever success the Veselovs enjoyed, they had achieved by honest, hard work. "It's not that we're hungry for material possessions," Lena said. "We work hard because we want our boys to have interesting lives – and because in the end, we'd like to see something of the world ourselves. We grew up in Soviet times, when we were so poor we stole potatoes from collective farm fields. You can't call that an interesting life."

Lena peeped through the drawn curtains to check on their car, parked in the yard. The family had recently bought a jeep, which they saw not as a luxury but as an essential because every summer they drove long distances on bad roads to reach their *dacha* in Karelia.

Lena was the one with the driving licence and she was effectively the family chauffeur. When she could, she drove Sasha to his job through the morning traffic jams. It should have been a 15-minute drive from the flat on Vasilievsky Ostrov (Island) to Ligovsky Prospekt, down by the railway tracks, where Sasha had his office. But if the traffic was heavy, the drive could take an hour or more.

When Lena was not available, Sasha had to do battle with the crowds on the municipal buses or queue for the minivans that took the proletariat to their various jobs. He set off for work at 7.30 am and officially finished at 17.30 but was often at his desk until eleven at night and sometimes worked weekends as well.

"The commuting is not so bad early in the morning but there is a terrible crush on public transport in the evening," said Lena. "He hates close physical contact with strangers and will often walk for an hour and a half to reach home rather than endure being packed in a sardine can on wheels. He's very tired, nearly dead when he gets home."

Being freelance, Lena wasn't on quite such a treadmill. If there was an order from a provincial theatre, she would work on costume designs and travel to deliver them but otherwise she could stay at home. Or rather, get behind the wheel again, for she was always ferrying the boys around.

When they'd been small, she'd taken them by metro to school and music lessons afterwards. As they grew, she found herself commuting with them regularly on the 10-hour drive down to the capital, where in due course they won places at a special school that aimed to get its students into the Moscow Conservatory or even prestigious colleges abroad. Basic education for the boys was free but Sasha and Lena had to pay big bucks for the music master classes that would give Fedya and Misha a chance of glittering careers.

It seemed that for years, Sasha and Lena put their own pleasures on hold as they built a future for their sons. But eventually, they were able to enjoy small treats, such as going out to restaurants, where they discovered they liked Italian food. They also caught the travel bug. The last time I saw Lena, she told me that for their wedding anniversary, Sasha had surprised her by presenting her with tickets for a trip to Budapest, something that would have been unthinkable when they were young, poor and stuck behind the Iron Curtain.

"The main thing is we are happy within our family," Lena said. "We know that happiness is not in having and acquiring things. And as you see, our lives are becoming very interesting now that we're middle-aged."

I was glad for them. It was rare to see such a good outcome. I know that Tolstoy famously wrote, "All happy families resemble one another. Each unhappy family is unhappy in its own way." That must have been because bourgeois happiness was the norm in his day. But my experience in post-Soviet Russia had taught me the opposite – that unhappy families were depressingly similar while happy, middle class families like the Veselovs were very much an exception to the rule.

PART FOUR

THE RETURN OF WINTER

1998

Superstitious Russians saw looming disaster in the omens for 1998. It was a tiger year, according to the Chinese zodiac system, which they had embraced along with their own Orthodox calendar, and they took that to mean that the Beast was going to roar.

In the children's park near my home, I came across a woman rooting around under the trees. At first I thought she'd lost her keys or something until I realised she was hunting for mushrooms – not a good idea, really, in central Moscow, where the concentrations of lead must have been off the scale. But Russians are obsessed with mushrooms and will hunt for them anywhere, even in the inner city if they have no alternative. "There's a glut this year," she said to me knowingly. "It's a bad sign. It means famine and war." Indeed, old people had often told me that the forests were thick with mushrooms before the Nazis invaded in 1941.

Even Russian "scientists" were doom-mongering in 1998. I interviewed Anatoly Votyakov, the author of a best-seller called *Theoretical Geography or Imminent Disaster,* who predicted that the Earth's crust was about to rearrange itself and cause an apocalyptic flood. The book mixed pseudo-science with the warnings of the 16[th-] century astrologer Nostradamus. "The process will begin when Greenland starts slipping towards the equator," he said. "The first result of this will be that a huge tidal wave hits the east coast of America, making clear to everyone the total irrelevance of the dollar." All the Western capitals were doomed and sinful Muscovites would only survive if they repented and fled to Siberia, according to this latter-day Noah.

So naturally we all approached the year 1998 with some trepidation…

What actually happened was that Russia defaulted on its sovereign debt. President Yeltsin said there would be no default, and the very next day there was a default. This caused a financial tidal wave that wiped out the profits and savings of millions of Russians, who were just starting to see something of a middle class lifestyle, and plunged them back into poverty, along with the poor who'd never really had their heads much above water. It also ruined Russia's international reputation.

In a panic, Yeltsin began changing his prime ministers as often as he changed his shirts. In retrospect, one can say that the default was the political death knell for Yeltsin, the first nail in his coffin, but he continued to rule, like a zombie, in the Kremlin. *Kukly*, the Russian equivalent of *Spitting Image*, created a very lifelike rubber puppet of him and satirised him mercilessly.

Meanwhile in Kolomna, another old man passed away. Vitaly's father Mikhail Matveyev died at the age of 65 from lung cancer, a predictable end, since as he said himself he'd "smoked and drunk like a real Russian". There was no hospital bed for him; no palliative care. He died in pain at home, looked after by his daughter Natasha.

But his funeral was not the bleak and awkward affair I had seen too often in Britain. Death is a part of life to the Russians, not a taboo, and they look it squarely in the face.

The Matveyev family, who were not rich, got limited help from the undertakers. Ritual, the Russian funeral service, provided the coffin and the bus that would take it to the cemetery but Natasha had to lay her father out herself. Older relatives were on hand to give advice about all the traditions. The curtains were drawn, of course, but Aunt Nina said the carpets should also be rolled back and a lock placed under the coffin. Why, she didn't know, but that was the way it had always been.

Coins closed the dead man's eyes and a glass of vodka with a slice of bread laid on top was placed next to the open coffin. The family could have had a *chitalka* or reader to sit up all night reading the Psalms while relatives kept vigil. But Vitaly and Natasha thought their father, who was not fanatically religious, would have begrudged the expense. Instead, they paid a small fee to have their father's name mentioned during a general memorial service in the local Orthodox church. The priest insisted on seeing the death certificate to be sure he was not being tricked into remembering a living person, which is a black magic practice.

Ritual had warned Vitaly and Natasha not to buy wreaths from street traders, as it said they were often stolen from graves. But after paying for the coffin and the bus, they had to economise on flowers, so they bought on the street anyway. The wreath frames were indeed old but fresh flowers had been put in. "Dad would just have thought it was funny," said Vitaly.

The burial took place in Kolomna's new cemetery. The dead man's sister-in-law, Aunt Vera, decreed that he'd forfeited the right to lie with his wife in the old cemetery because he'd had a brief relationship with another woman in his 15 years of being a widower. Aunt Vera herself would take the place with her sister when her time came. Old Matveyev would have laughed at that as well.

After the burial, the family had a wake at home. Dozens of neighbours crammed into the three-room flat to drink vodka and eat salads. An alcoholic, who had seen the coffin being taken out and knew there would be free drink later, gatecrashed the do. Uncle Yura got into a fight with him and Aunt Vera threw them both out. She would have to be on hand for two more drinking sessions that would be held on the 9th and 40th days after the death, when the soul is said to leave the place to which the person was attached in life.

"It's very shocking to see the person you have loved become a lifeless doll," said Vitaly on the way back to Moscow. "But the body of my dad was so unlike my dad that I concluded he simply wasn't there. And if he wasn't there, then he must have gone somewhere else."

Old Matveyev was free. The default didn't bother him; he was beyond omens and any more of his country's follies and disasters. We decided to take a detour via his *dacha*. Weeds were rampant and a strange quiet had descended over his garden, broken only by birdsong and the buzzing of flies.

Mikhail Matveyev

THE GODFATHER

Costya came home late one night in 1998, not just dumb from exhaustion as usual but covered with bruises along both forearms. "Some guy hit me with a baseball bat," he muttered before he collapsed into bed. I'd learnt to live with shocks like these, married as I was to a "New Russian" businessman.

About a year earlier, he'd rung me from the office to cancel an evening outing we'd had planned. "I can't get away just now," was all he'd said but I sensed that something was wrong. When he finally came home in the small hours of the morning, it turned out some protection racketeers had been holding him at gunpoint. His mafia godfather, to whom he paid a monthly "insurance premium", as was the way in Russia in the 1990s, had sorted that problem out by warning off the bandits. But Costya was worried about the baseball bat incident because he didn't know who had sent the attacker or why.

The assailant, a young man in baggy trousers and with a greasy ponytail, had hailed Costya as he got out of his Honda car to go into his office in the morning. "Are you Costya?" he'd asked. The second after Costya had answered in the affirmative, the stranger had lifted a blanket to reveal the baseball bat.

"I was carrying my briefcase in one hand and my mobile phone, my cigarettes and my lighter in the other," said Costya. "I dropped them and put my arms up to protect my head. He hit me on the arms several times before running off. I wish I had jumped on him like a bull terrier and found out who he was but it all happened so quickly. At least I managed to cover my head. Otherwise I would now be in the Sklif." He meant the Sklifosovsky Hospital, to whose famous accident and emergency department the victims of road accidents and violent crime were usually taken.

Given that Russian businessmen and bankers were often left lying in pools of their own blood, it had been a relatively minor assault, perhaps a warning. Costya couldn't think of any rivals who might have wanted to unnerve him or clients he had offended. "I got to thinking my secretary's boyfriend might have done it because I work her too hard," he joked. Colleagues suggested he start employing a bodyguard but not only did he find that solution too melodramatic, he couldn't afford one anyway.

Costya didn't think it worth reporting the incident to the police. The godfathers operated in their place. Often these were men who had been underground entrepreneurs in Communist times and done time in jail for "economic crimes". They were known as "thieves in law" and were figures of authority among ex-labour camp inmates, enforcing a moral code that boiled down to the tribal idea: "If you hurt one of ours, we will hurt you."

The newspaper *Moskovskaya Pravda* had run an interview with one of these godfathers. "The important thing," he said, "is not to be too greedy. The 'tax payer' should continue to work, make a profit, have an interest in the creative process of laying down capital, and not go and hang himself in the toilet from despair, or worse, report us to the police." Apparently, the mafia was generally satisfied with two to five per cent of profits.

Costya's godfather was called Uncle Boris. I never saw him. All I knew about him was that he was a small-time criminal from a provincial town; Russian, not Caucasian. Apparently, his initial charge for protection had been a modest 300 dollars a month, but after his intervention was required to warn off the gun-toting racketeers, his price had gone up to 1,200 dollars. "I guess you could say I used up my no-claims bonus," joked Costya.

Costya had needed to get protection because, after working for several years with his childhood friend Little Kostya in a modest flat renovation business, he'd gone into a slightly bigger league by launching a firm that sold youth fashions and rock accessories. It was more visible to the mafia because it had shop windows.

The new business had started when two young men came to Costya, asking for advice. One of them was a former policeman called Andrei Ognev, who was producing bandanas – all the rage among the kids in Moscow. The other was a former chef called Dmitry (Dima) Dashchenko, who had a hand punch that turned out metal rings with skulls on. Dima had been on holiday in London and seen a pub in Brixton with the sign of a goblin. They wanted to start a rock accessories business and call it Hobgoblin but they needed Costya on board to manage it.

The three partners began by renting a network of cellars that in Soviet times had been kept as a municipal bomb shelter, for use in case of nuclear attack. Gloomy, with lots of archways and tunnels, it was perfect for a shop selling gothic jewellery, T-shirts printed with skeletons and bats, and rucksacks with the logos of Western and Russian heavy metal, punk, rave and rap groups.

The business was an instant success. Kids flocked to the shop after school and on Saturdays; children as young as six dragged their parents there to buy them death's heads. Soon Costya and his team opened a wholesale warehouse too and before they knew it, they were supplying kiosks from the Far East to Belarus, from the Arctic to Astrakhan. The Astrakhan connection was particularly welcome because traders from there brought buckets of black caviar as gifts when they came up to Moscow to buy gear.

Costya established links with Britain's leader in the gothic jewellery market, Alchemy of Leicester, and ordered cloth badges from a firm called Razzamataz in the old Lancashire textile town of Colne. He also helped to revive an obsolete textile factory in the Russian city of Tver, asking them to sew rucksacks for him. Only one colour was required: funereal black. Looking east, Costya traded with Taiwan. In the very week that the Russian State Duma (lower house of parliament) curried favour with mainland China by declaring that Taiwan did not exist, Costya and Dima showed their superior grasp of economic geography by flying to Taipei and arranging the supply of silk flags and banners for Russian football fans.

Still Costya wasn't super-rich; he didn't have millions of dollars stashed away in an offshore bank account. In Russian terms, he might have been quite wealthy but by British standards, he was an ordinary middle class bloke. His 15 employees were on salaries that ranged from the equivalent of £50 to £600 a month. Costya himself could afford to take me out to restaurants or go away with me for a nice holiday abroad. One year we went to Barbados for 10 days. But had he cashed in his stake in the business, it wouldn't have bought him much more than a small flat in Russia. He owned no property and we continued to rent our Moscow apartment.

Hobgoblin made some errors of judgement. Partly because the residents in the flats above the cellar complained about the crowds of youngsters congregating there, but also because the founders overreached themselves, the shop moved to a location in the city centre, where it survived a mere month. The rent was far too high and the teenagers who had loved the bomb shelter didn't approve. The partners were left with only the wholesale business but they recovered and developed that. Soon one warehouse became three.

They still had the fun of retailing to the public once a week from the Gorbushka rock market, which drew thousands of Muscovites and foreigners to buy bootlegged audio and video tapes. A violent incident at Gorbushka, when Costya saw a black marine from the American embassy being beaten up by a group of skinheads, was decisive in persuading Hobgoblin to eschew racist insignia, even though the sale of swastikas would have been profitable. The goblins admitted to selling bootlegged items at first but they started to legitimise themselves by paying royalties. They sponsored young rock musicians and they paid tax. They tried to be good guys – or as good as it was possible to be in Russia at that time.

And then came the economic meltdown as a result of the default. For months, the rouble had been trading at around six to one against the US dollar. Suddenly the official rate was 16 to the dollar but on the black market it was as low as 30 to one.

To Costya, the economic hit was worse than the blow from the baseball bat. "We were stunned," he said. "We sat around in the warehouse, not knowing what to do. Many of our goods, like the T-shirts from Finland, were bought for dollars but we could only sell them for roubles. At first we didn't know what prices to put on them. When we worked it out, the prices doubled, tripled, quadrupled, and we knew nobody would be able to afford to buy. I had clients phoning from Novosibirsk, Tambov and Tomsk, all cancelling. Who needs pentagram pendants or coffin-shaped jewellery boxes when it's a matter of survival?"

The business still had valuable stock and not all its small investors – friends of the partners – were calling in their loans, so there was some room for manoeuvre. Hobgoblin would survive but difficult times lay ahead. They needed a break and fortunately the godfather Uncle Boris had said they could have a "tax holiday" until they started to make a profit again.

So I was surprised when, at home a few weeks later, the telephone rang, Costya picked up the receiver and I heard him say to some guy, "Look, I thought we had agreed that you were going to leave me in peace for a few months. Oh OK, I'll see you on the Old Arbat then."

"Who was that?" I asked.

"Slava, Uncle Boris's sidekick," he said.

Costya went to see him. "Slava took me to a café," Costya said after the meeting. "He doesn't usually do that. He usually comes to my office to pick up the money for Uncle Boris. He was trying to be nice to me."

Slava didn't demand cash. Instead, he told Costya a sob story. One of the "lads" had been injured in a shoot-out while protecting a business. The gangster's hospital treatment was costing the equivalent of £120 a day. "Donations would be gratefully accepted," he said.

"I refused," said Costya. "I'm broke. I told him, 'Listen, mate; you can't get blood out of a stone.'"

And so the Godfather had to accept that even for him there was a limit; in hard times there was the unexpected power of the little word "no".

Costya trading at Gorbushka market

TAMARA'S SALON

After the default, many Western business people packed up and left Moscow. "The party's over," one American told me curtly. Some had been carpetbaggers, out to make a fast buck in the Wild East, but others had genuinely believed they could make a difference in a decade. In retrospect, this was naïve. Russia needed Westerners who were there for the long haul. It demanded of its own citizens that they lay down their lives for the sake of the next generation. I began to suspect that although Russia would one day become free, fair and prosperous, it might not happen in my lifetime.

But life went on. Tamara Lavrienteva, the friend with whom I had gone on desperate shopping expeditions in Soviet times, decided to hold a musical salon in her own home to show that there was more to life than politics. She announced to all her friends that she was sick of people sitting round talking about the rate for the dollar, so we would have some culture instead. The default had impoverished us all, so no food would be provided but there would be music. About 30 guests declared their interest and Tamara began to tear her hair, wondering where she would find chairs and stools to seat us all.

From time to time, Tamara used to host these little private parties around her piano, the first one of the season often coinciding with her birthday on 4 November. Professional Russian musicians have an expression to dismiss this kind of amateur event: they call it "Aunt Sonya at a Namesday Party". But Tamara's salons were wonderful. She had that Russian ability to be serious without embarrassment and strove for the atmosphere of the society salons held on the Arbat in Pushkin's day. Not a musician herself but rather a social worker and ceramic artist, she nevertheless attracted good performers to open the concerts. Then the audience would join in. The children especially loved to do their party pieces.

When I first arrived in Russia in 1985, Tamara's home on Podkolokolny (Under the Bells) Lane had been like a lamp glowing in what seemed a grey, bewildering and hostile world. The star of the early salons had been a pianist from the Tallinn Conservatory called Irina Borisenko. Because she was as thin as a rake, everyone jokingly called her Pufik (Little Cushion), which she hated. Penniless and for a while homeless, Pufik lived at Tamara's, playing for her supper and giving music lessons to Tamara's daughter Dasha, who was then a little girl with a prodigious gift for drawing.

The salons gave Pufik a stage on which she played Rachmaninov and Tchaikovsky, and Dasha an opportunity to show her progress. Sometimes friends would sing. Often Tamara's husband Anton performed his own ballads to the guitar. As a young father, he'd penned a song we all liked that went, "love and garlic grow with the nappies in the kitchen".

Eventually Pufik left for Paris; she hoped that nobody would know her nickname there. But word leaked out on the Russian émigré grapevine and she continued to be Little Cushion even after she became a big star in France.

The salons were not the same after Pufik's departure. Other factors came close to defeating Tamara. Anton, an icon painter and Orthodox believer, went through a phase when he started to believe that singing for pleasure was a sin and he laid aside his guitar. Market reforms began and friends became too busy trying to make their fortunes, or just their livings, to care about music.

But the default helped to revive Tamara's salons – for her, the party was on again.

The gathering in 1998 took place on 7 November, which had been celebrated as the anniversary of the Bolshevik Revolution. Under Yeltsin, the public holiday was renamed the Day of Accord and Reconciliation and was supposed to bring old Communists and other elements of society together. Later, under Putin, the November holiday would commemorate an obscure Russian victory against the Poles (and by extension, all foreign enemies). But whatever the authorities called it, the *prazdnik* (holiday) remained an excuse to crack open the vodka.

Through the walls came sounds of Tamara's neighbours having a drunken good time before starting to argue and fight. By contrast, her salon was exploring the historical roots of pop music.

She had invited a musicologist, who sat in the rocking chair and explained to the audience – some on stools, some sitting on the floor – that music had always served the twin purposes of lifting the spirit and making the feet tap. The church and the opera really went hand in hand, he said. As for the Soviet state, well it had supported but also sought to control music. He quoted Lenin's famous maxim:

Every artist, everyone who considers himself an artist, has the right to create freely according to his ideal, independently of everything. However, we are Communists and we must not stand with folded hands and let chaos develop as it pleases. We must systemically guide this process and form its result.

And so, jazz was banned.

Dasha, now a young art student, floated around in a beaded dress from the 1920s while Tamara played old records of the first Soviet jazzman, Leonid Utyosov, as well as some LPs that a relative had brought home from Germany at the end of the war. Anton was back, strumming his guitar and singing without any conflict in his soul.

Then, as it was half-term, the kids were allowed to have a disco with Prodigy, which was pronounced by the musicologist to be a perfectly acceptable continuation of the great foot-tapping tradition.

The guests went away happy, even though they'd only been offered a few biscuits. "You must do another salon soon and we'll bring a cream cake next time," somebody promised.

"How do you find the energy to organise all this in the middle of an economic crisis?" I asked.

"Ah," Tamara replied, "when you have children, you are obliged to be an optimist. And besides, if there's no food, there's no washing-up afterwards."

THE FLAWED TSAR

While Tamara refused to give in to depression by reviving the tradition of her salons, down the road at the Hermitage Gardens the newly built New Opera opened with much fanfare in the autumn of 1998. It was a welcome addition to the musical landscape, dominated as it had been for years by the stodgy old Bolshoi Theatre. The New Opera chose as its first offering a production of Mussorgsky's *Boris Godunov*, about the Tsar who ruled in the "Time of Troubles". The parallels with the turbulent 1990s and another ruler named Boris were obvious to all.

Muscovites had their mayor, Yuri Luzhkov, to thank for the New Opera. He may have been a petty dictator in a flat cap who rode roughshod over individual rights, tore down historic buildings and gave lucrative contracts to his wife, but put him in charge of a new building project and he was your man. He'd presided over the construction and completion of the Novaya Opera (New Opera) in a mere two-and-a- half years. Apparently, Luzhkov had said he was "tired of seeing 50-year-old, bald Romeos with lousy diction" and he wanted opera to be fresh and accessible to the public.

In this, Luzhkov shared the dream of conductor Yevgeny Kolobov, who had so hated the Bolshoi's musty productions that he had walked away from the Soviet musical establishment and gone off into the wilderness to create something new. I had first met Kolobov five years earlier when he was working with a young troupe out of a dusty, disused cinema called Zenit. Cool in a black roll-neck sweater and jeans, he was like David taking on the Goliath of the Bolshoi.

The Bolshoi would eventually change, of course, and the Mariinsky in St Petersburg freshen its repertoire and become under Valery Gergiev a force to be reckoned with. But at the time Kolobov made his protest, Russian opera was stuck in a Soviet rut, repeating the same old productions year after year with fat, ageing singers who could not be fired because their jobs were guaranteed for life.

"Yevgeny Vladimirovich found it all so pompous," said Tatyana Roshkova, a musicologist who became chief administrator at the New Opera. "He gathered together a young company to inject some life back into opera."

In the cinema, Kolobov had only been able to put on concert versions of operas, without all the scenery and costumes. Even that had been refreshing because the voices and interpretations had been new. But now finally he could stage full productions. The New Opera had singers but no ballet dancers, which for all except ballet enthusiasts was a mercy.

"We're going to perform contemporary works or take a new approach to old favourites," said Ms Roshkova. "That may not sound very radical to you in the West but it's new for us. And of course, we have stripped away all the old political overtones of Soviet opera."

Naturally, I was keen to see what Kolobov could achieve on his splendid new stage. Unfortunately, I wasn't invited to the gala opening, when black stars from New York came to sing *Porgy and Bess*, a sensation for the lucky few who saw it. But I did have a ticket to hear *Boris Godunov*.

I remembered homeless Lydia as I walked through the gardens, looking up at the elegant art nouveau-style opera house that had been designed by Russian architect Igor Kotelnikov but built by Austrian and Yugoslav workers. Standing on the site of an old summer theatre, the New Opera mixed old and new. Its shiny foyer, with brass rails and chandeliers, brought to mind the first-class decks of the *Titanic*. The auditorium was very traditional, in red and gold.

The opera was well chosen for the difficult times through which Russia was passing. Boris Godunov was the Tsar who ruled in the chaotic interim between the death of Ivan the Terrible and the rise of the Romanov dynasty. The role of Boris was sung vigorously by Oleg Korotkov. The ragged masses pinned their hopes on this gold-clad monarch but he turned out to be tragically flawed. Of course, it set us thinking about Boris Yeltsin, who would have made an excellent subject for a modern opera.

He too presided over a period of transition and thus inflicted on his people what the Chinese would call the "curse of living in interesting times". He tried his best to be modern but he had one foot in the Communist past and so inevitably was dragged down, dragging his long-suffering nation with him.

Yeltsin it was – and who but Yeltsin could have done it? – who had leapt theatrically onto a tank to resist the hardline coup against Gorbachev. But then he had withdrawn, probably to drink, leaving the job half done, failing to dismantle the KGB that was at the heart of the rotten old system.

Yeltsin it was who had dared to bring in the free market overnight, something that had been beyond the courage of the more cautious, dithering Gorbachev. The result was raw pain for his people and Yeltsin must have known it. Was this one of the pressures that caused his heart to crack?

Yeltsin it was who restored to the Russians their God, their Orthodox Church, the memory of their royal family and their sense of history. Yeltsin it was who gave them freedom, failing to explain, perhaps because he was in the process of learning it himself, that the other side of freedom is responsibility.

Despite, or rather because of all his faults and flaws, Yeltsin was endearingly human, a kindly father figure who addressed his television audiences as "my dear Russians".

Yes, he invaded Chechnya and shed much blood but he also admitted it was his biggest mistake and allowed the "s" word (sorry) to pass his lips, something rarely if ever heard from politicians. He took the blame himself, rather than passing the buck to others, and he never clamped down on free speech, let alone murder his critics.

We laughed at him because we were free to do so and didn't realise a time might come when we would weep for the old buffoon and miss him. After all, who but a tipsy Yeltsin could have called the Queen and the woman Prime Minister of Norway (one wearing red and the other white at a state banquet) "raspberries and cream"? Or failed to get off a plane on an official visit to Ireland because he had overindulged (yet again) from the drinks trolley?

Perhaps as the years go by, history will be kinder to Yeltsin. For as his Prime Minister Viktor Chernomyrdin once famously said, "We did everything for the best but it turned out as it always does."

SPIES

Spy stories never really gripped me. Frankly I could take or leave the latest James Bond movie and I certainly wasn't interested in Russia's equivalent heroes, the agents who inspired Vladimir Putin as a little boy. Blofeld and his cat amused me but the antics of both fictional and real-life spies – indeed the notions of patriotism and treachery – struck me as puerile.

Unfortunately, the British press had an insatiable appetite for anything to do with espionage, so despite the fact that it wasn't really my cup of tea, I often found myself having to write about the old KGB. Over the years, and entirely without intending it, I became an "expert" on the organisation I had every reason to hate, since it had given me grief when I'd married a Russian.

I interviewed Trofim Molodiy, whose father Konon had spied in the West under the name of Gordon Lonsdale before being swapped in Berlin in 1964 for the jailed British secret agent Greville Wynne. Those were names to conjure with, if you were a spy buff.

I also met a woman called Nina Alexeyeva, who had been the mistress of Stalin's murderous henchman Lavrenty Beria and lived to tell the tale. And right under the noses of the KGB, I'd managed to interview Leyla Gordievskaya, the wife who was left behind in Moscow in 1991 when top spy Oleg Gordievsky had defected to the UK, apparently hidden in a diplomatic removal van.

All very cloak and dagger; all very exciting, you might think. But it somehow left me cold. Cold, that is, until I realised it wasn't the details of the spies' operations – their vehicles, their absurd exploding pens etc – that mattered so much as their motivation. I cared little for state secrets but I was interested in the secrets of the human heart.

So when George Blake, a British traitor who'd lived in Moscow since his escape from Wormwood Scrubs in 1966, suddenly popped up on Russian television, I found I did have some questions for him. He'd converted to Marxism during the Korean War and gone on to work in Berlin, from where he'd passed the West's secrets to Moscow. That was perhaps understandable in the context of fascism, the War and the Cold War. But what had his subsequent experience in the USSR really been like and did he have any regrets? That's what I wanted to know.

The TV programme showed him going to church with Russian *babushkas* (grannies) in headscarves and speaking of his life having been "determined by the universal force", which suggested some conversion in later life to religion. The church was in the village of Kratovo, just outside Moscow, so I went there looking for him. I waited outside the church for the evening service to end. Did anyone know an elderly Englishman called George? Perhaps he answered to the name of Georgy now? The members of the congregation shook their heads. The young priest claimed not to know him either. A man said gruffly, "He's not here today."

Neither could I spot the bearded Blake over the fences of any of the *dachas*. I fancied that he might have lived at the brown house with the foxgloves in the garden – very English – but it was probably my imagination. The makers of the documentary said later that Blake had gone away for the summer to Karelia, as if the pine trees of Kratovo were not enough for him. It was a cunning move. After the airing of the film, he must have known the British press would renew their efforts to track him down, and he gave us all the slip.

I had better luck interviewing Rufina Pukhova, the widow of Kim Philby, when she published *Island on the Sixth Floor*: her memoirs of life in a Moscow flat with the Cambridge spymaster who could never return to England.

"He did not feel he had betrayed England," Rufina Ivanovna told me. "He was fighting fascism and we were all on the same side in those days, weren't we?"

Philby's widow was particularly upset by stories about her husband's alleged depression after he saw the reality of life in the Soviet Union, which he had served through ideological conviction, not for money. One retired

KGB agent had gone so far as to suggest that Philby was disillusioned enough to take his own life.

"The suicide story is rubbish, to put it mildly," she said. Kim had died in a closed KGB hospital, where he was undergoing heart treatment. "I went to see him. He was very weak but brightened when he saw me. I wondered whether I should stay with him through the night but then thought if I did that it might worry him, so I left. I got home at eleven in the evening. I couldn't sleep; I was very nervous. I took sleeping pills. At two in the morning, I put out the light. The next day I rang the hospital and they told me he had died at exactly 2.00 am."

Rufina Ivanovna kept the "island on the sixth floor" more or less as it was when they lived there together, although financial need forced her to sell some items to Sotheby's. The KGB had allotted the Philbys, who feared pursuit by journalists, the perfect flat, hidden behind Tverskaya Street. Only invited guests were told which archways and doorways would bring them to the apartment.

Inside, Philby's study was as he'd left it, with his history books and detective novels for sleepless nights. In the living room, his old Riga radio with beautiful ivory buttons was still tuned to the BBC.

"There were two main myths about Kim," said his widow. "One had it that after he came to Moscow he lived in luxury, like cheese floating in butter, as we say in Russian. The other had it that he descended into degradation and poverty. The reality was less sensational."

Rufina Ivanovna admitted than when she'd first met Philby, he'd drunk heavily. But in 1972 he pulled himself out of his alcoholic depression and the KGB, which had kept him underemployed, found him work as a consultant. His children visited him from the West and he subscribed to all the Fleet Street newspapers; he liked *The Times* best for its cryptic crossword.

It was true that many aspects of Soviet life did disappoint him. "He was particularly irritated by Brezhnev," Rufina Ivanovna said. "Gorbachev raised his hopes at first but he got tired of his demagoguery. Of course, he would have been appalled by the poverty under Yeltsin; he had a great sense of social justice."

Philby was nostalgic for England, which he knew was lost to him for ever. "But he was also realistic," she said. "You know, he often used to say, 'The West has its defects too.' "

Perhaps it was my attempts to explore the psychology of Blake and Philby that persuaded a British publishing house that I would be the perfect person to ghost-write an English version of a book of memoirs that 12 retired KGB agents had brought out in Russian and rather wittily called *The KGB's Travel Guide to the Cities of the World*. Despite the promising title, it was a superficial book in which the Paris-based agent told his readers how he'd eaten *moules a la provencale* in Montmartre, and the London man recommended Russian vodka drinkers to persist with whisky, a taste that in his opinion was well worth acquiring.

The British publishers expected something more substantial than that; they wanted me to roll up my sleeves and interview all 12 agents to find out what they'd really been up to in their spying careers around the world. Thus, in 1998, I became the unlikely author of *Undercover Lives – Soviet Spies in the Cities of the World*. I didn't learn any Russian state secrets – I wouldn't have wanted to – but I did find out what made these men tick.

The agents had spied for the KGB in 12 cities – London, Paris, Berlin, Rome, New York, Mexico City, Rio de Janeiro, Cairo, Bangkok, Tokyo, Jakarta and New Delhi. Some had worked undercover as journalists while others had had diplomatic immunity. Only one, Oleg Brykin, who had been a translator at the UN in New York, had taken any real risks because if he'd been caught, he would have been tried and punished by the Americans. The worst that could have happened to the others, with their diplomatic and journalistic covers, was expulsion for "activities incompatible with their status".

Russians often say that there is no such thing as an ex-KGB officer. The agents themselves told me that the only way out of the KGB was "feet first, in a box". So I was keen to find out how and why these men had become involved with the organisation in the first place. It seemed some had been motivated by patriotism while others were working class lads who saw the KGB as their best chance of getting an education and a career. Leonid Kolosov, who'd been the "*Izvestia* correspondent" in Rome, told me how he'd been trained at a centre in the woods outside Moscow so "top secret" that the locals had scrawled "school for spies" on the wooden fence for all to see.

I learnt some interesting details about how the agents operated. The man who'd worked in Bangkok and New Delhi revealed the difficulties of finding suitable dead-letter boxes in Third World countries. You couldn't just hide a role of microfilm in an empty Coke can as you might have done in the West, he said, because the local people were so poor that they picked up and collected such pieces of rubbish. And then of course there was the danger of snakes, if you were rooting around in the long grass, trying to pick up some dropped message or other.

Brykin from New York revealed that his KGB masters were so stupid and racist that they assumed disadvantaged American blacks would incline to treachery and be easily recruited as informers. He also astonished me when he said that the "secret" reports he sent back to Moscow mostly consisted of summaries of the contents of magazines such as *Time* and *Newsweek*. They may have been publicly available in the West but in the Soviet Union, only top Communists were allowed to know what the Western press was writing. Information was power and the Soviet elite ruled by knowing just slightly more than ordinary citizens.

Several of the spies I interviewed had that particular snobbery that comes from knowing things, however trivial, that are off-limits to others. One was a dreadful gossip and filthy-minded too. One or two of them were gentlemanly, intelligent and modest but most of them, it seemed to me, had huge egos and were terribly pleased with themselves. Frankly, it would have been easier to interview the prima donnas of the Bolshoi Theatre. Only Brykin seemed to question in any way the purpose of what he had been doing.

I was glad, though, to have had the opportunity to meet these agents. It helped me to understand that the Cold War had to some extent been a game in which the two opposing sides mirrored each other. I did not, however, buy into the Russian notion of "equivalence" – that Russia may be corrupt, undemocratic etc. but then so is the West; that all politicians are basically the same. No, I believed and still believe that although the West does indeed have its faults, the scale of the problem is greater in Russia.

254

Meeting the secret agents also clarified my thoughts about my own profession of journalism. I saw that we needed the same skills of observation and used many of the same information-gathering techniques, but our motivation was completely different. They served a narrow audience of rulers while my job was to inform and thereby empower the general public.

Lastly, working with the agents brought me face to face with people I had regarded as my personal enemies. The KGB had certainly made my life a misery when I married Costya in 1987. I didn't change my mind about the organisation, of course, but I came to see that the individuals who worked in it were just cogs in a wheel. I didn't exactly befriend the men for whom I'd been a ghost-writer but I felt no animosity towards them either. They were sad old buffers, reminiscing about the adventures of their youth, and most of them are probably dead now anyway.

RAISA

Why is it that we never fully appreciate what we have until we lose it? When Raisa Gorbacheva was First Lady of the Soviet Union, Russians detested her to an irrational degree. When she fell ill with leukemia, they were full of pity for her. When she died in September 1999, there was an outpouring of grief for her that almost matched the mourning for Princess Diana two years earlier. Suddenly Raisa became Russia's Queen of Hearts.

I attended her funeral, at least the public parts of it, held first at the culture fund that she had founded. Then the cortege moved on to the medieval Novodevichy Convent for a Russian Orthodox blessing. Finally there was a private burial service in the convent cemetery, where all the most famous Russians rest.

Russian politicians were supposed to be stony-faced and their wives barely seen, far less heard, but Mikhail Gorbachev wept openly for the woman who had broken a taboo by showing herself as very much his partner during his time in the Kremlin. Flanked by their daughter Irina and their two granddaughters, the father of *glasnost* whispered to his wife in the open coffin and stroked her hair.

"The Gorbachevs were the nearest thing we had to a royal family," said the pensioner standing next to me behind the crowd control barriers at the convent. Like many in the throng of bereaved Muscovites, she was weeping unrestrainedly.

How different it had all been when Gorbachev was in power. Raisa, an educated woman with opinions of her own, was perceived then not as a role model for Russian women but as an arrogant "tsarina", who unduly influenced her husband in political matters. A Raisa joke that did the rounds in the years of *perestroika* went like this: Mikhail and the Tsarina are in bed together. "Misha," asks Raisa, "how does it feel to sleep with the wife of the leader of the Soviet Union?"

Everyone, it seemed, hated Raisa. Nancy Reagan, who'd been upstaged by her at summits, attacked the stylish Soviet First Lady in her memoirs, criticising her manners and dress sense. Boris Yeltsin accused Raisa of trying to create a "personality cult" and of taking too large a salary from her supposedly charitable culture fund.

Russian drinkers suspected she was behind Gorbachev's highly unpopular anti-alcohol drive. In her memoirs *I Hope*, Raisa mentioned the alcoholism of her brother which, she said, had been "a constant source of pain that I have carried in my heart for more than 30 years". It's likely she did indeed inspire the crackdown on Russians' favourite pastime of boozing.

Other Russians couldn't forgive Raisa when they saw her in a videotape, paying for furs and jewellery in London and Paris with an American Express card. Compared with the stout and self-effacing *babushkas* who had been the wives of past Soviet leaders, Raisa was too prominent, chic and intellectual for her own good and she provoked envy rather than public admiration. It seemed she knew this because in a television interview in the mid-1990s, she described how hard it had been to be the first visible First Lady.

It was said that Raisa suffered particularly during the coup in 1991, when hardliners tried to take over the country while the Gorbachevs were on holiday. Whether the stress of this contributed to her illness cannot be known. After the couple left power, Raisa began to devote herself to fund-raising for cancer research. This was before she was diagnosed with leukemia herself.

The news that Raisa was in hospital in Germany, waiting to receive a bone marrow transplant from her sister, shocked the nation and transformed Russians' attitudes towards their former First Lady. Suddenly, they were melting with pity for her. While Gorbachev kept a vigil at her bedside, the whole of Russia followed the saga and thousands of ordinary people sent letters, prescriptions for herbal cures and even offers of money. Sadly, Raisa succumbed to an infection before the transplant could take place and she died in the clinic in Münster at the age of 67. "Raisa Maximovna suffered very much in the past few weeks but her death was peaceful," said NTV.

Boris Yeltsin, once so bitter towards his old rival Gorbachev that he begrudged him the use of an official car, changed his tune and sent an aircraft to bring Raisa's body home. And Yeltsin's usually retiring wife Naina got a public role when she represented him at the funeral. The biggest foreign delegation came from Germany, which was grateful to Gorbachev for having allowed the Berlin Wall to fall. As Gorbachev nearly crumbled, former Chancellor Helmut Kohl embraced him in a consoling bear hug.

In his grief, perhaps Gorbachev found some comfort in the change of heart among ordinary Russian citizens, who had reviled him for breaking up the Soviet Union and scorned his wife for being smart, clever and always at his side. In 1996, when he'd stood in the presidential election against Yeltsin, Gorbachev had received a humiliating one per cent of the vote; that was how much they hated him and Raisa.

But over time, Russians came to reassess the Gorbachev legacy. Behind the crowd barriers at the funeral, the lively spirit of *glasnost* returned. I didn't need to interview people; they came up of their own accord to talk to me.

"It's how we are," sighed Olga Trubnikova, a secretary. "We envy other people their success but pity their misfortune. We used to find Raisa extremely irritating but at the end, we felt sorry for her and even sorrier for him, the loyal and loving husband, constantly at her bedside."

"I admit," said Tatyana Knyazeva, an art historian, "that I used to find Raisa hard to take. But now I realise that Gorbachev could never have achieved what he did without a woman like her behind him. He gave us freedom. I went on holiday to America, which for a Soviet person was like going to the moon. Today I have come to say 'thank you'. I don't have much money but I have brought these garden marigolds to say 'sorry' and 'thank you'."

TERROR IN MOSCOW

On the morning of 13 September 1999, Muscovites awoke to the terrible news that 45 bodies had been dragged from the rubble of an eight-storey apartment block in the south of the city following an explosion at 5.00 am. Altogether 120 people were registered as living in the flats and the death toll was almost certain to rise, the radio said. It did. The final toll from the blast at 6 Kashirskoye Shosse would end up at 119. This was the deadliest in a chain of explosions that killed Russian civilians in the one place they could have expected to be safe, fast asleep in their own beds in the middle of the night.

The 13th had been declared a day of national mourning for the dead of two earlier apartment block blasts, one in the Moscow district of Pechatniki and one in the Dagestani town of Buinaksk. But the requiems hadn't even been sung before the Russian people found themselves mourning fresh losses at Kashirskoye Shosse. The tower block had been built of bricks rather than concrete panels, and collapsed in small pieces, so it was clear that nobody was going to be found alive in an air pocket and miraculously rescued, as sometimes happens in earthquakes.

Events at Kashirskoye Shosse killed off the idea to which Russians had clung that the previous blasts had perhaps been the result of gas leaks. Now it was obvious to everyone that Moscow and other Russian cities (Volgodonsk was next on 16 September) were facing a concerted terrorist attack. The bombs left my friends and neighbours terrified – frightened to go out lest there were explosions in public places and even more scared to stay in their own homes.

Specialists said the explosive used – hexagen- was normally employed by the army and could have been stolen or sold by corrupt soldiers. It was planted in the basements of the buildings, guaranteeing complete demolition and suggesting that the terrorists had knowledge of the construction industry.

Although Chechen warlord Shamil Basayev denied his men were behind the attacks, saying it was "not their style to kill civilians", the Russian authorities immediately pointed the finger of blame at Islamic militants from Chechnya. President Yeltsin had a new prime minister, appointed in August 1999. His name was Vladimir Putin and he made clear he was not going to pussyfoot with the attackers.

"We will follow the terrorists wherever they go," he said in a soundbite that came to define his tough approach. "If they are at the airport, we will be there. Excuse me, but if they are in the toilets, we will go in there and blow them away. That's all there is to it; problem solved."

On 1 October, Russia sent troops into Chechnya, starting a second war with the restive Caucasian region. That autumn, Russian planes bombed the Chechen capital of Grozny to smithereens – its ruins resembled Stalingrad when the Russian Air Force had finished. In my view, NATO's bombing of Belgrade earlier that year gave Moscow food for thought when it came to punishing Chechnya. The NATO campaign in the former Yugoslavia had made the West many enemies in Russia. "How could we preach democracy and at the same time bomb Russians' Slav brothers, the Serbs?" ordinary Russians asked. So when they felt themselves under siege, no longer caring what the West thought, they embraced Mr Putin's bellicose rhetoric. As for the Russian military, they obviously got ideas from NATO's techniques of aerial attack that spared the pilots and made sure all the "collateral damage" was on the ground.

Now Russia was at war again. It was hard to believe because the Russians had been so tired of the first war with Chechnya, to which President Yeltsin had negotiated an end in 1996. Those with sons, like Vitaly, feared their boys might be conscripted. But the general mood turned rapidly in favour of Mr Putin's methods of dealing with the threat. Russians were said to be united in a way they hadn't been since they'd faced the Nazis. On red alert, Moscow was near psychosis, fearing further attacks, seeing enemies everywhere.

The authorities said they were studying the sophisticated anti-terrorist techniques used in Britain, France and Israel but it seemed to me they were falling back more on Soviet-era methods of public surveillance, relying on networks of "alert citizens" or busybodies who informed on others. After the Kashirskoye Shosse blast, hundreds of shocked Muscovites telephoned their local housing maintenance (GREP) offices to volunteer as "house seniors".

"We're making lists. If we get too many offers, we will have to choose," said a clerk in one office in the central district.

There was no question as to who should be the vigilant eye at 3 Nikonovsky Peryulok (Lane), a 14-storey block just round the corner from our house. Zoya Konstantinovna Baruzdova had been guarding the building on her own initiative since 1996, when somebody had stolen sugar and cooking oil from her flat. She sat on the ground floor in a little booth, watching the flickering screen of a closed circuit television for which the residents had had a whip-round. They also paid her a modest wage to act as their concierge.

"I went all through the Great Patriotic War [Second World War]," she declared. "I am not afraid of anybody, least of all a few terrorists. I know everybody in all 104 flats in our block. If any stranger appears, doing anything suspicious, you can be sure that I shall be on to him immediately."

Zoya Konstantinovna's motives might have been pure but there were worries that feuding neighbours might settle scores by making anonymous tip-offs about each other to the police. It seemed less like a Russian version of Britain's Neighbourhood Watch and more as if Stalin's ghost was patrolling the streets of Moscow. Immigrants were worried after Mayor Yuri Luzhkov issued an order that all the city's "guests" should reregister in the wake of the bombs. "We will see who needs to stay and who should leave," he said ominously.

"There's a foreigner living in there," I heard a man's voice say in the corridor outside my flat before, a minute later, the doorbell rang and I opened up to my local bobby, Constable Bocharev, who was accompanied by a criminal investigator in a leather coat whom I hadn't seen before. They asked to see my passport and a copy of my rental contract. Luckily I had this, as our landlady didn't evade tax and was scrupulous in providing written agreements with tenants. Also I was the "right kind of foreigner" –

Western – so they saluted and left. The visit might not have passed off so smoothly had I been a member of Moscow's Caucasian community, who had good reason to fear being turned into scapegoats.

It would be racist to say that all Russians were racist but the illiberal ones were certainly not particular in distinguishing between the Chechens, Dagestanis, Ingushetians and Ossetians, who came from the Russian-controlled north Caucasus; and Georgians, Armenians and Azeris, who were from independent states further south. Some were Muslim and some were Orthodox Christian but as far as Russian racists were concerned, they were all "black arses" and "bandits".

"I used to be a Soviet man. I went to university in Leningrad. Now I am an alien," said Ruslan, one of the thousands of Azeri stallholders without whose efforts Muscovites would not have eaten fresh fruit. "The Russians say, 'Mafia, mafia' but we are traders. The market is part of our culture. To us, the bazaar is theatre. To many Russians, it is still something dirty."

Ruslan condemned the bombs. "Not all Russians are bad. There are good and bad in all races. I would not wish these bombings on my worst enemy. It is complete savagery."

Worried about his future, Ruslan showed me the flimsy piece of paper that was his temporary residence permit. "It's still valid but now I will have to go to the police station and see if I can renew it. The police are always taking bribes from me. This time I'm afraid I will have to give a big one."

PC Bocharev had told me that he earned the equivalent of £25 a month and that for the duration of the bomb crisis, the police had been put on 12-hour shifts without a day off. Bocharev was perhaps honest but would it be any surprise if some of his colleagues sought to supplement their incomes by shaking down poor immigrants?

Apart from the pensioners, and police and army conscripts sent out to patrol the streets, workers in the GREP offices were bearing the brunt of the security operation. In one such office in central Moscow, four Russian women all called Tatyana and an Azeri guest worker called Eldar were taking a tea break. Their usual detective work involved investigating blocked lavatories and broken light bulbs or, in winter, smashing the icicles that hung dangerously from roofs.

"We were out all last night with the local police, searching basements and attics for explosives," said Tatyana Lishova. "After the bomb at Kashirskoye Shosse, Yeltsin gave Luzhkov 24 hours to check all Moscow buildings. Luzhkov in turn issued his orders and in the hierarchy, all the bosses kicked down until the poor people at the bottom were left to do the dirty work."

Ms Lishova was highly critical of the operation and especially of the use of "house seniors" for surveillance. "It's illiterate and unprofessional," she said. A Mum's Army rather than a Dad's Army had been created, as most of the volunteers were elderly women. "It's very dangerous for them to be out watching, especially at night, and what could they possibly do against determined terrorists?"

As I left the GREP office, I saw an old lady in conversation with a conscript. She was telling him that there was something fishy about an empty flat in her building. The grey-faced, underfed 18-year-old said he would report the matter to his superior officer but the blank look on his face suggested otherwise. As darkness fell, I saw the conscript again on the street near my home. He was still in uniform, on duty, begging cigarettes from passers-by.

Frankly, none of this inspired much confidence. We were no longer safe in our beds and I wasn't sure how far we could trust the people who were supposed to be protecting us.

RYAZAN

And what about Putin? Who was Mr Putin? That was the question we journalists were all feverishly attempting to answer after President Yeltsin appointed him, the latest in a series of prime ministers the Kremlin leader had been trying out as he continued his search for a possible successor. Up until this point, all the candidates the old man had put forward had been regarded with pity and contempt, as if endorsement by Yeltsin was the kiss of death for any aspiring politician. Putin just seemed like the next dull and dispensable little nobody – until the bombs; they changed everything.

When Putin threatened the terrorists, his ice-blue eyes lit up with inner fire. His response to the apartment attacks made him an overnight hero, Russia's avenging angel who would not only punish the Chechens but also heal all the hurts and humiliations the people had suffered through the difficult Yeltsin years. Putin was the clear political beneficiary of the terror and the new war. He was now seen as Yeltsin's most probable heir. So who the hell was he?

In my archives, I have a faded fax from a political analyst called Alexei Mukhin, who tried to answer that question for me in 1999. "Vladimir Vladimirovich Putin, born 7 October 1952, speaks perfect German (Hoch-Deutsch), master of sports in judo, runs and exercises for 45 minutes every morning, comes from a family of Leningrad workers, graduated from St Petersburg University, graduation reference described him as a 'man of exceptional honesty, integrity and responsibility', attended Moscow KGB school, was sent to the GDR in 1985, after the end of the Cold War this assignment was no longer a prestigious one etc., etc."

On my bookshelves, I have Putin's own "astonishingly frank" autobiography, *First Person*, published in 2000, in which he describes how his father hid from German soldiers during the war by diving into a marsh and breathing through a hollow reed and how he, Putin junior, spent his youth in a Leningrad slum, chasing rats with a stick in the stairwell. Other stories in the book are in a similarly gung-ho vein.

And I remember what the KGB agents I interviewed for my own book said about the KGB: "Once in the KGB, always in the KGB". That was their mantra.

The truth is I didn't know who Putin was back then and I don't know who he is to this day. I'm not sure we will ever really know the answer to the question: who is Mr Putin? All I can do is set down for the historical record the circumstances of how he came to power, as I observed them, and recount a very strange incident that happened in the city of Ryazan, 130 miles south-east of Moscow, in September 1999.

There has never been an independent inquiry into the apartment block bombings and pretty well everyone who tried to investigate them is now dead, including the journalist Yuri Shchekochikhin, who was apparently poisoned, and Alexander Litvinenko, who died of polonium poisoning in London in 2006.

Their suspicions were raised by the bizarre affair in Ryazan, which I happened to visit shortly after the wave of bombings. There I found the residents of 16/14 Novosyolov Street convinced they'd had a lucky escape from disaster. For after the Buinaksk, Moscow and Volgodonsk bombings, it looked as if they were next on the list to be blown up in their beds.

On 23 September, the residents of the tower block, which housed 250 people, noticed three strangers behaving suspiciously near the building and called the police. Officers found what they thought was a huge bomb in the basement and evacuated the flats. The residents were kept out in the cold all night. Only 24 hours later did the FSB at national level come out with the explanation that the emergency had been a "training exercise".

At first the residents' shock and relief at escaping the fate of those who had been buried under rubble in other cities turned to nothing more than annoyance with the FSB for using them in a bomb drill. But later, questions started to arise in their minds about the whole business. Was somebody really trying to kill them? Could it have been the very service that was supposed to ensure the security of citizens? Because normally, when there is a training exercise of any kind in Russia, different branches of the authorities have to be notified and advance warning of it given to the public. That hadn't happened in Ryazan; something wasn't right.

The block on Novosyolov (New Settlers') Street lay in the heart of a 1970s housing estate on the edge of Ryazan. It was easy enough to find but it took me a while to gain access to the building because since the scare, the residents had installed a new metal door with an electronic lock. Not knowing the code, I had to wait until someone came out before I could slip inside and start ringing doorbells at random.

The occupants all told me that the people I really needed to see were the Kartofelnikov family because they had been the main witnesses to everything that had happened. At flat number 19 on the fourth floor, the door was opened by Yulia Kartofelnikova, who said her parents, Alexei and Lyudmila, were out but she invited me anyway into their book-lined living room. Ms Kartofelnikova had just graduated from medical school. An intelligent and articulate young woman, she gave me a clear account of the disturbing events on 23 September.

"It was about nine in the evening," she said. "Dad had just come back from the garage [he was a bus driver]. He spotted a white car backed up to our building. A piece of paper with the number 62 [code for Ryazan] was pasted over the number plate. He thought it was odd. Most people would not notice such a thing but he is a driver, so such details catch his eye. I saw the car as well. I was looking down from the balcony. I saw one man from behind. He looked at his watch and got into the driver's seat."

Down at ground level, another witness, radio engineer Vladimir Vasiliev, also saw two passengers – a man and a woman – and he was adamant that they appeared to be ethnic Russians, not the swarthier-looking Chechens.

"Dad came up and rang the police," Ms Kartofelnikova continued. "The phone was engaged, engaged, but he persisted and got through. I was walking Malysh [their dog] when three policemen arrived. I showed them the way to the basement. The police were not keen to go down there but one young officer did, and he came rushing back up again, shouting, 'Bomb!' "

Bomb disposal teams were summoned. The police went after the white car, only to find it abandoned in a car park. The building was evacuated.

Use of the lifts was forbidden so residents, including elderly people and pregnant women, filed down the stairs. Several bedridden invalids had to be left behind. The residents stood in the cold until after midnight, when the nearby October cinema opened its doors to them.

"There was no heating and the water had been cut off," said Ms Kartofelnikova. "Then Dad had an idea. He fetched one of his buses and we spent the night in a warm coach. Early in the morning, on the radio, we heard that four sacks of explosives had been found, with a device set to detonate them at 5.30 am. Then it hit home. I felt afraid."

The next morning the residents were allowed to go back home. It was the head of the FSB himself, Nikolai Patrushev, who described the incident as a "training exercise". The sacks had contained sugar, he said. Not long after, the FSB announced it had found a "school for terrorists" in the Chechen town of Urus Martan with explosives identical to those used to bomb flats in Buinaksk, Moscow and Volgodonsk. Mr Kartofelnikov was declared a hero and given a black and white television set as a reward.

But questions kept on tormenting the residents. If it was a training exercise, who exactly was being trained? Why, after the residents had practised evacuation procedures, were they not reassured and allowed to go home? Why were they kept out of the building all night? And if, as Mr Patrushev said, this was a nationwide exercise, why hadn't there been similar drills in other cities?

The Kartofelnikov family was convinced Ryazan was next in line to be bombed but by whom, they couldn't say. A local FSB officer had told Mr Kartofelnikov privately that he'd been "born in a shirt", in other words been extremely lucky. I asked Ms Kartofelnikova whether she thought it was conceivable that FSB agents, rather than Chechen terrorists, were behind the bombings. "There is no proof but anything is possible," she said, adding that she did not blame the local police or Ryazan branch of the FSB for what had happened.

At that I left Novosyolov Street and, slightly nervous that I might be being followed, went to the police station. There Lieutenant-Colonel Sergei Kabashov told me, "Our preliminary tests showed the presence of explosives. We were not told it was a test. As far as we are concerned, the danger was real."

Another Ryazan police officer, Major Vladimir Golev, said a local telephone operator had intercepted a call to a known FSB number in Moscow in which the caller had sought instructions because the city's railway station was being watched. "Split up and make your own way out," said the voice on the other end, according to Major Golev, who said the call could perhaps have been part of the "exercise" to test police alertness.

Whatever the truth, the FSB was keen that the residents of Novosyolov Street forgot about the dark affair as soon as possible.

"At the very least, we were inconvenienced," Ms Kartofelnikova said. "Some of us wanted to take the matter to court. But Alexander Sergeyev of the local FSB paid us a visit. He said he understood our feelings but we should think of the situation in the country and be loyal."

When it came to fitting the new metal door and intercom system, the residents found they didn't have quite enough money of their own and were surprised when the housing authority stepped in and offered to give them the additional security features at a discount.

NEW YEAR

In the run-up to Novy God (New Year), it was almost impossible to catch the actress Yelena Dement at home. If I rang her at 8.00 am, her 12-year-old daughter Rada would answer the phone and say that mummy was already out. If I rang after midnight, her husband Vladimir would say wearily that she still hadn't come home. Ded Moroz (Grandfather Frost, the Russian equivalent of Santa Claus) was on his rounds and Yelena was assisting him in the role of Snegurochka (The Snow Maiden).

In late December, Russian actors and actresses can make a month's salary in a day by appearing at private parties as the seasonal pair. According to tradition, Grandfather Frost is big-hearted but prone to the foolishness of old age while his granddaughter the Snow Maiden is as bright as a button. In reality, the actress who plays the Snow Maiden usually holds the operation together; often, after a day in which Grandfather Frost will have had numerous glasses of vodka pressed on him, she ends up dragging her colleague home by the fur collar of his red or sometimes blue coat.

It was 29 December and I was still desperate to reach Yelena, who normally worked at Moscow's Theatre for Young Spectators. "OK," said the man at the Zarya (Dawn) agency that helped her get the New Year work and presumably took a cut of her earnings. "I'll let you into a secret. The Snow Maiden has a mobile phone." Yelena answered on the first ring and instructed me to meet her outside the metro station at Pechatniki, the working class suburb where three months earlier terrorists had blown up a block of flats.

I recognised her from her description of herself. She was a petite blonde, perfect for the Snow Maiden role, but the set of her shoulders made it clear she was not in a good mood. "He's late," she said through clenched teeth.

Not, as it happened, Grandfather Frost, who was played by a reliable young actor called Stas Klimushkin. With his red robe peeping from under his sheepskin coat, he was helping a driver to start a white Lada car. Rather, we were being kept waiting by Sasha Morozov, a one-man band from the circus who was also essential to the show.

"I'll kill him," said Yelena, who together with Stas had already visited three homes, making children believe that presents their parents had bought them were delivered by Grandfather Frost and his girl sidekick. "We've got 40 workers at a factory party. After that, we go to Gazprom (the state gas monopoly). Once we run late, the whole thing goes down like a row of dominoes."

Ten minutes later, sweating and breathless, Sasha arrived, loaded down with his costume bag, drum and violin case. It was a tight squeeze in their Lada, so I offered him a lift in my Niva jeep. "This is tiring work," sighed Sasha, "but it can be fun. The kids are the nicest. They believe until about age 10. Some of them are cynical, though."

At the Avtostamp factory, it looked as if we might have hit a snag.

"What do you produce?" I asked the director's PA innocently.

"Thermo something, something," she muttered, adding in an annoyed aside to the Snow Maiden, "You didn't say anything about bringing a Western correspondent with you."

I assured her that I was only interested in Russian New Year traditions, and hospitality won out over caution.

Inside, the workers, tired of waiting, had already started drinking heavily at a long table spread with salmon, salads, fruit and cakes. "A joke then," said Grandfather Frost, who was under orders to keep the show clean. "A man asks God, 'What are a thousand years to you?' God replies, 'They are but a minute to me, my son.' 'And what are a thousand dollars to you?' the man asks. 'They are but a cent to me, my son.' 'Give me a cent then, Oh Lord.' 'It shall be done, in just a minute.'"

It wasn't that funny but the workers, in their best suits, and secretaries, in satin blouses, wept with laughter. Then Sasha "the typhoon" entered, wildly playing his violin. The Snow Maiden led the audience in a song they had known since childhood:

In the forest the fir tree was born, in the forest
the fir tree grew,
Winter and summer delicate and green
the whole year through.

After party games, Grandfather Frost shouted, "One last drink for the road" and shared a glass of vodka with the workers. (He drank only half of it; Stas was not a soak, unlike many actors in that role.) The workers tried to kiss the Snow Maiden. Her lips smiled but her eyes showed exhaustion. And it was only 5.00 pm.

Outside, Yelena urged the others to hurry up, as they were now horribly late. "We should have a helicopter to fly us over the traffic jams," laughed Stas as they rode off into the night.

Then I went home to begin preparations for our family New Year celebrations. Several guests were coming and I wanted to give them a special treat by mixing Russian and Western traditions. Costya and his friends didn't know it but as well as all the ingredients for a Russian salad (tinned salmon, rice, peas, mayonnaise etc) I had managed to get hold of that rarity of rarities in Moscow – a packet of frozen Brussels sprouts!

New Millennium

But we never did sit down to enjoy the chicken and cranberries, Russian salad, cakes, vodka and champagne. Because at noon on the last day of the 20th century, I turned on the television to see a teary-eyed President Boris Yeltsin against a backdrop of the Kremlin Christmas tree, and this is what he was saying:

Dear friends, my dear ones, today I am wishing you New Year greetings for the last time. But that is not all. Today I am addressing you for the last time as Russian President. I have made a decision. I have contemplated this long and hard. Today, on the last day of the outgoing century, I am retiring.

Many times I have heard it said, "Yeltsin will try to hold on to power by any means; he won't hand it over to anyone." That is all lies. I would have liked the presidential elections to have taken place on schedule in June 2000. That was very important for Russia – we were creating a vital precedent of a civilised, voluntary handover of power. And yet I have taken a different decision. I [pause] am standing down. I am standing down earlier than scheduled. I have realised that I have to do this.

Russia must enter the new millennium with new politicians, new faces, new intelligent, strong and energetic people. As for those of us who have been in power for many years, we must go. Why hold onto power for another six months when the country has a strong person, fit to be President, with whom practically all Russians link their hopes for the future?

Today, on this incredibly important day for me, I want to ask you for your forgiveness because many of our hopes have

272

not come true, because what we thought would be easy turned out to be painfully difficult. I ask you to forgive me for not fulfilling some hopes of those people who believed that we would be able to jump from the grey, stagnating totalitarian past into a bright, rich and civilised future in one go.

I am not leaving because of my health, but because of all the problems taken together. A new generation is taking my place. In accordance with the constitution, as I go into retirement, I have signed a decree entrusting the duties of the President of Russia to Prime Minister Vladimir Vladimirovich Putin.

That was that, then. Our New Year party was cancelled because I suddenly found myself writing the front page not just of any old edition of *The Independent* but of *The Independent*'s Special Millennium Souvenir Issue. What the editors wanted was the reaction of ordinary Muscovites to the bombshell that the 68-year-old President had just dropped.

As you might expect, ordinary Muscovites were absorbed with last-minute preparations for their millennium celebrations and were taken completely off guard by Yeltsin's theatrical announcement. When Channel One ran the speech, most of them were in fact still doing battle in the shops.

"I feel a kind of weightlessness," one young trainee journalist told me. "Not the same shock as Russians felt on the death of Stalin, of course, but a milder version of that. We do not know the real motives of the people in the Kremlin. And we do not know whether for us this means positive change, or tragedy."

"I am shocked, I am stunned, I am bewildered," said a housewife who was scouring the city for tinfoil to decorate her home appropriately for the coming Chinese Year of the Dragon. "I cannot say I feel relieved by this news. While the rest of the world is worrying about computers [developed countries were unsure of the K2 changeover effect on computers], we are still living with our political chaos. People say Putin will be the next President but to me right now, our future looks quite foggy."

Attentive Kremlin watchers – and I couldn't claim that kudos for myself – might have sensed that the unpredictable and ailing President Yeltsin was about to deliver a millennium surprise because he'd allowed Mr Putin to preside over a New Year party for the political elite a few days earlier. And before that, he'd handed over the presidential prerogative of awarding medals to Mr Putin, involved as he was with pursuing the war against Chechnya. But most people were feeling rather tired of politics after the latest parliamentary elections and had taken their eyes off state affairs to concentrate on whatever was going on in their private lives.

NTV, which was still an independent channel then, said President Yeltsin, who'd sounded gruff but otherwise looked reasonably well, had made a sudden decision to retire on the day he'd sent Mr Putin to host the Kremlin party in his place. The President's New Year speech had then had to be re-recorded in great haste. I knew that Russians, drinking out the Old Year with vodka and drinking in the New Year with champagne, usually listened to the New Year speech with about as much attention as sated Britons listened to the Queen's speech on Christmas Day. But they were sure to be glued to their sets when the millennium speech was repeated, as it was several times through the day and, of course, again at the stroke of midnight.

Given the disappointments that Russians had suffered through the 1990s, of which President Yeltsin himself spoke with regret, I was surprised that more people didn't express joy that the sick old man they so hated was finally leaving.

Some did, such as Nina Alexeyevna, a pensioner who was selling eggs and yoghurt from a table protected only by an umbrella on the snow-swept street. "I could have had a quiet retirement if it were not for Yeltsin," she complained. "As it is, at 61 I have to sit here in the freezing cold until late afternoon on New Year's Eve. Good riddance to Yeltsin. I am glad to see the back of him."

But others had kind words for the President as he made history by becoming the first Russian leader to hand over power voluntarily. "You have to respect him for having the courage to admit to himself his own unpopularity. It was a beautiful gesture," said an art student called Masha.

"I am not one of those who has criticised Yeltsin," said Vera Belostatskaya, a doctor. "I have supported Yeltsin all along and put my trust in him. If he has chosen Putin, then now I will vote for him. But I am sad for Yeltsin. I had hoped to see him finish his term."

Some Muscovites, while welcoming the news, were annoyed by President Yeltsin's timing. "Did he have to do it today?" asked Valentina, a cook. "Couldn't it have waited until after Christmas [Russian Orthodox from 6–7 January]? To be frank with you, he has spoilt my holiday."

"I have mixed feelings," said Tatyana, a secretary. "At least with Yeltsin always 'working on documents' [the euphemism when he was ill] there was a kind of stability, but now we are going into the unknown."

Others thought there was nothing at all "unknown" about the situation. An artist called Viktor said Yeltsin's resignation was nothing but a "cunning trick" to give his chosen successor the best possible springboard for the presidential elections, which were scheduled for March 2000.

And indeed, as "acting President", Prime Minister Putin now had a built-in advantage against all the other candidates. Despite casualties that were starting to come in from the new war in Chechnya, his forthcoming victory was pretty much a foregone conclusion. As for Yeltsin, around whom the whiff of a corruption scandal had recently hung, he secured immunity from prosecution in retirement.

WRITTEN IN THE STARS

Over the years in Russia, I came to understand that friendship was a full-time occupation. If you had a Russian friend, you couldn't just pencil him or her into your diary for lunch two weeks next Tuesday. When Russian friends phoned, they wanted to see you the same day and real *druzhba* (friendship) demanded that you met at least once if not several times a week. In an extreme situation, a friend would "give the shirt off his back" for you and expect you to do the same. Russians would have said it was because they had broader souls than petty and calculating Westerners. Whatever the reason, Russian friendship was as tight and binding as a bear hug.

In March 2000, my Russian friends were losing patience with me. They kept ringing up, wanting to meet, and getting the reply that I was busy.

"What do you mean: busy?"

"Well, it may have escaped your notice but the presidential election is in 10 days' time and so I am rather busy at the moment."

"Yeltsin, Putin, Futin. That's only politics. When does real life start again?" said my old friend Vitaly. "By the way, do you need anything?"

Foolishly, I mentioned that I was running out of washing-up liquid. "I'll get some for you and bring it round," he said. "I'm just going to the market now anyway."

Half an hour later, the phone went again. It was Vitaly, ringing to tell me that in his haste to fulfil "my commission", he'd fallen down the stairs and "broken his leg", so I ended up rushing round to his place instead. It turned out he'd fallen off one step and twisted his ankle. "You'd better have an X-ray to make sure it's not broken," I said but he didn't want to get involved with doctors. We had a cup of tea and I left him whining but apparently recovering.

Next day he rang to say he was in agony and I must come over with a bottle of vodka to kill the pain. "I spared nothing to buy your washing-up liquid," he said, and indeed I remembered all the times he'd made heroic efforts on my behalf. So I went over with the vodka and left him to get happily drunk.

On the third day, his ankle was as swollen as ever. He rang a medical friend, who repeated my rational Western advice about the X-ray but added her own Russian diagnosis: "You know, a broken limb is usually a sign of something changing in your life. You should go and see an astrologer as well."

Thus began an idiotic little adventure, with me playing chauffeur to the man who was supposed to be my driver. I took him first to outpatients at the Sklifosovsky Hospital, where we sat in the corridor while road and assault victims were wheeled past. A nurse had given Vitaly a piece of paper describing his injury as a "self-inflicted trauma, a fall from a height of the patient's own height". In a pause between less absurd cases, a kind radiologist X-rayed him for a small payment on the side. "No break – you'll live," she pronounced.

The next thing was to find the astrologer. "There's an Age of Aquarius exhibition down the road near the old KGB headquarters," said Vitaly, no longer limping but leaping. We entered a hall smelling of joss sticks, where New Age types were selling everything from essential oils and crystals to Buddhist texts and tarot cards. Wedged between a stand offering buns and a counter with Chinese snacks sat a golden-haired lady, bespectacled, wearing purple and looking suitably mystical. Here was the very person we needed.

Tatyana Gorbunova, "independent astrologer", took the details of Vitaly's Scorpio birth and invited him to collect his horoscope a few hours later. When we returned, she told him the first half of his life had been a disaster but everything was going to improve and he might end up rich and famous. He was so pleased, he persuaded me to make an appointment to have my fortune told. That was how life worked in Russia. One thing led to another and you got sucked in to an endlessly entertaining soap opera, if only you remembered that Putin was just politics and the real action happened with your friends.

When I went back on my own to see Tatyana Gorbunova, I discovered she was a "trainee astrologer". She reckoned to see in my birth chart not only the usual freedom-loving and altruistic characteristics of an Aquarius but also "unrealised occult powers" that could make me an astrologer too. She gave me some books and promised that if I did my homework, she would take me with her to her next class at the Astrology Academy. "But, the presidential elections..." I protested weakly. To be honest, I was already hooked.

The scepticism of the journalist lost out to the thirst for new experiences that is typical of those born under the sign of the water carrier. I plunged into the books. I couldn't understand a thing about the "aspects of planets" or why the moon "exalted" in Taurus, and found myself seeking clarification during further visits to Tatyana's incense-filled home.

There was something attractive about her searching spirit. She told me that in Soviet times, she had studied French and worked as a librarian. *Perestroika* had liberated her spiritually rather than politically, enabling her to read books on comparative religion. At first she'd studied Russian Orthodoxy. Then she became interested in Hinduism and went to live for a while in India. Her fascination with psychology drew her to astrology as an instrument for gaining insights into the characters of other people.

The question that lay people always asked, she said, was how much room there was for free will and how much life was predetermined by fate. It was a mystery that applied also to countries, which had their zodiac signs just as people did. Like me, Russia (and also Australia) were Aquarius – impractical idealists, believing in human equality, and perhaps about to come into their own in the Age of Aquarius.

By this point, I was dying to go to the Astrology Academy but Tatyana had one more lesson for me. "Remember," she said, "the astrologer should always be motivated by goodwill. You should always emphasise the positive and weigh the dangers of revealing anything negative, as what you say can become a self-fulfilling prophecy." At that, she said I was ready to join the evening classes at the small, fee-paying school that had been founded a decade earlier when astrology came out of the closet thanks to Gorbachev's reforms.

The academy was in a building belonging to the Ministry of Economics. In one room, the Association of Taxpayers was holding a meeting. In another sat the astrology students, listening intently to the lecturer, Dr Mikhail Levin, a mathematician. "Astrology is a science," he was saying as I took my seat. Then I noticed that almost every one of the 30 or so people in the stuffy room was a forty-something, bespectacled woman like Tatyana and me. I nearly fled in horror.

It was a good thing I stayed because after some esoteric stuff, the students gathered round a computer and began charting the horoscope of Vladimir Putin, the "balanced" Libra widely tipped to take over from the "unpredictable" Aquarius, Boris Yeltsin. With three days to go before the election, they foresaw for him "career changes, an improvement in his social position and opportunities for work-related travel".

"There you are," said Tatyana. "Now you don't need to worry about your election coverage. It's all written in the stars."

And of course it was. Putin won. Who had ever doubted it?

Afterwards, I had to tell Tatyana that astrology was probably not for me, as my irreverent streak was stronger than my occult potential. She said she'd known all along I would say that. "As an Aquarius, you are ruled by Uranus, the anarchic planet of laughter."

EUROVISION

It was just something I mentioned in passing. Discussing pop music with Vitaly's teenage son Cyril and his friend Mitya, I said that at their age I'd liked to get together with friends, drink beer and laugh at the Eurovision Song Contest.

Before I knew it, they had spread the word that I was holding a "Eurovision party" and on the night of the marathon competition, they and their mates Veronika, Olya and Borya descended on me.

The Iron Curtain had cut off Russians and East Europeans from many things, not least the joys of Eurovision. When Russia was just starting to take part, it sent its ageing Soviet-era diva Alla Pugacheva to Dublin, where she went down like a lead balloon.

In May 2000, at just about the same time that President Vladimir Putin was inaugurated, it seemed Russia might have a better chance on the Eurovision stage. The country was being represented in Stockholm by a sexy young thing called Alsu and there was lively interest.

In my living room, we opened the beer and settled down to wait for the new star to appear. Compared with Pugacheva, Alsu was *koolnaya* (cool), said Mitya, beginning what for me was to turn into a crash course in Russian teenage slang.

Before the competition, I'd tried to interview Alsu but found she did not live permanently in Russia. Her father was an oil tycoon and she went to a private college in London, where she was not to be tracked down either because on the eve of Eurovision, she was resting in Malta.

Alsu was her real name. It means "pink water" in the Tartar language. She was from the Muslim region of Tartarstan which, unlike Chechnya, had been wily and managed to achieve a considerable degree of autonomy without enraging Moscow. She'd become popular all over Russia after appearing in a pop video as a Lolita-like waif, singing "Winter Dream", a song about adolescent love.

In Stockholm, she was going to sing a song called "Solo", with lyrics in English, which her fans said would increase her chances of appealing to an international audience.

An Israeli group opened the show. "Uh, uh, be happy; uh, uh, be happy," they sang. Immediately, an argument broke out around the television set. "That's cool," said Borya. "They're singing out of tune to get a deliberate punk effect."

"No they're not," sneered Veronika. "They're just singing out of tune." Cyril said "*otstoi*", which probably best translated as "stagnant".

We were out of the room, getting more beer from the fridge, when Britain's Nikki French came on and performed her number. I heard the Russian commentator say that her song sounded a lot like Abba but I didn't know if that was a compliment or a weary expression of déjà vu.

We were back in time to hear the Romanian group Taxi sing "Moon". Olya liked the folk rhythms but Cyril said the entry was stagnant. Mitya went further. "*Masdai*," he said, in a corruption of "it must die".

Alsu's moment of glory was approaching but before that there was the "fat woman from Malta", as the teenagers put it. I thought she was quite good – at least she had a voice. We all agreed that the three Valkyries from Norway, singing "My Heart Goes Boom", were deeply stagnant and must definitely die.

Then Alsu came on, a vision in shimmering peach trousers. "*Rulis, rulis, rulis*," chanted the teenagers, using a corruption of "she rules".

Alsu sang sweetly, even confidently, but failed to inspire my young guests.

"Stagnant," said Cyril. "The usual *popsa* [commercial pop music]."

"At least she's *nasha* [our own]," said Veronika.

The general verdict was "*Nasha popsa*".

After this, the rest of the song contest became a beery blur. For part of it, we turned the sound down so that the lads, who were really rap fans, could put on some of their own CDs and make a real racket.

Veronika came into the kitchen for a quiet talk. She said she liked The

Cardigans, "you know, especially that clip where the girl is driving fast with a stone to hold down the accelerator and she gets killed when the stone flies up and hits her in the head".

Somewhere on the edges of our awareness, the Danes were making their contribution to the Eurovision evening. "Disgusting ****", said Mitya unprintably. What a sobering moment it was, then, when the disgusting **** won the competition.

"*Otstoi!*" they all shouted in disbelief.

But Alsu came second – a creditable result for *Rasha* (Russia), which in Eurovision terms was a young country, and for Alsu herself, who at only 16 years of age was the youngest contestant.

We were all bound to agree that was pretty cool. "*Nasha Rasha rulis, rulis, rulis!*"

THE KURSK

The nuclear-powered submarine *Kursk* was no ageing, Soviet-era vessel but a state-of-the-art cruise missile carrier built during President Boris Yeltsin's rule. On its black conning tower, it bore the two-headed eagle, the symbol of the new Russia. It was the pride of the Arctic-based Northern Fleet and regarded, like the *Titanic*, as quite simply unsinkable. On 12 August 2000, to quote President Vladimir Putin's famous phrase when asked what happened to the *Kursk*, "it sank".

Eight days later, I was sitting in the Nightingale Grove Café in Kursk, drinking coffee and listening as the other clients talked in subdued voices about the tragedy of the submarine, which was named after their city. Even though tapping had been heard from the sunken submarine for at least 48 hours after the initial accident, Russia had delayed accepting foreign offers of help. Now finally, on 20 August, Norwegian divers experienced in repairing oil rigs, and an LR5 British mini-submarine, reckoned to be the most advanced underwater rescue craft in the world, were about to go down under the Barents Sea, attempt to dock with the *Kursk*, and see if there were any signs of life.

The television in the corner of the café was showing an old Jacques Cousteau film about underwater wonders. The café customers gazed at the fish without seeing them, apparently impervious to the curious programming choice of the pro-Kremlin First Channel. Their anxious conversation was all of oxygen and whether, by some miracle, the 118 submariners, who included 7 men from the city of Kursk, might possibly still be breathing.

The assistants at the counter had no milk for my coffee. When the ladies at the next table heard my foreign accent, they offered me milk from their own shopping bags. When they learnt I was British, they came over to my table. "We want you to know that we are very grateful to Britain," said

Galina, a pensioner, who was wearing a black and white polka-dot dress. "The British are our only hope now. We will be glued to the television, watching them go into action."

The overwhelming popular view was that human lives mattered more than possible exposure of Russian naval secrets or loss of national pride. "We are all for saving lives," said Sergei, the waiter in the Nightingale Grove. "If foreigners can make a difference, why not? We will be only too happy."

The rare Russian voice that expressed xenophobia was quickly silenced. On a radio phone-in I'd picked up back at my hotel, during which listeners had been asked to choose between the values of life and patriotism, one woman had voted for national pride. She was verbally savaged by the next listener, who said, "Don't you understand that caring about people *is* national pride? We have lost too many of our people. Last year the bombs in Moscow, and now this."

After finishing my coffee, I walked out into the "Hero City of Kursk", which had suffered its greatest losses in a famous tank battle during the Second World War. The main feature of the grubby, industrial city, 500 miles south of Moscow, is a giant war cemetery. Nightingales sing in the willow trees there each June. A popular wartime song asks the nightingales not to wake the sleeping soldiers. The people of Kursk were all praying they would not have to add another verse about sleeping submariners.

Some people were still clinging to hope. Down at the market, where the fruits of late summer – corn on the cob, water melons and peaches – were abundant, a forward-thinking trader was laying out and combing her range of fur hats. "I've not given up hope for the sailors yet," she said. "We must hope until the last."

Another trader, selling nylon aprons and pellets to kill cockroaches, was beside herself over the submarine tragedy. "Our poor boys," she cried. "We have been waiting and waiting. I could strangle our government over this."

Deep down, everyone knew it was probably too late to save the crew, who ranged from the lowliest conscripts to some of the top brass of the Northern Fleet. "We will most likely have to say that our worst fears have come true," Vice-Admiral Mikhail Motsak warned television viewers. And indeed, when the Norwegian divers reached the submarine escape hatch and opened it, they found the *Kursk* completely flooded and knew there was no chance any of the sailors could have survived. The Norwegians swam out again and to the disappointment of the British, the waiting rescue mini-sub never went into action at all.

The fact that the Norwegians managed to do in a day – albeit a calm day – what Russian rescuers had failed to achieve in more than a week of stormy weather only further inflamed public anger. The inescapable conclusion was that had foreigners been brought in sooner, at least some of the crew might have been rescued.

The still-free Russian press fired off a barrage of articles, raising embarrassing questions. Why, when the submarine had sunk on Saturday 12 August during exercises, had we not heard about the accident until Monday 14 August? Why did the Navy initially say there had been a collision (presumably with another submarine, possibly American) when in fact there had been an internal explosion? What was this internal explosion? The *Kursk*'s own torpedoes? And how did that happen? Above all, why had Russia wasted time making six failed rescue attempts using diving bells before accepting foreign aid that had been on offer all along?

"Russian rescuers who went down repeatedly into the cold sea to try to open the submarine hatch did all they could but the country will never forgive those who pretended Russia was a superpower," thundered the daily *Izvestia*.

Public anger was now directed at President Putin, who through all this drama had remained on holiday in Sochi on the sunny Black Sea coast. Russians had been particularly offended by one TV appearance he made, wearing a beige, open-necked T-shirt and looking tanned, in which he said that the submarine situation was "critical" and "every effort" was being made to save the crew. People just couldn't understand his failure to break off his holiday and show some concern. Had he so quickly gained a taste for the political high life that he was now indifferent to ordinary citizens? Many put his poor sense of public relations down to his inexperience. The press printed derisive pictures of him wearing naval uniform, for it wasn't so long since he'd had a photo opportunity on board a nuclear submarine himself.

Certainly, it wouldn't have been a good idea for Mr Putin to show his face in Kursk that August. Actually, he'd been in the city only three months earlier – to open a new war memorial, a triumphal arch almost as large as Moscow's copy of the Arc de Triomphe in Paris. Crowds of women had screamed in ecstasy at the newly-elected President. But the mood had made a 180-degree turn against him since then.

"How dare Putin swan around on holiday at the Black Sea when our boys are trapped up there in the Arctic? Well, I mean to say, they're dead now," complained Leonid, who eked out a living by using his car as an unofficial taxi. "Those in power care more about a lump of metal and their stupid secrets than human beings. Mind you, I never liked Putin. I didn't vote for him. What can you expect from a former KGB agent?"

Natasha, a student who said she had voted (although not screamed) for Putin, was just as angry. "I certainly wouldn't vote for him again. He has lost my trust. He has dithered instead of acting, and waited far too long before accepting foreign help. It is simply indecent that he did not go straight up to Severomorsk [the submarine base] when he found out that the boat had sunk."

Once the deaths were confirmed, my editors in London, of course, wanted me to find the bereaved families in Kursk. That was easier said than done, even with a list of surnames from the official death toll. How do you find seven families in a city that has one million people but no telephone directory? I'll let you into a journalistic secret: you ask the taxi drivers; they know everything.

The cowboy taxi driver Leonid didn't know but he introduced me to colleagues who did. Most of the sailors' relatives, I was told, had already taken a third-class train, laid on specially by the local authorities, for the gruelling 45-hour journey north to the Arctic garrison town of Vidyayevo, where they would join a vigil for the dead. That was a shame because I'd been hoping to interview Valentina Staroseltseva, the mother of conscript Dmitry Staroseltsev, whose story was already out on the news wires and was rather a touching one.

Apparently, as a boy, Dmitry had been crazy about swimming in the river in landlocked Kursk. He'd had to compete for the perceived prestige of doing his military service in the Northern Fleet. His mother had been relieved that he'd not been sent to Chechnya. Before the submarine sank, she'd had a premonition that something was wrong. There was a photo of her on the wires, wearing her best white blouse, with her sad little suitcase packed for the rail trip north and her eyes closed in pain.

But there was one Kursk woman who hadn't gone on the train because she was too ill. Her name was Olga Kuznetsova, mother of 28-year-old Viktor Kuznetsov, who'd been a junior officer on the doomed submarine. Once we pinned down her address, Leonid drove me to visit her. She lived in a small, shabby flat in a typical Khrushchev-era block. She was sitting on her sofa-bed, wearing a yellow candlewick dressing gown. She'd just come out of hospital after an operation for breast cancer. "She just keeps crying and crying," her daughter Lyuba whispered to me.

When she saw me, Mrs Kuznetsova pulled herself together. "Hope is fading," she sighed. "I feel as if I have a huge stone in my soul. I would rather have died on the operating table than have this happen to my poor Viktor."

She didn't waste much emotion on Mr Putin, saying only that he'd been "indecisive and insensitive".

Mrs Kuznetsova had seven children. Her youngest son, 16-year-old Timur, led me to a table with cheap cardboard icons surrounding photographs of Viktor: Viktor as a schoolboy; Viktor as a young seaman; Viktor with his wife, Svetlana, and their son Dima, 3. "As you see, we are a large family," said Mrs Kuznetsova. "My father is 100 years old. He doesn't know his grandson is on the submarine. The news would kill him."

Mrs Kuznetsova, a retired postwoman, spoke of Viktor as a calm, restrained man. He'd dreamed of the sea and when he saw it for the first time as a conscript, he loved it so much he decided to make his career in the Navy. He joined the crew of the *Kursk* when it was first launched in 1994.

"I wanted to serve on the *Kursk* too," said Timur who, after finishing school, would be liable for conscription. "But I'm not so sure about the Navy now. Perhaps I'll be a fireman instead."

I didn't know what to say to that and left soon afterwards, making awkward apologies. After I'd gone, the daughter Lyuba phoned to thank me for having come. My visit and the "attention" I'd given the family had helped them, she said.

I remembered then what the editor of the *Bradford Telegraph and Argus*, my first employer in journalism, had told me when I'd shown reluctance to go and put my foot in the door of a home where the son of the family had just been killed in a motorbike crash. "They'll want you to be there," my boss had said. "The vicar, the undertaker, the journalist – they're all part of the ritual. It will give them some comfort."

Over the years, I'd often found that people in distress regarded me as much as a psychological therapist as a reporter. I did sympathise but I had to remain detached for my own sanity. I couldn't take the grief of all the people I interviewed onto myself or it would have made me ill.

But Mrs Kuznetsova was already ill. Not long afterwards, her daughter rang again to say that the trauma of losing Viktor had brought back her cancer and she too had died. It was a very bad business indeed.

Finally it seemed that President Putin recognised the depth of the tragedy because he flew up to the Arctic to meet the grieving relatives of all the 118 lost submariners. Irina Lyachina, widow of the vessel's commander, Captain Gennady Lyachin, received the Kremlin leader in her poor apartment and other relatives gave him a hearing but they refused to mourn with him. Given Russians' tradition of forgiving all hurts and grievances at funerals, their refusal to include him in their ceremonies effectively meant that they were withholding forgiveness. Mr Putin made a grovelling apology and left a wreath behind when he departed.

Orthodox Russians prefer their dead to rest in the earth, not at sea, but the weather was turning autumnal and there was no immediate prospect of bodies being brought up from the wreck of the *Kursk* for reburial on land. (Some bodies were later recovered and buried in cemeteries across Russia.) Instead the relatives, having boycotted Mr Putin's "national day of mourning", laid their own memorial stone at Vidyayevo and then took a boat out to sea to the spot below which the submarine lay. NTV, which had been aggressive in its criticism of Mr Putin throughout the crisis, covered this last elegiac chapter.

The relatives threw wreaths onto the waves, including the one left behind by the embarrassed President. Something was missing. Had they been at a graveside on land, they would have had the traditional drink with the dead by pouring vodka into the soil. Suddenly, slyly, a man produced a bottle of vodka, decorated with a bunch of plastic grapes, and tossed it overboard into the water. Then he turned and smiled at the camera. For a moment, on board the boat there seemed to be a mood of grim satisfaction.

All of this left Mr Putin with a choice. Commentators said that after the humiliating drubbing he had received from the press, he could either dedicate himself to genuine reforms that would ultimately make Russia an open and humane democracy. He could, for example, abolish conscription and create the professional armed forces that Boris Yeltsin had promised Russia would have by the new millennium.

Or he could revert to Soviet ways of thinking, turn his back on the interfering West, and seek the easy comfort of nationalism. He could get tough and nasty, cracking down on the media and ensuring that nobody dared to portray him as an incompetent weakling ever again.

In retrospect, we know the choice he made. He chose to be a "strong" leader of a "strong" Russia. With the sinking of the *Kursk* rose the Vladimir Putin we know today.

SINKING

When the *Kursk* sank, something in me sank too. There were many things that were impossible or at least very difficult to change in Russia. The harsh climate, for example, always had to be reckoned with and the poor housing and other infrastructure obviously couldn't be renewed overnight. The Orthodox Church preached *smirenie* (humble acceptance) and it was true that stamping your feet in frustration got you nowhere. And yet, it seemed to me, there were some things that could easily have been improved.

I'll always remember arriving at Sheremetevo Airport in 1985 with six suitcases (I was coming to stay for a long time) and finding that the Russians had no concept of baggage trolleys. Now that wasn't rocket science or even particularly costly but you'd be surprised how many years it took for the airport to provide luggage carts. Most of all, I thought, Russian life could be transformed if only people would put a smile on their faces and be nice to each other. A can-do attitude can achieve wonders and win-win is always better than lose-lose.

But when the *Kursk* sank, it dawned on me that these "simple" attitudinal changes were actually the most difficult of all and Russians had to make these inner shifts themselves; there was nothing I could do to help them. By playing a jolly, encouraging figure to my impoverished, complaining friends, I was actually delaying the moment when they stopped whining and understood their own power to change their lives. I took to heart what Russians were saying about "interfering foreigners" and realised that with my comments and advice, given both privately and in print, I was a voice in a Western chorus that was part of the problem, not the solution.

On a personal level, I began to feel insecure. The *Kursk* reminded me that life was cheap in Russia and that meant my own life was cheap too. Russian family, friends and culture were dear but the ways of the Russian state remained unacceptable to me. I realised that my attempt to make Russia my "home" had been naïve and doomed. I might have wanted to integrate but the Russian state showed me over and over again that I was an outsider, an observer, a guest on a yearly renewable visa who would one day have to leave.

In this, I was no different from millions of Russian emigres, who knew the sorrow of feeling spiritually at home in a place that politically did not suit them at all. The music of Rachmaninov had first drawn me to Russia and it was only much later that I discovered he wrote most of his wonderful "Russian" music while living in forced exile in America.

I remembered then the wise words of my old Swedish friend, Tore Persson. He was an "expert" on Russia and had first inspired me to go to Moscow by giving me Hedrick Smith's groundbreaking book *The Russians*, which described ordinary Soviet life rather than the intrigues in the Kremlin. "Go to Russia, enjoy yourself by all means," said Tore, "but never forget who you are and where you come from."

And so in autumn 2000, I decided to leave Moscow. At the new millennium, my parents had given me £2,000 (a pound for every year since the birth of Christ), which at first I'd just banked. Suddenly, I got the bright idea to spend this windfall on a trip to Australia.

Before I left Moscow, the last thing I did was to help my friend Vitaly to buy a small flat for himself as he was going through a difficult divorce with his wife Marina and was in danger of ending up homeless. Buying that flat was one of the most bizarre experiences I had in Russia, which was par excellence the realm of the bizarre.

Vitaly didn't have much money, so he was looking for the cheapest one-room flat he could find on the furthest edge of Moscow. In the end, an estate agent called Yegor, who sported an avocado-coloured jacket, found a suitable apartment for him in a satellite town called Balashikha. It was at the end of "civilisation"; it was so far out that from his balcony, Vitaly could see the start of the forests stretching all the way to Siberia, or so it seemed.

In the absence of mortgages, Vitaly was paying cash – not quite a suitcase but a plastic bag of cash. The vendor, a timid pensioner called

Kirill Andreyevich, trusted neither our estate agent nor Vitaly. He was afraid the dollars he laid on the table might have been forged and wanted them processed through a Russian bank. But reminding him how millions of Russians had lost their savings in collapsed banks in 1998, Yegor said Kirill Andreyevich would be mad to allow a local bank to hold the money for even a day.

Finally, the vendor's estate agent came up with a solution. She would photocopy the dollar notes, every one of them, and the old man would show the serial numbers to the bank and if and when he was satisfied they were genuine, he would hand over the key to the flat.

Thus Vitaly became the depressed rather than proud owner of a God-awful box in an urban wasteland, but I felt able to leave knowing that at least he wouldn't be homeless. It took him a while but he went on to pick himself up, restore contact with his children and shine in his musical career.

Free and refreshed in Australia, I soon found a new life for myself in the Outback. I fell so much in love with the red desert that I stayed on to become, if not quite an Aussie, then certainly more than a tourist Down Under. It was not until 2003 that I returned to Russia, no longer as a representative of the British press but as a contributor to *The Sydney Morning Herald*. I came back because I missed my friends and because I was curious to see how Russia was developing, but my connection to the country was now a looser one.

While I'd been away, Costya and I had divorced. We'd drifted apart and the time had come for a new approach. Since we were childless, it was not difficult to split and we were not the kind of people to argue over sofas and television sets. Without any animosity, we had a long-distance exchange of legal paperwork and then transformed our marriage into a friendship. Russians say friendship is the "highest form of love" and I'm proud that Costya and I, through good sense and kindness, reached this level of pure mutual acceptance. Back in Moscow, I moved into a small flat on my own and Costya jokingly gave me "custody" of Blackjack the cat. He came to visit us sometimes.

Starting to write about Russia again, I took nothing for granted. I was well aware that what looked familiar might be deeply changed on the inside; that what seemed different might simply have had a new coat of paint. Certainly, the centre of Moscow looked richer and trendier than I remembered it; almost like Berlin or Paris. But it was enough for me to ride out on the metro to the ends of the lines to see that an awful lot of poverty remained. For me, the bottom line had always been: "Are ordinary Russians living better? If yes, great; if not, why not?"

After an absence of three years, I couldn't see any startling breakthrough, although many Russians spoke of the relief of a new stability that allowed them to prosper. My old friend and colleague, the photographer Viktor Korotayev, told me, "In Soviet times, most Russians lived in exactly the same way. Now Russians live in all sorts of different ways. Some are rich; some are poor. Some drink themselves to death; some take their holidays in Dubai. It depends much more on the choices of the individual."

I kept an open mind; I was willing to give Mr Putin more time and the benefit of the doubt.

But I'd only been back a few weeks when the oil tycoon Mikhail Khodorkovsky was hauled off his jet at an airport in Siberia and thrown into prison, ostensibly for economic crimes, more likely because he'd dared to challenge the Kremlin. After that, I was covering Beslan, the mishandled "rescue" of hostages in a Caucasian school that left 334 people including 186 children dead; the Orange Revolution in Kiev, sparked by Russian interference in Ukrainians' electoral choices; the Kremlin's creation of the youth group Nashi in a paranoid attempt to stop a similar "colour revolution" happening in Russia; the murder of the journalist Anna Politkovskaya in Moscow; the scandalous polonium poisoning of Alexander Litvinenko in London and Russia's refusal to extradite the suspects. And so it went on...

Heaven knows I wasn't an enemy of Russia. I didn't set out to look for bad news; I always welcomed the chance to tell my readers something positive. But apart from the story of undoubted economic growth – and even that had more to do with the price of oil than any significant reform or modernisation – the news coming out of Putin's Russia seemed to be bleak and discouraging, to say the least.

THE SNOW REVOLUTION

Fast-forward to 2011. For what more, really, can I say about Vladimir Putin's first eight years in the Kremlin or the four years during which Dmitry Medvedev kept his seat warm for him until, following the letter but not the spirit of the constitution, he could return as President for a third term? When, in September 2011, the tandem admitted this had been their cynical arrangement all along, the scales began to fall from people's eyes. After it emerged that December's parliamentary elections had been fixed, Moscow witnessed a winter of discontent, the season of the "Snow Revolution".

Time, which had stopped, started to tick again; the times once more became "interesting". On 10 December, some 30,000 people came out onto Bolotnaya Square in the biggest protest Moscow had seen since the break-up of the Soviet Union. As the first snowflakes of winter swirled in the air, the square turned white with people carrying white chrysanthemums, wearing white satin ribbons on their coats, or holding white balloons. Significantly, the majority of them were not opposition regulars but ordinary citizens who had not attended a demonstration before.

"Our patience has snapped," an engineer called Yaroslav Rogozin told me. "I didn't vote for United Russia (the pro-Putin party) and neither did any of my friends or relatives or anyone I know. So I don't see how they can say the party won 50 per cent."

"White is the colour of purity and truth," said Ekaterina Danilova, an independent journalist who attended the demo as a citizen rather than in her professional capacity. The protestors said white also represented the people whose opinions had been blanked out by the regime. "We're sick of it," said Alexei Kozin, an IT specialist. "They're reconstructing the Soviet one-party state."

The authorities had previously cracked down on small demonstrations

294

held on the last day of 31-day months to draw attention to Article 31 of the Russian constitution, which guarantees freedom of speech and assembly. But seeing the number of people signing up on Facebook to attend the meeting at Bolotnaya Square, they wisely decided to allow it. The demo passed off peacefully and revealed two things: that a new generation that got its information from the internet rather than state-controlled television had come of age; and that the growing middle class wanted not only economic but also political freedom. The notion that "Asian" Russians would be satisfied with a Chinese model of economic growth but political control was disproved.

First-time demonstrator Viktor Sokolov, a financier sporting a mink hat, complained about corruption. "We are normal people; we are tax payers," he said, "and we see our money being stolen to feed an army of corrupt bureaucrats."

Banker Yaroslav Gryaznov objected to the idea that Mr Putin could just impose himself on the Russian people, whether they liked it or not. "It would be one thing if he was returning with a programme of real reforms – judicial reform, for example. But he is coming back with the same old ideas that only benefit impudent bureaucrats."

A woman called Marfa, whose dog Mucha wore a white ribbon on her collar, said she didn't mind whether or not Mr Putin came back. "The point is he should be legitimately elected. If he really has a majority, then fine, but the trouble is we cannot be sure of that."

Mikhail Gorbachev, by this time 80 years old, expressed support for the protestors and said he was glad he had lived to see the ideals of *glasnost* come alive again. I felt the same – somehow vindicated, as if all my years in Russia had not been in vain.

A crack had certainly appeared in the Putin façade. The myth of the universally popular superman had been exploded. It turned out many Russians were tired of him and wanted a change.

Putin tried to brush off the new opposition with crude jokes. He said he mistook the demonstration for an anti-AIDS rally and thought the white ribbons on people's coats were condoms. That turned the tide against him. If at Bolotnaya Square, the people had been complaining mainly of election violations, by the time they demonstrated again, on Academician Sakharov Avenue on Christmas Eve, their numbers had quadrupled and they were openly calling for Putin's resignation.

"We want free elections. We want this corrupt system to become a thing of the past. We want to live honestly," said two young women called Alla and Irina. Not only were they wearing white but they were also carrying a stuffed purple snake. In reference to wily Kaa from *The Jungle Book*, the opposition had started calling Putin Python Puu. They were hissing and booing him now.

One man, a manager called Konstantin Samarin, held up a placard with the words: "Putin past his sell-by date".

"Putin is sneering at innocent people," said Sergei Kolpakov, a factory worker who said he'd seen with his own eyes how ballots had been stuffed at his polling station during the parliamentary elections. "This scandal was bad enough but then Putin uses language so dirty that I can only describe him as that object he said was on our coats."

Placards showed Putin's face inside a condom, with the slogan: "We don't need used contraceptives". Up on stage, one of the speakers was dressed from head to foot in white, like a sheath.

"Other countries have orange revolutions and tulip springs but we have a condom revolution," said one protestor. It was obvious that Putin wasn't going to be allowed to forget his unfortunate innuendo. Former President Gorbachev said he was ashamed of the man whose political career he'd once supported.

The Snow Revolution put Russia back on the front pages of the world's newspapers. Russia was waking up, it seemed, and that aroused the West's flagging interest in what had been largely written off as an incorrigible country, important to us only as a supplier of oil and gas. Suddenly, all the talk was of Russia again.

None of it made any immediate difference, of course. On 4 March 2012, in an election that observers said was heavily weighted in Putin's favour, he was "chosen" in a single round of voting to be Russia's President for a third term and for at least another six years. Despite serious violations, it's probably true that the majority of Russians still preferred him. Putin voters whom I spoke to said he was the lesser of the evils on offer. Their thinking seemed to be: "Always keep tight hold of nurse for fear of finding something worse".

Commentators noted that in most countries, the outcome of an election is uncertain but the future is reasonably clear once it is known which party has won. In Russia, it was the other way round. The outcome of the election was a foregone conclusion but which way Mr Putin intended to take the country was anybody's guess.

Some predicted he would preside over a liberalisation and finally go down in history as a true reformer of Russia. Others said he would become a new Stalin. Still others thought he wouldn't do much at all but try to preserve the corrupt status quo from which he and his cronies benefited.

I doubted that a leopard could change his spots. New restrictive laws brought in after the election and the inquisition against the punk group Pussy Riot, which had performed a protest in Moscow's main cathedral, didn't inspire confidence.

After Putin's "re-election", friends who had attended the snow demonstrations fell into depression. There was a danger that bright young people might either emigrate or go into what Russians call "internal migration": sitting round the kitchen table at home and moaning.

But Yulia Kolesnichenko, a young woman who volunteered as an observer at a polling station, cheered me when she said, "It's not over. It's up to each of us now to become more civic-minded." Yulia had recently taken responsibility by adopting a child. She urged fellow Russians not to despair but to "volunteer, engage in charity, monitor and challenge the activities of the authorities, be more active. Only when each one of us changes ourselves can we hope to change our society".

COSTYA AND VITALY

Costya didn't attend any of the demonstrations of the "Snow Revolution". He'd long ago voted with his feet and he spent his winters relaxing on the beach in Goa, running his business from a laptop computer.

On what would have been our silver wedding anniversary, he invited me to join him on holiday in India and, under the palm trees, I saw for myself how Costya had taken the average Russian's *pofigism* (don't-give-a-fig philosophy) to a whole new level of enlightenment. Costya's motto was "Why worry?" and he certainly wasn't going to trouble himself over Putin or the future of Russia.

Vitaly did care. Still not very well off despite all his musical talent, and disenfranchised into the bargain, he donned a white woolly hat and went to one of the marches. "I'm going as a concerned citizen," he said. "I just want to see what this is all about."

But he was put off by the disunity of the opposition and the rabble-rousing of some of their leaders. He was particularly critical of Boris Nemtsov, a liberal who conveniently forgot that he'd once urged Russians to support Putin. "When I heard that hypocrite Nemtsov shouting down his megaphone, that was enough for me and I decided to go home."

Vitaly and I met for a meal later, when the demo was over. I forgot to mention that he was my new husband by now. We'd married in 2008, on 22 February at 11.30 am to be precise. There were any number of times and places the wedding could have taken place but I had resisted remarrying for a long time. In fact, on the very morning of the wedding, I still wasn't sure.

"Look," said Vitaly, "we'll just do what suits us." And when he said that, I decided to take the plunge and go with him to the registry office.

"Do you want any flowers?" he asked, as we got out at the metro station.

"On any other day but today," I said.

For the "ceremony", we both wore jeans and our scruffiest jumpers. The registrar was taken aback when we told her we didn't have rings and didn't want any music either. We just signed a piece of paper and that was it.

Afterwards, we went home and wolfed some sausages before we both had to go to work. Vitaly never remembers the wedding anniversary; he has to look in his passport to check the date.

But we do go out to restaurants when the mood takes us. With his regular salary from his job as a piano accompanist at a state concert agency, Vitaly can certainly afford that much. And when we sit down together to pasta and a bottle of red wine, we still have plenty of things to talk about.

"The conditions are difficult. At first, one must move warily, like an old fox walking over ice. The caution of a fox walking over ice is proverbial in China. His ears are constantly alert to the cracking of the ice, as he carefully and circumspectly searches out the safest spots. A young fox who as yet has not acquired this caution goes ahead boldly, and it may happen that he falls in and gets his tail wet when he is almost across the water." (From the I-Ching or Chinese Book of Changes, translated by Richard Wilhelm.)